To Matt,

Keep working hard and have fun!

# HEART & HUSTLE

—

# HEART & HUSTLE

AN UNLIKELY JOURNEY
FROM
LITTLE LEAGUER TO BIG LEAGUER

# Frank Catalanotto

with

Diane Montiel and Steve Alexander

# Foreword by Michael Young

An imprint of Bantry Bay Media, LLC
Chicago

Printed in the United States of America.
For information, address Bantry Bay Media, LLC.,
1340 N. Astor Street, #1007, Chicago, IL 60610
bantrybaymedia@gmail.com


ISBN 978-0-9850673-0-4

Photo credits:
Rob Cuni Photography, Nesconset, NY  www.robcuni.com
Matt Walbeck  www.walbeckbaseball.com
The Catalanotto Family

Jacket design:
Anthony Paolillo
www.acdesignny.com


To schedule Frank Catalanotto
for a speaking engagement or appearance:
(516) 768-1950

For more information about the author, go to
www.frankcatalanotto.com
Or follow him on Twitter @fcat27

# DEDICATION

To Mom and Dad;

Thanks, Mom, for being so loving and teaching me how to love. I am so grateful to have had such a strong, beautiful role model in my life. You have shown me how to be diligent and always prepared and for that, I will forever be thankful. Knowing you were there to support me and guide me as I followed my dreams brought me comfort, and I cannot begin to express how much I appreciated that.

Thank you, Dad, for teaching me so much both on and off the field. You taught me that whatever I do in life, I should have fun and do it to the best of my ability. I admire your love and dedication to our family and pray that I can be as good of a role model to my children.

I cannot emphasize enough how much I treasured both of you being so involved in my young life; all the games you attended, all the fields you drove me to and all your encouragement along the way. You both instilled a work ethic in me that helped me achieve my childhood dreams. Thanks for being there every step of the way.

# CONTENTS

# INTRODUCTION

I was thinking about titling this book, "Everything I Needed To Know About Life, I Learned In Baseball". The lessons seem endless. Success, failure, courage, accountability, ambition, assertiveness, rejection, empathy, cooperation, commitment, patience, honesty, integrity, persistence, loyalty, thankfulness, selflessness, tolerance and devotion are just some of what the game of baseball taught me.

Baseball changed my life. That's why I wrote this book. It changed me in ways that I never would have imagined and I want to pass along what I learned to anyone who has ever felt the sting of being overlooked. This book is for the Little Leaguer who is just getting the hang of the game. It's for the parents who don't yet know just how vital they are to their child's development. It is for the high school player who dreams of getting into college or professional baseball. It's for the minor leaguer who is looking for that one last piece to the puzzle that will get him into the big leagues.

I don't think anyone thought that I, a scrawny little kid from Long Island, would ever have the chance to be a Major League Baseball player. Even I had my doubts and after reading this book, you will understand why.

There were no pro scouts or college coaches drooling over my skills. In fact, I wasn't blessed with many that were eye opening. However, I did have desire and drive or, as some would say, "heart and hustle". I became a student of the game and wrote everything I learned in a little black book that I studied every night before going to bed. I worked every day of the year on hitting and fielding drills and did it all because I thought it was fun. And the more fun I had, the better I became.

It wasn't until late in my senior year of high school that a local scout told me I might have a chance to play pro ball. When I was drafted, I dedicated myself to the game and to becoming a better player. I soon learned that if I wanted to succeed in the competitive environment that is professional baseball, I would need to change my approach. And once I did, everything changed.

My hope is that the readers of this book take the lessons I've learned from my experiences and use them in their approach towards success in sports or life.

"Heart & Hustle" is my love letter to baseball and to my family, whose support made my success possible. I hope you enjoy the read.

# ACKNOWLEDGMENTS

I never really intended to write a book, but every now and then, my cousin, Bobby Vanderhoof, would encourage me to jot down what I saw, experienced and learned in my nineteen years of professional baseball. He seemed to enjoy my stories and felt that other people would as well. Thanks, Bobby. Had you not encouraged me, there's no way I would have completed this book. A special thanks to Diane Montiel and Steve Alexander of Bantry Bay Books for their editing and layout skills and for interviewing the people who allowed their thoughts and memories to be included in this book. I am grateful for my team of proofreaders, including Alexandra Busa. Rob Cuni deserves big thanks for all of his help with the book and its photos, as does Anthony Paolillo for his work on the cover design.

On the baseball side, I was influenced by many people over the years, but without Larry Parrish's coaching, mentoring and friendship, I never would have made it to the major leagues. Thank you, L.P. Also, I would like to acknowledge my agents, Alan Nero and Scott Pucino, for their guidance and advice over the past twenty years.

None of what I accomplished in baseball would have been possible without the love and encouragement of my family. The words "thank you" don't seem adequate to express my appreciation to my parents Frank and Sharon, my sister Christa and my brother Michael. Their unwavering support and belief in me made it all happen. They were always there for me, and for that I am grateful beyond words. I especially want to thank my wife, Barbara, and our four girls, Morgan, Camdyn, Karson and Gracyn. Their love and devotion provided me with the drive I needed to push through the tough times. I appreciate them for putting up with the baseball lifestyle. I love them all.

# FOREWORD

In late September of 2000, I walked into the visiting clubhouse of Safeco Field in Seattle as a big leaguer for the first time. I was excited, confident, nervous, happy, and scared. As a rookie, first order of business: meet my new teammates. I approached every guy with my standard, yet apparently unimpressive introduction. "Hi...I'm Mike." In return, I was greeted with a couple lukewarm responses. But, this group generally struck me as a bunch of guys with better things to do, utterly oblivious to the new guy with not much to say.

Suddenly (and I can remember this vividly), I found myself in the middle of a warm exchange.

"Hey Mike...I'm Frank Catalanotto, good to meet you."

"Nice meeting you too."

"Congratulations kid....you excited?"

"Yeah, I'm pumped."

"Good for you. If you need anything at all, let me know. Enjoy yourself. Happy for you, buddy."

"Thanks. I appreciate it."

Just like that, I had my first true teammate in the big leagues... Frank Catalanotto.

Since that day Frank, or, "Cat" as he's known to us, has not only been a terrific teammate, but a trusted and loyal friend. I've developed a great admiration for his dedication to family, friends and to the manner in which he approached his job. Throughout my career, I've always had a tendency to gravitate toward players who best exemplified "blue collar" ideals. Players who were talented, but relied on heart. Players who were given a great opportunity, but maximized it through hard work. Players who enjoyed performing at a high level, but took an equal amount of satisfaction in seeing their teammates do the same. I recognized these things in Frank.

The greatest compliment I can give Frank is that he earned everything he received in his career. He developed himself from a young kid out of high school to one of the game's most respected players. He learned to play multiple positions, ran the bases aggressively and intelligently and developed a fantastic approach to hitting. In short, he was a player that you wanted on your team. When guys were hurt, tired, and enduring the late stages of a physically exhausting season, Frank was one of the guys we could depend on to lead with his toughness and grit.

If you're a parent, as I am, I'm sure you're looking for ways to keep your children healthy and happy. This book can serve as a useful guide to teach kids important life lessons through sports. You can learn from the examples set by Frank's parents to be supportive, encouraging, and to teach proper perspective. If you're a young athlete, you can learn about specific parts of the game in which Frank excelled. You will learn to master the fundamentals, condition your mind and body to achieve success, and develop an understanding of proper technique for hitting and fielding. Frank will help you become a better player.

Since the day I met Frank in Seattle, I've valued my friendship with him. He was a fantastic teammate and even better friend. I can only hope I've had as great an impact on him as he's had on me.

Michael Young

Seven Time All-Star (2004–2009, 2011)
Gold Glove Award winner (2008)
2005 American League batting champion
2006 MLB All-Star Game MVP
Marvin Miller Man of the Year (2008, 2011)

# HEART
# &
# HUSTLE

"Love the game. Love the game for the pure joy of accomplishment. Love the game for everything it can teach you about yourself. Love the game for the feeling of belonging to a group endeavoring to do its best. Love the game for being involved in a team whose members can't wait to see you do your best. Love the game for the challenge of working harder than you ever have at something and then harder than that. Love the game because it takes all team members to give it life. Love the game because at its best, the game tradition will include your contributions. Love the game because you belong to a long line of fine athletes who have loved it. It is now your legacy. Love the game so much that you will pass on your love of the game to another athlete who has seen your dedication, your work, your challenges, your triumphs...and then that athlete will, because of you, love the game." ~ Unknown

*I loved baseball at an early age.*

## 1

# A SLOW START

*"I think Little League is wonderful.  It keeps the kids out of the house...and parents off the streets." ~ Yogi Berra*

**"W**hat do you want to be when you grow up, Frankie?" My answer, each of the dozens of times I was asked, was "a baseball player". If given the chance, I would add that I was going to be a New York Yankee.  Following the Yanks as a kid on Long Island, I looked at them as if they were not human.  Even though the 1980s teams had misplaced the luster of the Yankees' dynasty years, they seemed like robots in pinstripes that, at the very least, entertained us and always had the potential to thrill us.

Although I was sure that I wanted to be a Major League Baseball player, I never really stopped to connect the dots from where I was at age nine in Smithtown, New York to the dugout at Yankee Stadium. Just how would someone like me become a Major Leaguer? How would skinny little me become one of those freakish heroes who made it all look so easy?  Rather than spend much time considering the unknown and the improbable, I focused on just playing for fun.

Much of the credit for keeping it fun goes to my parents, Frank and Sharon. Some parents make their kids miserable by pushing them too hard in athletics. Some parents are the other extreme, not involved at all. Mine did everything right. There is no way I can overstate the importance of their support and involvement. And that included the power of positive thinking. "Frankie", they would tell me, "you're going to be a major leaguer one day. You're going to play with the Yankees." My typical response was "Yeah, right" and a laugh. I have never asked them whether they really believed that or wished for it, but it was *my* wish and hearing that they shared in that, or at least made me believe they did, was ultimately a lesson for me in how to be a great parent. There was never any pressure from them to be a baseball player, just support for my ambitions. Playing and practicing baseball was the most fun I could have and, with their support, I pushed myself to be the best player that I could be.

As young as age three or four, my dad took me into our backyard, put a bat in my hand and flipped me ball after ball. I would swing away and every ball I hit, I would run to first base and back, as fast as I could, for another swing. I didn't want it to end and dreaded the inevitable moment, usually when it got dark, that we had to go inside. As I got older, I would go out back and throw a tennis ball off the chimney and practice fielding the unpredictable bounces for hours. Dad worked long days as a Certified Public Accountant and I could hardly wait until he got home each night around six o'clock.

*FRANK, SR.: Early on it was always fun playing baseball with Frank and our other kids. Great enjoyment. I did see that Frank had a special ability when it came to baseball, could see it in the way he swung a bat, caught a baseball, the way he ran and his overall enthusiasm about the game showed up very early. Even if he was all alone outside, throwing the ball against the exterior of the fireplace, he seemed to enjoy it. In fact, we had to drag him in when it got dark and even then, we would make up games. I would sit in my den; our kitchen and den were situated so you could run around from one through the other. When he was three or four*

*years old, he would run into the foyer, through the kitchen, around into the den as I would throw a ball up against the wall. It would come back to me right as he was sliding into "second base" and I was applying the tag. We did it so often, he wore a hole in the carpet.*

Mom, who worked as a secretary for an engineering firm, and Dad would shuttle me from sport to sport, game to game. I was a good athlete, but not the best on my teams. Until eighth grade, I went to a small Christian school that didn't have much of a sports program. My parents decided that if I were to have a chance at getting an athletic scholarship to college, I would have to switch to a large public school and compete with better talent.

It didn't start well. I tried out for the basketball team, but didn't make it. Basketball wasn't my best sport but I knew that I was better than some of the guys who made the team. That was the first time I became aware that pure talent isn't the only factor coaches use in choosing their teams. The basketball coaches didn't know "the new kid" and that worked against me. I was hoping that wouldn't be the case when it came to baseball. Baseball was my passion. I *had* to make the team.

When spring came and it was time for tryouts, I gave it my all. I thought my baseball talents shone through and made some coaches open their eyes. They put me at second base—but only on the freshman team. Some of my classmates were on junior varsity, but maybe because the coaches didn't know me that well, I was left behind. I had a solid year as the freshman team's second baseman, but the next year, while many of my friends were promoted to varsity, I was placed at the junior varsity level.

Well, okay, I thought. Maybe I just wasn't as good as I thought. Maybe my friends were better. When summer came that sophomore year, I was excited to play for the elite summer travel team that my buddies and I were trying out for: the mighty Bayside Yankees. I got cut from that team, too!

Was I disappointed? Of course. But, I wasn't crushed. In fact, it only made me more determined to get better and prove to every coach I played for that I belonged. Plus, I felt that the better I played the more fun I had, and I wanted to have fun. So, I started doing a lot more hitting drills on my own. I bought a Wiffle golf ball, tied a string to it and hung it from the ceiling in our basement. I would take a broomstick handle —a bat would have been too easy—and hit that golf ball for hours each day. Just like my mom didn't love that I ruined her carpet in the den, she also didn't care for the constant banging sound the golf ball and broomstick made. But, she didn't stop me. She understood and was proud of my determination to improve at the sport I loved.

*SHARON: You have to instill a healthy self-confidence when they are young. Be interested in what they are interested in. Then, if they go on to do well, respect and honor their ability so they feel good about themselves. In sports, if you aren't well grounded mentally, it is hard to succeed.*

A big moment in my development was when I started getting hitting lessons from Al Mar, a local scout. Once a week we would meet up at a local batting cage and he would help me with my swing, stance, hands and approach. I mixed in weightlifting and running and, sure enough, the better I got the more fun I had. I wasn't even focusing on getting a scholarship or getting drafted, I was just busy having fun.

I was ready for my senior year in high school, but my journey to the dugout at Yankee Stadium was about to hit a few more bumps in the road.

# *Sports*

## The Smithtown News

# *Hear Him Roar!*

# East Grad Inks Name On Tigers Contract

**MAJOR LEAGUE PROSPECT:** Recent Smithtown East graduate Frank Catalanotto Jr. inked his name Friday night on a professional baseball contract with the Detroit Tigers. On hand for the signing were (l. to r.) his father, Frank Catalanotto Sr., sister Christa, brother Michael, Detroit scout Ramon Pena, and his mother Sharon Catalanotto.

*Photo by Pat Colombraro*

# HUSTLE

*"I don't think I can play any other way but all out. I enjoy the game so much because I'm putting so much into it." ~ George Brett*

I n my senior year of high school, we had an excellent varsity baseball team. Major league scouts would attend our games, but not to watch me. We had three players who were considered professional baseball prospects: catcher Mike Ciminiello, pitcher John Forneiro and first baseman/pitcher Steve Reduto. These guys were great and received a lot of attention. I wasn't jealous, but I definitely wanted to make someone notice me. When I asked my dad what I had to do to get noticed, he said, "Always hustle on and off the field, around the bases, whenever you have the chance. Just hustle! That's the way to stand out, Frankie. When everyone else is lollygagging it, you hustle".

*FRANK, SR.: I remember telling him that hustle means running out every hit no matter where you hit it, to the infield or to the gap, you always play the game hard. For the most part I didn't have to push Frank because it was innate in him. Anything that he did, any sport, any game he played he would play it to win. I told the kids...play the game to win but it's important to know how to lose. That's one of the attributes Frankie had; he was able to lose with dignity. That really stood out when we watched him.*

*SHARON: You learn things from losing. Sometimes more than you learn by winning.*

Of all the great advice my dad has given me over the years hustling may have been the most important. I ran from the dugout and to the dugout. Whenever I was on the field, I was hustling. But as my senior season was nearing its end, it seemed as if my dad's advice wasn't working. The other players were still getting all of the attention. That didn't stop me, though. In fact, I hustled even harder. Finally, a local scout, Larry Izzo, approached me and said, "You know Frank, all these scouts are here to see these other guys but I think you're the player here that we need to keep an eye on". Sweeter words had never been spoken to me.

*LARRY IZZO: I almost missed Frank. I was scouting for the Major League Scouting Bureau and all twenty-eight (at that time) clubs got my report. Smithtown East had a very good team, but the kids getting scouts' attention were two pitchers and a catcher. Those are always the positions scouts see standing out right away. Frank was at second base and although I could see he played hard and hustled, he was fairly well hidden there. I couldn't see whether he had an arm because all he did was flip the ball to first base.*

*Toward the middle of the season, I decided to go back and take a closer look at him. He was okay at second base, but when he got to the plate, I saw that he had a good stance, a good swing and unlike most hitters that age, he used the whole field. He did the things that good hitters do. And, he hit left-handed, a big plus. One other thing that surprised me was how fast he was. He was 4.2 to first base, which was the MLB average. Frank could run. So, I started to think that I had something there.*

*What got Frank to the big leagues was his bat. And, he had one other thing that every scout searches for: makeup, which is the word scouts use to measure the personal qualities of a player. He had great makeup, came from a solid, supportive family. He played the game the right way. He hustled. He respected his coaches and umpires. He was a kid that you'd pull for because of his makeup. But, you didn't have to because he was a major league hitter. (See Larry's report on the next page.)*

Larry told me that he noticed my passion for the game and the way I always hustled even if I hit the ball right back to the pitcher. He

## M.L.S.B. FREE AGENT REPORT

PLAYER _Catalanotto_ ___Frank___ ___John___ OFP # _44.5_
last / first / middle

Date of Birth _4-27-74_ Ht. _5'11_ Wt. _165_ Bats _L_ Throws _R_ Pos. _2B_

School/Team _Smithtown East HS._ City _St. James_ State _N.Y._

School Type _HS_ (HS, JC, 4YR) Stat _____ (5YR, DO, NS) Grad Date _6-92_ Class _Sr._

Comments _____

Curr Add _____ Perm Add _Same_
(if different)

City/St _Smithtown, N.Y._ City/St _____

Zip _11787_ Telephone _____ Zip _____ Telephone _____

Scout _Larry Izzo_ Report Type _INT_ (INT, CHG) Report Date _5-6-92_

Games _3_ Inn. _21_ Eye Test _no_ Comments _eye test will follow._

A.M.I. _no_ Date Mailed _____ Filmed _no_ Comments _____

| RATING KEY | NON-PITCHERS | | Pres. | Fut. | PITCHERS | Pres. | Fut. | USE WORD DESCRIPTION |
|---|---|---|---|---|---|---|---|---|
| 8—Outstanding | Hitting Ability | ★ | 4 | 66 | Fast Ball | ★ | | Habits _good_ |
| 7—Very Good | Power | ★ | 3 | 4 | F.B. Movement | | | Dedication _good_ |
| 6—Above Average | Running Speed | ★ | 4 | 4 | Curve | ★ | | Agility _fc_ |
| 5—Average | Base Running | | 5 | 5 | Control | | | Aptitude _good_ |
| 4—Below Average | Arm Strength | ★ | 3 | 4 | Change of Pace | | | Phys Maturity _good_ |
| 3—Well Below Average | Arm Accuracy | | 4 | 5 | Slider | ★ | | Emot. Maturity _good_ |
| 2—Poor | Fielding | ★ | 4 | 5 | Other | ★ | | |
| Use One Grade | Range | | 4 | 5 | Poise | | | Date eligible |
| Grade On Major | Baseball Instinct | | 5 | 5 | Baseball Instinct | | | _6-92_ |
| League Standards | Aggressiveness | | 5 | 5 | Aggressiveness | | | Worth Figure |
| Not Amateur | Pull ___ Str. Away _X_ Opp. Field ___ | | | | Arm Action ___ Delivery ___ | | | _8-11_ |

### Physical Description
Shade above avg height. Physically very young. Still maturing.
Lots to go.

### Gls/Contacts _Yes_ Injs/Medical Update
Wears contacts. As of this report no known injuries.

### Abilities
Excellent hitting mechanics. Makes consistent contact. Project
above avg hitter. Shows soft hands, future avg fielder. Runs well
once under way. Adaquate arm strength for pos.

### Weaknesses
Still lacking needed strength. Lacks pop and needed arm
strength.

### Summation and Signability
Young man just starting to come into his own. Good hitting prospect
with good eye hand contact. Shows adaquate range and soft hands
needed for pos. Has problem out of box but once under way runs well.

liked the way I swung the bat and said I was very "projectable", which is "scout talk" meaning I showed promise. He saw skills that he thought could get me into professional baseball. Over the course of the final month leading up to the Major League Baseball Draft I had greatly improved my play and turned some heads.

Word must have traveled fast because I received a call from Ramon Pena, a Detroit Tigers scout who said he wanted to see me play. He was coming from New York City. It was fairly simple to tell when the scouts showed up at our games, they tend to stand out with their clipboards and stopwatches. While I didn't know what Ramon looked like, I didn't see a new face in the crowd before the game. After a couple of innings, I scanned the crowd again and still didn't notice anyone new. I started to fear that he may have changed his mind. We were beating the other team badly and my coach pulled me out of the game in the fourth inning. As I took my seat on the bench, I was told that Ramon had still not arrived. I was disappointed.

However, my luck soon changed. In the fifth inning of a seven inning game, I noticed a black vehicle with tinted windows driving toward our field. It came to a stop and I waited for the door to open. It seemed like forever, but the door eventually opened and out stepped Ramon Pena. He had gotten lost. After the game he asked if he could put me through a workout on the field. Of course, I agreed. He brought a friend to throw batting practice. I stepped up to the plate, but right before we started Ramon walked up to me and took the aluminum bat out of my hands and handed me a wood bat. I had never hit with a wood bat! It felt so heavy, and I was nervous to have to use it for the first time in front of a pro scout. All eyes were on me. Many of the adults and some of my teammates stayed around for the workout. I got the hang of the wood bat quickly and the session went well. Next would be ground balls. I started to run out to second base but Ramon stopped me halfway and said, "Go to shortstop. We want to see your arm". Uh-oh. Shortstop? I hadn't had to make the long throw in years. Fortunately, I got through it with no problem. After fielding, they timed me running sprints. I ran as hard and fast as I could and that was the end of the workout. I was happy with how I did and felt like I had made a good impression. Ramon approached my dad and me and said, "You should hear from me Monday". Monday was the first day of the 1992 MLB Amateur Draft. I couldn't believe it. It was happening so fast! I didn't want to get my hopes up because I knew if I expected to get drafted and it didn't happen I would be disappointed. I had also heard the horror stories of players who were told by scouts that they would be getting a phone call on draft day and they sat by the phone all day, but the scouts never called. Then the second day of the draft came and went and, again, no phone call. I didn't want that to happen to me.

Monday approached and I told my dad, "They only do the top ten rounds on Monday. There's no way I'm going to get drafted in the top ten rounds."

"Well, don't be disappointed if you don't get a call", he said.

I was so nervous I could barely eat. Sunday night, I hardly slept. Monday morning, I went to school, but nothing there could take my mind off the draft.

That afternoon, shortly after I got home, the phone rang. My stomach was doing flips as I looked at my mom.

She picked up the handset. "Hello?"

Was it the Tigers? Had I been drafted? No. It was my aunt.

Minutes went by and it rang again. This time, it was a friend of my dad's. Finally, one of the times the phone rang, my mom answered and held the receiver toward me.

"Frank, it's for you."

It wasn't the Tigers. It was Al Mar, the local scout who'd given me hitting lessons.

"Frank, I just heard from another scout that you were drafted in the tenth round by the Detroit Tigers. Congratulations!"

I got the chills, I was so excited. I said goodbye and yelled, "Mom, the Tigers took me in the tenth round!" I called my dad and told him. And then, nothing. The Tigers still hadn't called to make it official, but I was pretty sure that Al knew what he was talking about. It was just Mom and me at home. I didn't know what to do with myself. I thought, "Alright, this is the best news ever and I don't have anybody to tell". I wanted to tell my buddies, including a couple of guys who were supposed to get drafted, but they hadn't been called and I didn't want to put a damper on their day. Plus, the Tigers still hadn't called.

I was so antsy and Dad hadn't gotten home yet, so I drove to get gas. My car didn't need gas, but I needed to do something. I was so excited. Finally, later in the evening, the Tigers called and told me that I had been drafted.

As for the other guys on my high school team who the scouts had spent so much time on all season: they weren't drafted. No one in school could understand how I got drafted and those guys didn't. Frankly, I couldn't either. It was kind of awkward when I saw them, but they were happy for me.

Now, I had a decision on my hands. I had a scholarship to play baseball at Seton Hall in New Jersey. Do I go to school like the rest of my friends or do I try to live out my childhood dream? My parents would support either decision I made. My dad was leaning toward signing. Mom wanted me to go to college.

*SHARON: I was leaning that way because I never had the opportunity to go to college. My husband was leaning towards baseball because that was always his dream. So we both had to realize it wasn't about us and that it was Frankie's decision.*

Everyday, the three of us would talk about the pros and cons of each. Ramon Pena came to the house a couple of times to try to convince me to sign. The Tigers were offering $25,000. That was my first taste of the "business" of baseball. He was telling me what I wanted to hear—but didn't quite believe: that I'd be in the big leagues within three years. At some level, I probably knew better, but it sure sounded good at the time. He was very convincing and made it sound like going to college would be a waste of my talent. And, what if I got hurt playing college ball? This great opportunity, "the one you've dreamed of your whole life, Frankie", would be gone and I would live a life of regret.

*FRANK, SR.: I think it all came down to posing the question: Why do you want to go to college? His answer was to play baseball and to get signed to a big league team. I think we had our answer at that point, but we were going back and forth. The college coach called us and told us he needed to go to college and that they were going to make him the number*

**SIGNED, SEALED:** Frank Catalanotto is in the Tiger mode already as his son, Frank Jr. (l.), signs a pro contract with the Detroit Tigers. Tiger scout Ramon Pena joined the Catalanotto family at their Smithtown L.I. home Friday night for a celebration.
**CARMINE DONOFRIO** DAILY NEWS

# Yankee fan gets deal from Tigers

*one pick in a few years. Of course, the scout who signed him said, "What? Are you crazy? We're going to give him the opportunity to make it to the big leagues. If it doesn't work out, we'll pay for his education". It was very tough and at one point Frank said, "Listen, I don't want to think about it for a week or so. I'm going to Cooperstown to play ball in a tournament with my friends". He did and after a game we brought him to the hotel room and told him we needed to let the coach and scout know. He made the decision there...I want to give baseball a shot. He left the room and my wife started to cry. The tears may have been the realization that she was losing her little boy. He was going away to play minor league baseball.*

In addition to being talent evaluators, scouts are also paid to be salesmen. They promise you the world and make you believe that you're better than you actually are, or have proven you are. That is, until you ask for a larger signing bonus. Only then do they start to discuss your inabilities. It was the first time I had been treated like a piece of property. It was as if I was being haggled over like a used car. Ramon was the buyer and he really wanted this shiny new model with low miles, but his job was to buy low, and if that meant pointing out a fleck of rust on a wheel well or a dent in a fender, so be it.

*BARBARA CATALANOTTO: When Frank was drafted, people around Smithtown were excited, but many thought the chances of him making it were slim to none. We'd only been dating six months at the time he was making his draft/college decision so I didn't feel that I could encourage him one way or the other. He really deliberated about it and thought it out. I think it took him a month to six weeks to think about it. It wasn't a rash decision. His dad is so realistic, practical and grounded. They discussed all the options and his parents told him if baseball didn't work out, he could go to college. I thought at the time that he'd made the right choice.*

It was frustrating but money wasn't the biggest factor for my parents and me. It was more about making the right choice. We didn't want to have any regrets. Pulling me the opposite way from Ramon was the head coach at Seton Hall, who said the right decision was to come play for him and he would help me become a higher round pick. My draft advisor, who became my agent after I turned pro, was telling me that I should probably go to school because I wasn't ready for professional baseball and the punishing lifestyle that low-level minor leaguers are subjected to.

*ALAN NERO, AGENT, OCTAGON (then CSMG): In our business, most of our clients fail. And because we view our clients as family and want them to not only make a lot of money, but also be prepared for life's curve balls, we place a high value on education. Now, if Frank had been drafted in the first round where the signing bonus would have made him a millionaire, the decision would have been easier. But, by the tenth round, there were over two hundred fifty players the major league clubs chose instead of Frank. The odds of a tenth rounder making it to the big leagues and staying there for more than a cup of coffee are really slim. I never doubted Frank's baseball ability, I just thought his chances of success would be better after a few years in college, plus he'd have most of his degree work done to prepare him for life after baseball. Of course, I am thrilled with how his career played out and it's been a privilege to be his agent.*

All of them were probably right. Getting a good education was very important to me and I agonized over the decision for a month. But when the Tigers put a clause in the contract that said they would pay for most of my college education if I decided to quit baseball, my mind was made up. That made my decision easier. I had to give it a shot because I may never have gotten that opportunity again.

With the gift of 20-20 hindsight, I made the right choice. But, I was lucky and I often tell parents who want my opinion that I think their sons should go to college. Coming up through the minors, I saw hundreds of guys who signed out of high school and never made it beyond AA or AAA. They may have spent several years trying, but never even got a "cup of coffee". Some even called it quits, or were released, from A ball. What often happens is a guy will spend ten years in the minors, meet a girl along the way, start a family and when he washes out he has to find a job. Even though he may have a College Scholarship Plan from Major League Baseball, he's too busy trying to feed his family to take advantage of it. There is no one-size-fits-all answer, but if you're playing the odds, college is the way to go.

*CHRISTA CATALANOTTO OLSON (SISTER): I was in college at the time, but I was home for the signing party. I think I was leaning towards him going pro. I loved college but I thought, what's the harm in signing? Of course, he could have gotten stuck in the minor leagues for ten years and gone nowhere, but I thought it was definitely a once in a lifetime opportu-*

nity that he shouldn't pass up. Frank was kind of living our dad's dream. Dad had to step back and really think about it but he (and our mom) did a great job trying to guide him in the right direction. It was a trying time for everyone knowing that this meant that Frankie would be away from our family. When the decision was made, we had a big signing party, and the journey began!

Ramon Pena came to the house for the party and I signed the contract in front of family and friends. After playing in the All-Long Island game at Yankee Stadium—a game that the Tigers were not happy I played in because they considered me their property and didn't want me to get injured—I was off to the Tigers' rookie league affiliate in Bristol, Tennessee.

*The Smithtown News - June 18, 1992 - Page 27*

## SPORTS
# Detroit Tigers Pick East Senior!

**By Tony Bellissimo**

Smithtown East senior Frank Catalanotto had his childhood dream become a reality on June 1.

Catalanotto, an All-League second baseman on the Indians varsity baseball club, was drafted that day in the 10th round of the Major League Baseball Draft by the Detroit Tigers.

"My entire family and all my friends are excited for me," said Catalanotto, who was scouted on numerous occasions by the Tigers, Milwaukee Brewers and Toronto Blue Jays. "Getting picked in the top ten rounds is nice, but it's created a lot of decision making."

Catalanotto batted .448 this spring with five homers, 28 runs scored and 14 stolen bases. He committed only one fielding error in two seasons in helping East to a combined 39-8 mark.

"He's the best second baseman I've ever coached," Smithtown East coach Al Chandler said of Catalanotto. "He got physically stronger after his junior year and that made a big difference in his game, especially offensively," Chandler explained.

After hitting a highly respectable .375 last season, Catalanotto improved by 73 points.

"The representatives from Detroit said they drafted me for my defense, hustle and speed," he said.

Having drafted him, the Tigers own the rights to Catalanotto for five years, unless he elects to attend Seton Hall University this coming fall. Contract negotiations between the two parties are underway. If he signs to play professionally, Catalanotto will be promptly assigned to the Rookie League in Virginia and forfeit his collegiate baseball eligibility.

"I have a full scholarship waiting for me at Seton Hall. But I can't say I'm leaning a particular way right now because I'm still undecided," Catalanotto explained.

The two-year varsity player also noted that if he were selected a few rounds earlier, or later, his decision would be easier. He was the 250th player selected in the draft overall. "It's a tough round to have been chosen," he said of the tenth. "I should be making a decision in the next week or two."

For now, Catalanotto is content playing summer ball with his friends and former teammates on the Smithtown Cardinals.

"He's a great kid and a great leader," noted Chandler. "I'm confident that he'll be successful no matter which road he decides to choose."

**BIG LEAGUE PROSPECT:** Smithtown East second baseman Frank Catalanotto was selected in the 10th round of the Major League Baseball Draft by the Detroit Tigers on June 1. The senior now must choose between Rookie ball in Virginia or a full scholarship to attend Seton Hall University.    *Photo by Pat Colombraro*

*Turning two in Rookie Ball at Bristol.*

# 3

# LIFE IN THE MINORS

*"One of the beautiful things about baseball is that every once in a while you come into a situation where you want to, and where you have to, reach down and prove something." ~ Nolan Ryan*

My first season in the minor leagues did not go as well as I had planned. I thought I was going to Bristol to be the starting second baseman. However, I arrived to an older player, Tim Thomas, batting third and playing second base everyday. Tim was signed by the Tigers out of college and was having a good start to his season. So, I sat a lot. That was quite a brush back for a guy who thought that the team was anxiously awaiting my arrival and would exhibit the appropriate amount of enthusiasm when I showed up. But there wasn't a lot of fanfare on the bench, and the few times I got in the lineup, I had trouble adjusting to the wood bat. Wood bats aren't as forgiving as aluminum bats. The sweet spot on wood bats is much smaller, which gives you less margin for error. They also weigh a lot more. I felt like I was hitting with a tree trunk. In my rookie season, I had fifty-eight plate appearances and batted .200 with eight walks and eight strikeouts.

Another adjustment involved being away from home. Ramon

Pena, the scout who drafted me, had painted a much better picture of the minor league lifestyle than I saw. I was an eighteen-year-old kid, living in a strange town, in an apartment, with three other guys. Breakfast was fast food. Lunch was fast food. For variety, I had fast food for dinner. And I had to learn how to do my own laundry.

*SHARON: We drove Frankie to Bristol, Tennessee. We were worried about the things parents worry about and just hoped he would be safe. But, he met up with the nicest players. It seems like wherever he went he hung with the crème of the crop. Eventually, we understood that he would choose the right path. We were more worried that he would get hurt and may not get the right medical care. Would his housing be safe? Would he eat good food? But when he picked roommates, they seemed to be the guys who knew how to cook.*

My mom and dad had done pretty much everything for me up until Bristol, and they paid for it, too. I was making the standard rookie pay of $850 per month. (By 2011, Major League Baseball had mandated that clubs raise Rookie Ball pay to $1000, still not within a long fly ball of the poverty level.) Out of that $850, which was about $275 every two weeks after taxes, I had to pay rent, utilities, food and other necessities. More often than not, my paychecks were spent well before the next one came. When we went on the road, each of us got a whopping $9 per day for meal money. That might cover a couple of meals at McDonald's or Taco Bell, but forget about anything more substantial. Eventually my roommate and I figured out a pretty good system. Before we would go on long road trips, we would pack a cooler with sandwich meat, peanut butter and jelly, bread and drinks. For some variety, and a "hot" meal, after a lot of games we would buy the leftover hot dogs from the concession stands at ballparks for around fifty cents each. We were definitely not eating like kings. That changed, for a day or two, when my mom and dad would visit. They would take me out for some good meals at restaurants I couldn't afford on my own. Dad would always slip me a wad of money before they returned home.

In our cramped, un-air-conditioned clubhouse, we had to compete for space with roaches and mice. Whenever we walked in after a road trip, mice would scurry behind the lockers. We took showers in dirty water up to our ankles because the drains were clogged. In the bathroom, the single toilet stall didn't have a door so everyone could see you do your business. I was miserable.

I began second-guessing my decision to go pro. My friends who had gone to college were telling me how great it was and how much they were partying. I felt like I was missing out. When September came and the season ended, I knew I had to decide if pro baseball was really what I wanted to do. First, though, I would have to go to the Tigers' Instructional League in Lakeland, Florida. Instructional League was for guys the organization wanted to look at more closely. It started in mid-September and went until November. There, I met Larry Parrish, the roving minor league hitting instructor. He played for fifteen years in the Major Leagues and not only knew a lot about the game, he knew how to teach it.

*LARRY PARRISH: Frank was just a skinny little high school kid when I saw him in September of that first year. He was so weak and overwhelmed by the Florida heat and humidity that he couldn't take more than four grounders without getting winded. The Tigers' farm director didn't have any patience for this tenth-rounder who wasn't that great on defense and didn't show that he could hit very well in his first shortened season. He wanted to release him. We had a meeting where a friend of mine in the front office, Joe McDonald, told the farm director, "We don't release a high school kid after the first year. He needs to have time." Then, I spoke up for Frank. I said, "Yes, he's weak and needs to get stronger, but his hand-eye coordination is great. You can't teach that. He's got a God-given gift. He never misses if he swings at it. It may not go very far, but he can hit from the top of his cap to his shoestrings." Well, the farm director got mad because he didn't like Frank. So, he said, "I'll tell you what. You've got him, but you don't work with him until you're done with all the other guys."*

Had it not been for Larry, my life may have taken a far different path. "L.P.", as he was known, made me his project. He took me under his wing and worked with me day and night. I knew that I was on thin ice with the Tigers and that motivated me. I learned a lot in my short time with Larry—things that made me feel more comfortable and confident at the plate. Instructional League days were long and grueling in the early autumn Florida swelter. We were supposed to be on the field for stretching at 8:30 a.m. and rarely finished before 6 p.m. Larry had me show up at 7 a.m. for early work and in the late afternoon and evenings after he was done with all the others, he worked me again. I would go back to the dorm absolutely drained and there were a couple of times that I asked Larry if I could sleep in an extra thirty minutes the next morning. "You can sleep when you're dead," he growled. "See ya at 7 a.m. sharp!"

*LARRY PARRISH: There were times when Frank would be in the batting cage as they were serving food in the dorm and he was missing the evening meal. This was when he was an 18-year-old and he kept that top of the line work ethic all the way through the game. He gave you what he had. Those after-hours sessions gave us a chance to talk about things that he needed to do over the winter to improve, like lifting weights. He came back in the spring (of 1998) a lot stronger. He went back to Bristol and hit .300 and from that time on, he always hit.*

As I was making my way toward the big leagues finding success at each level, it made me realize that you should never let anyone tell you that you can't do something. If they try, work your butt off to prove them wrong.

Even after meeting Larry and feeling better about myself following that rocky first season, I still agonized over whether to chuck it all and go to college. My dad and I talked about it during the off-season and we decided that I should give it another try. I felt that I needed to play a full season from spring training in March until September before making such a major decision.

*SHARON: I don't think he ever would've thrown away his gift. He had hard times and missed important events like weddings and funerals of beloved family members. But he realized he had this gift and to throw it away because it was difficult was just not Frank. He was determined to show that he was grateful and preparing himself and playing hard is just who he is.*

*FRANK, SR.: Frank had great determination. He was always trying his best. He gave one hundred percent of himself and always had a good attitude. He just loved the game of baseball.*

Spring Training, 1993 started in the beginning of March at Tigertown in Lakeland, Florida. That was the name of the complex built on a World War II airbase where fighter pilots were trained. It included a dormitory that all of the minor leaguers had to temporarily call home: Fetzer Hall, a three-story concrete dormitory built in 1971. It looked more like a prison cell block than a temporary home to prized athletes, some of whom had been paid hundreds of thousands of dollars before they played an inning of baseball for the Tigers. There were two guys to a room and there was no choosing your roommate. Players came from all over the world and generally ranged in age from seventeen to twenty-two. Many were kids fresh out of high school, while others were college guys from across the country. There were also Dominicans, Puerto Ricans, Mexicans, Canadians and Japanese players and one from Long Island. A lot of them could not speak English. The only thing we had in common was baseball.

We had a cafeteria and a game room in a nearby building. Curfew was 11 p.m. although guys often missed it and snuck in through windows late at night. Those who were caught repeatedly would sometimes get a one-way ticket back home. When you are in the low minor leagues and not a top prospect, the teams didn't need much of a reason to release you. I've even seen prospects who were troublemakers released just so they didn't bring anyone else down. As I look back, we had some great times in that dorm. A lot of funny memories, including the old guy stationed at the front door who may have been there since it was built. None of the rooms had phones, so whenever a parent or girlfriend called, he would page us over a loud speaker. The sound of his voice would echo through the hallways. "Frank Caff-uh-luh-netti, Frank Caff-uh-luh-netti, telephone call." A lot of people have butchered my name, but that one took the cake.

The travel, which Ramon had made sound exciting, was brutal. Many of our games were hundreds of miles away, and we traveled by bus; crowded, uncomfortable buses. Trips were often thirteen or fourteen hours long. The bus was packed so no one had their own seat. It was often so hot that guys would strip down to their underwear just to try to get comfortable. Passing the time included doing crossword puzzles, listening to our headphones or playing cards. Every now and then there would be a fight on the bus, usually about someone playing his music too loud or being inconsiderate in some other way. Guys would line the aisle with towels so they could lie down and sleep. Others, those who were small enough, would go up top in the luggage racks to sleep. Anyway you tried it, sleep wasn't easy nor very comfortable.

Those bus rides are probably the major reason why I have back problems today. I remember one trip when the bus broke down out in the middle of nowhere. It was too hot to stay in the bus, so we all got off and hung out along the side of the highway for hours in one hundred degree heat waiting for a mechanic to come. After he realized that he couldn't fix it, another bus was sent out to pick us up and take us to the game. By the time we finally got on the road again, there was no way we were going to make it in time for the 6 p.m. first pitch, so our general manager asked the opposing team if they would wait for us. They agreed and when we got off the bus at almost 9 p.m., we had only enough time to put on our uniforms and walk into the dugout before the ump yelled, "Play ball!" There was no batting practice, no loosening up. We were stiff as boards and starving—we didn't have time to stop for dinner. Another time, our uniforms somehow didn't make it on the bus with us on a road trip. When we got to the field, all we had were our workout clothes, tee shirts and shorts. That's how we played the game.

Even when everything else went right, there were other problems. The hotels were nearly always terrible with plumbing problems and lumpy, hard mattresses that made your body ache. Most of the clubhouses were appalling and must have been in violation of nearly every health code in the books. Fields were atrocious, worse than nearly every field I had played on since Little League. Every grounder was a bad hop. (Of course, right after I got to the major leagues it seemed that most of the minor league parks were renovated and I'm told that they're now beautiful.) And, to top it off, the weather was nearly always extremely hot and humid; thick, wet air that made it difficult to catch your breath. And the reward for all of that? A paycheck that didn't cover expenses. My trek through the minor leagues was bumpy, but I wouldn't change a thing. The ups and downs are what helped make me the player and the person I became.

Living with three or four other guys in a cramped apartment could get annoying at times but we all made the best of it. Out of sheer boredom, I guess, we played many pranks on each other. When one of the guys would be out at night, we would put cellophane on the toilet. Usually, if a guy was out late, it meant he'd been drinking, so the first thing he did when he got home was rush to the bathroom, only to have that see-through barrier cause the expected mess. One of my roomies who I had pranked got me back good. While I was gone, he sprinkled a bottle of talcum powder on my white bed sheets. When I hopped in bed, I was covered in a cloud of powder. I never saw the powder but in hindsight I should have known by the powdery smell of the room that something was up. You always had to be ready for retaliation. Teaming up with a guy was always a good way to make sure you wouldn't get it from him. Pitcher Scott Norman and I decided to start a water war. We put a cup of water on top of the door to our other two roommates' room. When they opened the door to go in they'd get a head full of water. That progressed to buckets of water that were rigged with rope on an elaborate pulley system. We created a trip wire that would cause the bucket to tip over and drench the unlucky guy who was walking up the stairs. No one was safe and you always had to watch where you were walking. Sure, sometimes it started fights but it was all in good fun and no one got hurt.

After my short season in rookie ball in 1992, the Tigers sent me back in 1993. I was more comfortable and it went more like I expected my first season to go. The wood bats no longer felt like logs and I adapted to the minor league lifestyle. In two hundred-twenty plate appearances, I hit .307.

*LARRY PARRISH: Going back to Bristol gave him a chance to grow up a little bit. The thing about Frank was that he was so coachable. He'd listen, he'd try things. I think that had a lot to do with the way he was raised. I saw that a lot in the minor leagues. Kids who came from supportive families were more likely to try things, like changing their swing. Frank understood constructive criticism and that I was just trying to help him. Some other kids, a lot of times when you tried to correct them they felt that you weren't trying to help, you were just being critical. Throughout his early years, whatever you told Frank he needed to work on or should try, he did it. That continued through his major league years.*

In 1994, while playing with the Fayetteville Generals in Low A (one level above Rookie League), I had over 500 plate appearances for the first time, batted .325 and made the All-Star team. I was leading the league in batting for most of the season, but with just a couple of days left, Ben Boulware of the Hickory Crawdads collected just enough plate appearances to qualify for the batting title. He beat me by a few points, but I felt like I had put myself on the map and was very happy with my season. Apparently, the Tigers were too. In 1995, they sent me to AA

Jacksonville, skipping High A in Lakeland.

The biggest change as you move up from class to class is the pitching. For the first time, I was consistently seeing breaking balls in 2-0, 3-0, or 3-1 situations. I had a tough time making the adjustment. Time after time, I came up empty and felt like I had no luck. I couldn't get anything going. It was a frustrating season and my average dropped back to .226 but, once again, I was learning from my struggles. I learned that baseball isn't always fair and that I had to be able to separate games from games and at-bats from at-bats. I learned that I needed to just relax. I learned the importance of focus. Too often, I would be thinking about what happened at the plate and not focusing on the matter at hand. I would take my at-bats into the field with me and lose focus on defense. Those lessons, as difficult as they seemed at the time, helped me accept failure more easily and may have helped shape my career.

# 4

# "MOM, DAD...I'M GOING TO THE SHOW!"

*"It was all I lived for, to play baseball." ~ Mickey Mantle*

You may have noticed a pattern in these first few chapters. I didn't make junior varsity as a high school freshman. I didn't make varsity as a sophomore. And, in the pros, I repeated a level more than once. It was hard for me because as a competitor I wanted to move up every year regardless of how I did. I did not want to be seen by friends back home as struggling or failing. But I had to swallow my New York pride. During my second season in Bristol I learned from my rookie mistakes and got better. My second year at AA in Jacksonville allowed me to make adjustments and gain confidence. It helped me see that my hard work was paying off. I was able to learn from my failures and was able to conquer the level before moving on. It was the right path for me.

After repeating AA, I headed for AAA Toledo in 1997 and I knew I was close to making my dream come true; only fifty-two miles separated Toledo and Tiger Stadium. I got off to a good start, made the All-Star team and started hearing rumors that I might be called up to the big team when the minor league season was over. On September 1st my manager Gene Roof called me into his office. I had a feeling it was going to be a good conversation, and sure enough, it was. Finally, my dream had come true! The first thing I did was call my mom and dad to tell them the good news.

I had always imagined how gratifying it would be to be able to make that phone call. It was a proud moment for me, and I had long planned what I would say. Years earlier, there was a television commercial for a phone company that I had loved and kept in the back of my mind. It was pouring rain outside a baseball stadium and a minor league umpire, soaked to the bone, scrambled into a phone booth, put his coins in the payphone and dialed. When there was an answer, he said, "Mom, Dad...I'm goin' to the show!" That was such a cool commercial. I decided that if I ever had the chance to make that call, I would use those same words.

*FRANK, SR.: The first thing out of his mouth was..."Mom, Dad...I'm goin' to the show!" That was a thrill and a half.*

*SHARON: That call was just amazing for all of us; you could hear the excitement in his voice. Frank and I just rejoiced for hours. We were so happy for him. I felt that our prayers were answered. It was so nice to see his goal achieved after he worked so hard for it. We were extremely proud and couldn't wait to call everybody. Even a week in the big leagues would give him the opportunity to know what it was like. Who ever knew it would be fourteen years?*

*FRANK, SR.: To know that after all of the hard work he put in to get to this point...Just to make it to the big leagues...it was so exciting and I couldn't wait to get off the phone to call Christa, Michael and our other relatives and friends to tell them.*

The next day, I flew to Atlanta where the Tigers had an interleague series with the Braves. When I walked on the field for batting practice I flashed back to when my dad took me to Yankee Stadium as a kid. I breathed in the familiar smells of fresh-cut grass, hot dogs and pretzels. Atlanta had an organ player, just like at Yankee Stadium. I looked across the field and saw Chipper Jones, Fred McGriff, John Smoltz and Greg Maddux. I was not only in awe of them, but of being at the same playing level. Some guys get to the major leagues and automatically think they are great players and that they belong there. Not me. I kept thinking, "Am I dreaming? I can't believe I've done it!" It was surreal.

As happy as I was to be there, I was shaking in my boots, or cleats, I should say. I was thinking, "If I have to play today, how am I going to do this?" I had never played in front of so many people. In the minor leagues, we had maybe 2,000 people in the stands, tops. That day, there were 36,556 fans. I wanted to make a good impression, and while I had a great season at AAA, I didn't know how my skills would translate to the big leagues. Was I good enough to be there? There was a lot of doubt and anxiety and I remember being about as nervous as I had every been when manager Buddy Bell put me in to pinch-hit for Mike Myers. There should have been no pressure because we were leading 12-3. Stepping into the on-deck circle, I felt as though my entire body was filled with concrete. I didn't want to screw up; it was a terrible feeling. I remember thinking, "There's no way I can deal with this stress every single day!" I was trying to play it cool, like it was a piece of cake, so maybe no one realized how scared I was. There were two outs, nobody on. Chad Fox, a righty, was the pitcher. I swung and missed at one pitch, but the other four pitches were balls. My first big league appearance was a walk.

After the game when the bus let us off at the hotel, I picked up my luggage and took it to my room. Later, one of the veterans grabbed me and said, "Don't ever let me see you carry your bags again. This is the big leagues. You have a bellman take your bags".

Major league travel is first-rate all the way. A bus takes you from the ballpark right to the plane, usually a private jet with big, first-class type seats throughout. You never have to wait in a concourse or in long security lines.

*BARBARA: Traveling as a family with Frank in the last few years had some funny moments, because all of that airport security stuff was for-*

*eign to him—let alone going through it with four little girls. Little girls just take a long time, getting their coats off, their boots off, and then their coats and boots back on again. Poor Frank would get so impatient, we'd just tell him to go ahead to the gate and we'd meet him there. I joked with him how spoiled he'd gotten, that it'll be good for him to have to fly coach.*

Every couple of hours during my first few days with Detroit, someone was coming up to me and giving me money. "This is your meal money." "Here's your hotel money". I remember calling my dad and telling him that everybody was throwing money at me. Suddenly, there were people doing things for me. When I got to the ballpark, there was a guy at the clubhouse to shine my shoes. I never had to worry about anything. I never had to go the store if I needed something. Whatever it was, a guy from the clubhouse staff would take care of it and, the next thing I knew, it'd be in my locker. Even my personal laundry and dry cleaning was taken care of if I wanted. When I traveled, I didn't have to carry anything other than what I wanted to have with me on the plane. And there were no more crummy motels. I stayed at the best hotels in every city. It was a different world.

When people ask me if it was what I had imagined, I tell them it was so much more and so much better than anything I could have dreamed. That includes the food. In the minor leagues, when we arrived at the park, the clubby gave us peanut butter and jelly sandwiches. For dinner, just before the game, we got peanut butter and jelly sandwiches. Sometimes, a clubhouse would have cold cuts, usually turkey and ham. If we were lucky we would get pizza, but PB&J sandwiches were the norm. In the big leagues, we were eating spreads from Outback, P.F. Chang's, Cracker Barrel, the local barbecue joint or other good restaurants that would cater, a different one each night. We had Chinese, Japanese, sushi or even the best local Mexican food. And after the games, we would be starving, so it was nice that there was always great food waiting for us. Many times I could barely wait until the game was over so I could eat.

Our families were treated well, too. The teams always had someone who watched over the families, took them where they needed to go and showed them the places to visit in different cities. In the minor leagues, there was none of that.

*BARBARA:  It was fantastic for families in the major leagues.  Most ball clubs provide a family room and within that room there is a nursery and the club hires babysitters for free or a small charge.  In Texas, we had no family around for the first time ever and I was with Morgan all day long, so the ballpark daycare was my break.  We would go to every game and I would drop her off for two hours and spend time with other wives.  And I made such great friends during our time in Texas.  They were genuine, down to earth, not what you see on the TV shows.  Morgan had a great time with the other kids and, of course, didn't realize that it was a big deal.  All her friends' daddies played baseball and were on TV.  She thought everybody's daddy played baseball.  Favorite story: at four, she came home from school and told me her friend Erica's daddy played baseball too.  He was actually a fireman and played softball, but Morgan didn't see a difference.*

Everything changes when you get to the big leagues.  The paycheck, of course, but the lifestyle is so different.  There are perks the family never dreamed of.  It is such a change and takes getting used to.  It is a good getting used to, but it is an adjustment.  Once in a while, there would be a family trip where the wives and kids could fly on the team plane with us.  In the minor leagues, if the families wanted to go on road trips, they always had to find their own way.

*MICHAEL:  I was playing fall baseball at Salisbury College in Maryland when Frank was called up.  It was my first semester and while I loved baseball, I didn't think I would have the same opportunity to turn pro that he had, so I decided to stop playing.  I called my parents and Frank to say that I had a chance few people would ever have; to watch my brother play Major League Baseball, and I was going to want to do it every year, travel to his games as often as possible and experience the lifestyle.  So, I did.  No regrets.  I took off as often as possible; maybe fly to Seattle for a weekend series against the Mariners.  Wherever I met up with him, I got to meet amazing people and Frank always made sure I could get into the clubhouse, hang out with guys and he would take me to dinner with players.  Just great experiences!*

## THE CLUBHOUSE

Sometimes, just looking around the clubhouse, I would have to pinch myself to make sure it was all real. I was in awe, playing with guys I had watched on TV as a kid. It was like some of my baseball cards had come to life. It was a little nerve-wracking at times and I would question whether I belonged. You try to fit in the best you can when you're a young guy, but I was always a bit shy and wasn't very talkative. That actually served me well. Some rookies let it all go to their head, thought they were the toast of the town and were loud and obnoxious. The veterans really got on guys who were full of themselves.

*BARBARA: In the beginning, Frank was enamored by it all. How can you not be? He went from eating at Arby's and staying at bargain motels to dining at Morton's and staying at the Ritz-Carlton. He was only about twenty-three at the time so it is hard to keep a rein on that. He was excited by it and thought it was cool. And it was cool! But because of the way he was raised, he did a good job of putting things into perspective. For a year or two he did feel a little overwhelmed. But you gradually adjust to it without losing a sense of appreciation for it, or forgetting where you came from.*

Baseball has a way of knocking you down a little bit when you start thinking too highly of yourself, or think you're better than you are. When you started to get a big head, before you knew it, you were 0 for your last 20 and now had your tail between your legs. I was always careful to respect the game and the players around me and never think I was bigger than the game. I never got too big for my britches and never forgot where I came from or the people back home.

*SHARON: He married his high school sweetheart and they've maintained relationships with all their old friends. He still plays cards with his high school friends at his house on Monday nights.*

*BARBARA: We met at a summer party before my junior year in high school. I was sixteen and Frank was a year ahead of me at Smithtown East High School. I knew practically nothing about him, not even that he was on the baseball team. He had gorgeous eyes; big, brown eyes with long lashes. If you ask my mom, she'll say that when I came home that night, all I could talk about were his eyes.*

*FRANK, SR.: He's never let any of this go to his head and I give him a lot of credit because if it were me I'd be wearing my major league jersey all the time. You know who got all his sweatshirts and jerseys? Me! Whenever I would meet any of the coaches from the teams he played on, they all praised him and said what a great guy he was. That is a great feeling as a parent. He established The Frank Catalanotto Foundation and raised a lot of money for the Vascular Birthmark Foundation and others. We couldn't be any prouder.*

*BARBARA: Our family and kids helped keep him, and me, pretty ground-ed. If we looked to make an extravagant purchase his parents would look at us like we had six heads! Frank's mom is very practical and would ask, "Really? You really need...?" It made us realize how dumb and unneces-sary that was. We have developed more expensive tastes along the way, but he stayed true to who he was.*

Another thing that changed in the big leagues was the equip-ment. In the minors, other than bats, which the team provided, you were mostly paying for your own shoes, gloves, batting gloves, sliding shorts, etc. Once I got to the big leagues, one of my agents, Scott Pucino, called me and said Nike, Franklin and Louisville Slugger wanted to give me equipment to use and would pay me to use it. Once again, people were throwing money at me! I loved it. Nike gave me a nice contract. It was great being able to order whatever I wanted off the Nike web-site. There was a Niketown in nearly every big league city and I would schedule visits where I was allowed to shop and pick out some cool products, all for free. Believe it or not, that is one of the things I miss the most! I always had brand new Nike shoes and my wife and kids would always be decked out as well.

## THE GRIND

I understand how lucky I was to be able to play a game for a living, and was reminded of it often by people who rightly shook their heads at the crazy amount of money that players were getting. But I worked hard at it and never treated it as just a game. Multiply the ten-hour days by one hundred sixty-two games, add in spring training, which begins in the middle of February, and – if you're lucky – add on another month for playoffs and you have nine full months of ten-hour days. It is a grind and you have to be committed to it, and committed to your team. For those eight or nine months, other than a couple of hours a day, your focus has to be on baseball. It is physically demanding and mentally draining. When Larry Parrish was managing me at Jacksonville, he called me into his office at the end of our AA season.

"Frank, we changed your swing around earlier this year and you had a real good season. How do you feel?"

I said, "Physically, I feel fine, but mentally, I'm drained."

He said, "That's the answer I was hoping for. You should be mentally drained. It's a long season and that tells me you were using your brain."

You owe the team your full dedication and focus. It is a huge commitment. You have to be a strong person to endure the grind and manage not only your job and yourself, but things outside of the game, like what's going on at home. That's why, if you're going to have a family, marry well! I was lucky because a lot of guys got flack from their wives about being on the road so much or going to the ballpark early. Barbara was always great. She knew that family came first with me, but she also knew there would be a lot of times I could not be around. It's a shared sacrifice. It's a partnership and you need a very strong partner. I couldn't have asked for a better one than Barbara.

When you start having children, the big league life gets even more complicated and having a strong partner becomes even more important. Over the years, baseball hasn't looked kindly on players leaving for the births of their children. It was not until the 2007-2011 Collective Bargaining Agreement that baseball added a Family Leave clause. Even though it is a federal law, it is sometimes frowned upon when players have taken advantage of it. You never wanted to be the guy who took too much time away from the team, but I was there for all four of my daughters' births. We got lucky with Morgan. She was born in January. Camdyn was due in April, so Barbara and her doctor arranged for her to be induced on April 2nd, right at the end of spring training and a couple days before opening day. The team allowed me to be gone for two days to be there for her birth. With Karson, Barbara was induced on August 28th and that was scheduled around an off day. Gracyn was born on December 3rd during the off-season.

Players often had to walk a tightrope between team and family, with people on both sides pulling at them. As I am writing this, I understand that there are those who believe family comes first, period. But there's also the argument that baseball is a job and with the window of opportunity to be a major league player so very small for most guys, it is hard to miss a day for anything personal, even a birth or death. Guys counted on each other and even though we wanted our teammate to take time off if he needed to, there were always some players who would gripe about it and make comments if the were gone too long. "When will he be back?" "Why does he need to be gone so long? *He* isn't having the baby!" Players never wanted their commitment to the team to be questioned, but there would always be teammates talking when a guy left.

## PAYDAY

Big paychecks were not among my main reasons for wanting to make it to the big leagues. What drove me were the dreams that started when I was running the bases around our family room. The dreams that grew each time my dad would take me to Yankee Stadium or bring baseball cards home for me. I just wanted to be one of those guys. I ate, breathed and slept baseball. It's all I ever wanted to do and the fact that I was getting paid an enormous amount of money to do what I loved most was like gravy.

In 1997, the average major league salary was $1.3 million, but rookies' paychecks were based on the MLB minimum salary of $150,000. I was up for only twenty-six games that year, so I made approximately $23,000. I was making more in one game than I did in a whole month of playing rookie ball in 1992! In 1998, I made slightly less than the $170,000 minimum, because I spent twenty-eight games at AAA. The next year, I was up the full year and probably made a little more than the $200,000 minimum. In my wildest dreams, I never thought I would get paychecks with all those numbers on them. There was no direct deposit back then, so I would put my paycheck in an envelope and mail it home to Mom and Dad. They opened up a joint account and as the years went by and the checks got bigger, Dad would say, "I don't believe this. You're in your twenties and you've probably made more money than I have in my whole life."

On one hand, the money was motivating because it made me want to work harder to avoid being sent back to the minor leagues where the most I had made was $10,000 a season. But it was also a source of stress because I wanted to prove I was worth all that money. I wanted to prove it to the club, my teammates and the fans. When I would see guys signing three- and four-year deals for $10 million and more, I would think about what a relief it must have been for them because the pressure was off. They were guaranteed more money than they would need for the rest of their lives. When I signed my first three-year deal, my first thought was that I, too, could just relax. I was later surprised to learn that I was under even more pressure. Sure, the financial pressure was gone, but I needed to live up to that paycheck. I put a lot of pressure on myself. Money did not eliminate stress; it just created a different kind.

It also created a little fun later in my career when I was making a lot of money. When I would get a very large check, I would take it to the bank, wait in line for the teller and when I pushed the check and my deposit slip across the counter to her, I would wait for the inevitable wide-eyed expression on her face. The biggest check I did that with was when I got a $2,000,000 buyout of my contract. After taxes, it was $1,400,000. The whole bank kind of shut down. But I always kept the money in perspective. I carried a deep appreciation for all that baseball had given me, including the ability to earn an amazing amount of money while doing what I had always dreamed of.

*My first major league hit.*
*September 9, 1997—Tigers' Stadium*
*Texas vs. Detroit*

# LIFE AS A ROOKIE

*"Every day is a new opportunity. You can build on yesterday's success or put its failures behind and start over again. That's the way life is, with a new game every day, and that's the way baseball is." ~ Bob Feller*

Every baseball player looks forward to his first hit and always loves telling the stories that go along with it. For instance, when it was, where it was, against whom, what the pitch was and whether it was a single, double, triple or a home run.

After my first big league at-bat ended in a walk on September 3, 1997, I got another chance to get my first hit on September 4th against Anaheim at Tiger's Stadium. In the bottom of the ninth, the score was tied at four and I pinch-hit for Marcus Jensen. The pitcher was Mike James. I fouled off a couple, took a ball and on the fifth pitch with the count 1-2, I swung and missed.

My next opportunity to get that first hit didn't come for three more days. I sat on the bench for games two and three against Anaheim. On September 7th, I was starting at second base in place of Damion Easley and was batting second. Jason Dickson was the Angels' pitcher. In my first at-bat, I walked on four pitches. In the bottom of the third, I led off and on the first pitch, I got hold of a fastball and hit a fly ball deep into left field, where Garrett Anderson made an easy catch. My next try at my first major league hit was in the bottom of the fifth, when on two pitches, I connected again: a screaming line drive into right field, where Tim Salmon barely had to move to make the out. After the sixth inning, my day was done. Buddy Bell put Damion Easley in for me at second and I watched as it took fifteen innings for the Angels to beat us, 3 to 2. Three games, two walks, a fly out, a line out and a swinging strike out, but still, no hit. In five plate appearances, I was batting zero.

The next day, September 8th, I sat as we beat the Rangers, 6-2. On Tuesday, September 9, 1997, a cloudy, cool day, the stands were mostly empty as 9,139 fans gathered for an afternoon game against the Rangers. I was on the lineup card again, this time as the designated hitter. I was batting sixth. In the second inning, I dug in at the plate against Rick Helling. No outs, Tony Clark was at third and Travis Fryman was at first. I got a pitch I liked and connected for a single to right field! Tony scored and I had both my first hit and first RBI in one swing. What a relief. The pressure was off and it was such a load off my mind. A lot of guys who are called up in September don't get a hit, are sent back and never get back to the big leagues. In my next trip to the plate against Helling (with whom I became really good friends when I was traded to the Rangers and I reminded him of that hit from time to time), I struck out and in my final at-bat for the day, I flied out, but I was thrilled. I had my hit. I wanted to get that one out of the way.

Standard procedure when a rookie gets his first hit is that the ball will be thrown into the dugout for him to have as a keepsake. Someone from the team will inscribe the details of the hit on the ball. I remember standing at first base, relieved that I had finally gotten it out of the way. I couldn't wait to get the ball so I could give it to my dad because I knew he would want to proudly display it. After the umpire was alerted that it was my first hit, he threw the ball to our dugout. Phil Nevin was standing at the top of the steps with his arms out to make sure the ball was thrown to him and would be in safe hands. Or so I thought. I watched Phil as he turned to the fans in the stands and threw the ball more than ten rows up! I was thinking, "Oh, no! That's my first hit ball!" My heart sank and the whole time I was on the base paths I was wondering if I was ever going to see the prized ball again. After I scored and trotted to the dugout, he played dumb for a minute, but finally said, "No, no, I've got it for you," and plopped it into my hand. I was so relieved, until I saw that he had sloppily scribbled the details, misspelling my name and the pitcher's name! Even the date was wrong. I couldn't believe that he had ruined my ball. I was thinking to myself, "What a dumb ass", but, sure enough, the joke was still on me. The clubhouse already had the real ball and was taking care of it. The next season, after I got my first home run (on May 8, 1998, off Ken Hill of the Angels), Luis Gonzalez took both balls and my bat and had them mounted for me. It is a beautiful piece and I gave it to my dad to put above the mantle. There's a nice shot of it in the center color photo section.

Going from AAA to the big leagues is thrilling, humbling and scary. It's kind of like going from junior high to high school. Maybe you were king of the hill in junior high, but in high school, you were at the bottom of the heap. In the big leagues, there were continual reminders of the rookie's lowly status, including from umpires. As a rookie, I didn't get the benefit of the doubt when it came to the strike zone. Borderline pitches were almost always called strikes. And I didn't dare think of arguing or asking where the pitch was. The umpire didn't want to hear it. Often, even if you looked back at him while you stepped out of the batter's box after a questionable call, he would snap at you and yell, "Get back in the box, Rook!" or, "Don't you even think about showing me up or you are gone!" A lot of the older umpires seemed to have chips on their shoulders for some reason or another. Before long, you figured out who you could talk to and who you should leave alone. I was lucky to be breaking in at the same time that a lot of the umpires I had in AAA were coming up. I had a good rapport with many of them my first year because I tried to keep to myself and not overreact when things didn't go my way.

Once you got to the big leagues, your job just got a lot harder.

Rather than feeling that you're on Easy Street, the pressure was as high as ever because you must now be a productive player against the best players on some of the biggest stages in the world. This was your dream and you wanted to stay there as long as possible. But the odds are stacked against you. Consider these numbers:

Percentage of high school players drafted: .6%[1]

Percentage of high school players who make the big leagues: .015%[1]

Percentage of minor league players who make the big leagues:  17.2%[2]

Percentage of players who play more than three seasons in the big leagues: 10.4%[2]

[1]www.ncaa.org
[2]Based on analysis of 15,660 players drafted in rounds 1-20 from 1965-1995

One of a rookie's biggest fears – next to being sent down – is trying to fit in and prove that he belongs, not only on the field, but in the clubhouse. The biggest mistake you can make is to act like you're hot stuff, to gloat about a good game. The veterans will quickly and gruffly let you know when you're out of line. Rookies need to watch what the veterans do, listen to what they say and learn what not to say and do. Rookies need to learn how to act toward and how to deal with the media. You must watch what you say to the reporters because it can be taken out of context and you may come off sounding arrogant, cocky or even insulting to a teammate or opponent. Boring, typical answers to reporters' post-game questions were usually the best way to go, such as, "I just hope I can keep helping the team win ball games". "God willing, I'll take advantage of the opportunities that the team gives me." "The team has shown confidence in me and I hope to be able to contribute for years to come." Comments like those were safe and never got you in trouble. I know that athletes are often criticized for bland "player speak", but it's the safest way to go if you don't want to incur the wrath of teammates, opponents, your manager, owners, umpires and fans. And if you say something wrong in the heat of the moment, you can't take it back; everything that you say during an interview is on video or audio tape.

Each rookie can count on being a victim of the veteran players' jokes and pranks. The veterans had it happen to them when they were rookies and they make sure the new guys are welcomed appropriately. Usually, the shenanigans are a rite of passage, part of the initiation into an elite club. But, occasionally, they serve as a lesson in how the rookie should behave. One of my teammates told the story of how he was schooled by a veteran. He had been getting on the vet's nerves and didn't take the hint to knock it off. One day, the rookie showed up at the ballpark wearing some expensive, new clothes and changed into his uniform. As we all did, he left his street clothes in his locker where anyone could get to them. When the team went out on the field for batting practice, the veteran stayed behind, got some scissors and cut all of the rookie's clothes to shreds. Everything! Pants, shirt, underwear and socks. When batting practice was over, the rookie returned to a clubhouse full of laughing teammates. He had to wear some of the Tigers' workout gear home. Needless to say, he got the message and he didn't test the veteran anymore. They went on to be great friends and still are today.

Unfortunately, even though I was well liked by the veterans, I didn't escape the pranks, although compared to what happened to some of the other rookies, I guess I got off easy. My most embarrassing moment happened before a game where I joined the rest of the guys in the starting lineup on the field to stretch, run sprints and get loose. While I was getting ready down the third base line I noticed a lot of fans waving, smiling, laughing and pointing in my direction. I was feeling good about myself thinking that these fans loved me and wanted my autograph. I continued to get loose, but my teammates smirked at me as they passed by. Something was up and I kept wondering what was so funny, but carried on with my stretching. Before heading into the dugout, minutes before the first pitch, I figured I'd stop and sign some autographs for the fans who clearly wanted mine. As I signed, several of them said, "Thanks, Cruz". Cruz? Finally, someone clued me in that I had the wrong jersey on. I checked the back of my jersey and, sure enough, I was wearing Deivi Cruz's jersey. The fans and some of my teammates had a good laugh at my expense, but I was so embarrassed. Here I was, thinking that these people were big fans of mine and little did I know that they were laughing at me. Deivi had the locker next to mine in the clubhouse and one of the veteran players had switched the jerseys. I should have realized it because his jersey was two sizes smaller than mine. So not only did I have a jersey with only four letters as opposed to eleven, but I was also busting out of it. That was a lesson for me: always check the back of your jersey before you put it on. From then on I was paranoid about it. I wouldn't step on the field without checking my back at least five times!

Another prank they pulled on me was very frustrating. We flew into Chicago very late one night. It was almost 4 a.m. and when I got to my room I just wanted to take out my contacts, brush my teeth and go to bed. I called down to the bell stand to have my luggage brought up. I asked them to please bring up number 27. Each player's luggage had a team tag on it with his number, so when you called down for your bag, you could just tell them your number and how many bags you had. When I finally got my bag, I couldn't open it. Every bag had a built-in combination lock on it. My combination was 0027. It wouldn't work. I tried it over and over. Nothing. I called our team equipment guy. He wasn't happy to have to come to my room at that time of the morning, but I needed to figure out why my bag wouldn't work. Long story short, we figured out that someone must have switched the tag on the bag. I went down to the lobby and there were thirty-plus team bags still there. Most of the guys just got to their rooms and crashed; they'd get their bags in the morning. So I had to try to figure out which bag was mine, and not only were there a few dozen of them, but most of them looked alike! I assumed that it must have been switched with another rookie's. Whoever had done it would not inconvenience a veteran. It took a while to try my combination on bag after bag before I got the right one. It was after 5 a.m. when I finally got to bed.

I've seen veterans soak a rookie's street clothes in water and put them in a freezer during the game. After the game, to the delight of the veterans, the rookie would find frozen-stiff clothing hanging in his locker. Some rookies would take the pranks in stride and laugh them off. Others would get pissed, which would only make matters worse. You never wanted to show the veterans that you were upset. If you couldn't take a joke, they would get you again and again. It was all in good fun and, if something was ruined, the veterans would replace it with something much better.

There were other parts of being a rookie that I could have done without, like carrying the beer. On road trips, the rookies would have to load up a couple of coolers full of beer and carry them from the club-house to the bus, then from the bus to the plane. And once we landed, we had to replenish the coolers and carry them from the plane to the bus and then from the bus to the hotel. And God forbid the beer wasn't ice cold! You would get an earful from the veterans. You were always hoping another rookie would get called up to the team so you could be relieved from your duties or at least get some help.

Getting harassed or embarrassed by pranks behind closed doors is one thing but embarrassing youself on the field during a game is much worse, especially if you're a rookie trying to get noticed. In early April, 1998, we went to Texas to play the Rangers for a three-game se-ries. The team was off to a slow start and manager Buddy Bell was getting tired of the lackluster effort. I got the start at second base in the final game of the series and was hoping to impress the manager and help infuse some youth and energy into the lineup. I singled to left in the seventh inning and moved to second base after a single by Joe Randa. We were having trouble scoring and I was looking to be aggressive on the base paths and put a run on the board. I got a little too anxious. There were no outs when Joe Oliver hit a soft liner off the end of his bat up the middle on the second base side of the bag. It looked like the ball would fall and hit the ground before second base-man Mark McLemore would catch it. I took off immediately, stopped, took a couple steps back and then sprinted to third base. When I heard the roar of the stadium crowd, I knew that McLemore had caught the ball and doubled me off second base. McLemore made a great play to catch the ball, but it didn't matter. In that situation, I must see the ball hit the ground before heading to third base and even if I can't advance to third, I can at least stay at second base and there will only be one out in the inning with a runner still in scoring position. Instead, there were two outs and no one on base. Not a good way for me to impress my manager. I jogged back to the dugout with my head down and tail between my legs. As I walked the length of the dugout to put my helmet in the rack, I noticed Buddy waiting for me. He didn't want to just talk to me; he wanted to get real close to my face and scream at me in front of the whole team. I remember hearing things like, "What the hell were you doing?" and, "What were they teaching you in the minor leagues?" and, "What a stupid play!" Each was laced with colorful profanities. I felt terrible and hoped it wouldn't cost me a trip to the minors. But the story gets worse. After we wound up losing that game, Buddy called a meeting in the clubhouse and ripped us all. The next day was a scheduled off day in Detroit, but Buddy said that we were having a practice at 9 a.m. to work on base running among other fundamentals of the game. In the major leagues, you don't get many off days to yourself, so they were very precious, especially since we wouldn't be getting back to Detroit until 2 a.m. Some guys wanted to sleep in. I didn't feel like it was all my fault that we were having this practice, that is until we were on the plane and some of the veteran players had some beer in them. Pete Incaviglia was screaming at the top of his lungs, "Thanks a lot Cat, we all have to wake up and practice tomorrow at 9 a.m. because you were running pass patterns out at second base tonight! What were you doing"? Others piled on and that went on for basically the whole three-hour flight back to Detroit. I just sunk into my seat and pretended that I was sleeping. I couldn't have felt worse and Pete and the others made sure of it. There is a silver lining to the story, though. We got a call early in the morning from the clubhouse manager to tell us that practice was cancelled because it was pouring rain. Phew! I lucked out.

One of the first times that I came back to play in New York against the Yankees in front of my family and friends proved to be embarrassing, as well. Very rarely do you see a base runner get picked off at first base. Well, I didn't just get picked off once, I got picked off twice! The first time by Roger Clemens and the second by Mike Stanton. I wasn't even a base-stealing threat. I was going nowhere and still got picked. There was no excuse for it. Talk about a rally killer. I was totally embarrassed and had to jog in my shame all the way across the field to the third base dugout. Sometimes, we just can't explain some of the bone-headed things that we do.

Even with the embarrassing mistakes, my rookie year was an incredible experience. I learned a lot from some great players and made friendships that will last forever. Having a no-nonsense manager like Buddy was an advantage. Not only was he a colorful curser, he was a great baseball man, approachable and expected his players to play hard for him and to play fundamentally solid baseball.

*Grabbing a pre-game snack with some Rangers teammates in the visiting clubhouse at Tampa Bay.*

# A TYPICAL DAY IN THE BIG LEAGUES

*"When they start the game, they don't yell, 'Work ball'. They say, 'Play ball!'"*
*~ Willie Stargell, 1981*

The late Willie Stargell was right. We did *play* ball, but it was a lot of work and the days were long. I'm not complaining because I would never trade a day working at baseball for a day working in an office or in a factory.

**10:00 a.m. – 10:30 a.m.** After about eight hours of sleep, I would get breakfast, run errands and spend a little time with the family if they were around.

**1:30 p.m.** There weren't many people—players or coaches—who got to the park earlier than I did. If we were at home, I would drive. On the road, I would take a cab. Quite often on the road, I would have lunch with one of the other guys and we'd share a cab to the park. Once there, I would go into the hot tub for ten to fifteen minutes to warm up my body and then get my treatment in the trainer's room. For most of my career I had lower back issues, so the trainer would focus on that. Any other aches or injuries would be taken care of too. After the trainer finished with me, I would go to the weight room to do a core routine with my abs and lower back and maybe a stretching routine to get loose.

**2:30 p.m.** Most of the other guys would show up. A lot of them would be in the weight room or getting treatments. Others, especially pitchers, would be out on the field running. Some guys would be playing cards in the clubhouse. There was always music playing, the type usually depending on who was pitching. The starter got to pick the music, like it or not. Sometimes, I would wish there was a different pitcher that day because I didn't like his choice of music. Occasionally there would even be fights about music. A player might walk over and turn off the music and the next thing you know, you've got an argument going on. Music often caused controversy and as insignificant as you think it would be, it sometimes created the most discord in the clubhouse. Sometimes, a player who was very religious would object to music that had curse words in it. Latin players wanted salsa, merengue and similar music, American players preferred country, rock, rap or pop. It was impossible to please everyone.

**3:15 p.m.** I would be in the video room watching video of the pitcher for that night, maybe his last outing or maybe the last time I faced him. I might have watched some video of myself, especially if I was struggling at the plate. Old video of me when I was hitting the ball well could be very instructive and motivating. The video rooms were typically very big, with ten to fifteen TV screens and DVD players in the early days. Later on, the video was all on computers. It wasn't mandatory for players to watch video, and I was often confused as to why more guys didn't take advantage of it. It was a great tool, but there weren't a heck of a lot of guys who used it. That surprised me.

**3:45 p.m.** The hitting coach would come around to guys who were interested in seeing the scouting report. I would go through it because it provided me with valuable information including what pitchers throw in specific counts and situations. Every now and then, I would see something that would be significant, like eighty percent of the time in a 2-0 count, the pitcher throws a change-up. I would file that away and be looking for a change-up if I got into that 2-0 count.

**4:00 p.m.** I would go to the batting cage and do some hitting drills with the hitting coach. I wanted to warm up a little and get my swing going before batting practice.

**4:30 p.m.** All of the players would head out to the field to do our team stretch. That was when the stadium was just waking up. The stands were empty, but the vendors were getting set up. It was mostly silent as we sat on the field and stretched, but random noises would carry and echo around the park. A clang here, a crash there. You could hear what people a couple of hundred feet away, talking in normal voices, were saying. There was laughter. It was a happy, serene time in the park, which was especially nice after a loss. The sting of the previous night's failure had been swept away with the beer cups and hot dog wrappers. It was a clean, fresh start and it seemed that even the stadium seemed to know it. Some guys didn't like stretching and just sat there on the grass. Sometimes, the coach running the stretching didn't care and let them sit there, but others would be tougher and made sure no one was slacking off. I loved the stretch time and viewed it as necessary and beneficial.

**4:50 p.m.** We paired up for long toss, where we'd loosen up our arms by playing catch at increasingly longer distances, up to about one hundred twenty feet.

**5:00 p.m.** We began batting practice. We were split into four groups and when you weren't hitting, you'd be in the field working on your ground balls or fly balls, or just shagging, which meant catching the balls hit into the outfield and throwing them back to a guy near second base who was manning the bucket. During BP, infielders were busy getting their ground balls hit from the coaches and the outfielders were busy fielding fly balls and line drives, but there wasn't much for pitchers to do, so they usually had to shag. Most of them hated doing it, but we needed guys out there to throw the balls back in.

If you were a veteran, or if you were in the starting lineup you could head to the clubhouse after you finished your specific work on the field. If you hadn't, you had to stay out there. It could get tedious as you were on your feet the whole time.

It was interesting to see how different managers operated during batting practice. My favorite managers communicated with players. They would walk around in the outfield, go to each player, take his temperature, so to speak. "How's it going?" "How are you feeling?" "How's your arm?" "I know you're in a bit of a slump, so you've gotta come out early for BP and make some adjustments." That's what the really good ones would do. Others would just stand behind the batting cage and watch. Some wouldn't even come out for BP. They might be inside talking with the media or going over the scouting report on the opposition.

**6:15 p.m.** Batting practice ends. We had about a half hour to change into our game uniforms and get a quick bite to eat. Different guys had different pre-game routines. Some would play cards and some did crossword puzzles. Some had headphones on, listening to their favorite music, while others chose to watch TV. I spent the time getting mentally prepared and locked in on my game plan. I would generally sit at my locker and have some quiet time. I didn't like talking much during that time. I would run through my plan, reinforcing what I would do if this happened or that happened. When it would get too loud in the clubhouse and guys would be horsing around, I would go elsewhere to find some quiet. Sometimes I would simply find another room, or even a bathroom stall. I wanted to get my breathing under control and try to minimize my anxiety. It was always there. I would get butterflies just before game time, even during my fourteenth year in the big leagues. Somebody told me early on that getting nervous wasn't a bad thing. It's just the way we're built. It's your mind and body's way of amping up for a performance. I would be nervous until my first at-bat or first play in the field. Once that happened, I was good to go.

**6:40 p.m.** The starters usually stopped what they were doing, got focused and ready to hit the field.

**6:45 p.m.** Walking into the dugout from the clubhouse and stepping onto the field never got old. By this time, the stadium was usually filling up, but you never really knew how many would show. I was always in awe, just amazed and proud. I was among the lucky few to see a ballgame from the inside looking out. When I was growing up, I was one of 55,000 fans watching players at Yankee Stadium. Now, I was looking up and seeing all those people looking at me. It was awe-inspiring and could be a little nerve-wracking too, until I got into my zone. Once I stepped into the on-deck circle or up to the plate, I couldn't hear anything. Everything but the job in front of me was blocked out. People would tell me later that they yelled for me from the stands, but I never heard them.

**6:55 p.m.** The ceremonial first pitch, which was often a wild throw by a celebrity standing in front of the mound. Players would take turns as the catchers. I caught a few of them over the years, but I don't recall anyone famous. Few things compare with being on a Major League Baseball field. In fact, now that I think more about it, there's nothing that compares. From a sensory perspective, there was the meticulously manicured and uniformly green outfield grass with its laser-straight foul lines; the perfectly smooth, flat-as-a-table infield dirt with its pleasant, earthy smell in the first inning just after it had been watered down; the singing of the national anthem; the slight echo when a bat hit the ball just right; the surround-sound roar of the crowd and, depending on how hot it is and whether there was a breeze, the characteristic smells of the ballpark. I felt so blessed every time I set foot on a field.

**7:00 p.m.** We'd line up for the singing of the Star Spangled Banner, the managers and umpires would meet at home plate to shake hands, crack jokes and trade lineup cards.

**7:05 p.m.** Play ball! (Give or take a few minutes. When we played in Chicago against the White Sox, first pitch was always at 7:11 because it was sponsored by 7-Eleven.) I had the best "seat" in the house, especially when I played the outfield. I could see the catcher setting up, fielders positioning themselves, the contrast of the beautiful grass with the triple-decker stadiums packed with fans looming in the background. But I wasn't there to sightsee. Instead, I would see little things, like the runner at first leading off the base, noticing that he did something a little different and I would try to figure out what it meant. Whether one little half step or the position of his feet or the lean of his body meant he was going to steal. I would see how the pitcher would set up a hitter and how a hitter would take a swing on a ball because he thought it would be a fastball, but it was a change-up. I watched how his body posture changed.

In the dugout, I learned early on that it wasn't a time to be sitting back and not paying attention. I studied the pitcher, looking for his tendencies, like whether he was doing something particular on a pitch. Maybe the way he held his glove or where he came set on particular pitches. I watched the opposing third base coach give his signs. Anything I could pick up that we could benefit from. I was watching the game within the game. It was always different, but it was always the same: three outs per half-inning, at least eight and a half innings, unless it was shortened by weather or lengthened by a tie, but it seemed that there were as many possibilities of how the game unfolded as there are stars in the sky. And I loved every moment.

**9:15 p.m. – 10:00 p.m. or ??** You never knew how long a game would last. That's one of the great things about baseball: there's no clock. The team with the lead can't run out the clock like they can in football. The pitcher has to throw the ball. The average length of a major league game has gradually gotten longer over the last several years, but for most of the years I played, it was around two hours and forty-five minutes. After the final out we filed back to the clubhouse, victorious or beaten by the other team or the weather. I know that fans often bust players for seeming not to care whether they win or lose, that they're just in it for the money, but it isn't true. We care, we just don't show it on the field because you never want to let the other guys know that they got to you. Of course, the clubhouse mood varied greatly, depending on whether we won or lost.

If we won, music was blasting. If a guy had a walk-off hit we might give him a beer shower. He would probably have a TV and radio interview on the field just after the game and we would be waiting to pour beer on his head when he walked in.

If we lost...crickets. No music, very little, if any, conversation for the first ten or fifteen minutes, then some guys might start talking about the game. Everyone was different, though. And you had to remember who had a good game and who had a bad game. Even if you won and you went 4-4, your buddy sitting next to you might have gone 0-5 and he'd be angry, at least on the inside. You had to be sensitive to the different moods. That was all part of respecting the game and your teammates.

**Fifteen minutes after the game ends** The media enters the clubhouse. We had fifteen minutes until reporters and photographers were allowed in. Sometimes, that wasn't enough time to cool down if you were mad because you blew the game, made an error that lost the game or the umpire blew a key call and you were screaming about it. But you would have to get yourself together because you knew that when that fifteenth minute passed, the doors would fly open and there would be twenty people at your locker asking you questions, many of them the same ones that only made you relive your mistake. Naturally, if you had a good game, you were excited and eager to talk about it.

The manager doesn't say much after the game. He might make a brief appearance and say, "Keep your heads up, we'll get 'em tomorrow" or, "Great game, guys". He'd go right to his office because he had media coming to him as well.

As for the media, when the clubhouse door was opened, they could stay as long as they wanted and they'd usually go straight for the starting pitcher's locker. Or they would go to the hero of the game or the goat of the game. Especially for the goat, some questions were tough and a few of the reporters were ruthless and brutal: "How did you miss that ball (that cost the game)?" "What happened?" I learned which reporters to give good answers to and which ones would get a one-word answer. Some reporters would bash you and only say or write nasty things about you. They were the ones who got the one-word answers. Other reporters were fair and professional. For them, you wanted to stick around and answer all their questions. The interviews usually took half an hour. Sometimes, you would do your interviews, shower, dress and there'd still be reporters there when you left.

Some players, when they had a bad game, would hustle into the clubhouse and leave before the media got in. I didn't believe in that. Whether you had a good game or bad game, it's part of your duty as a professional baseball player to answer the questions. The media are one of your connections to the fans, and the fans pay your salary. Still, you needed to be careful about what you said, or even what reporters could see in your locker. There was a saying that was posted in a lot of clubhouses: "What you see here, what you hear here, stays here". But not everyone would take it seriously, and if the wrong guy saw or heard something interesting, he would leak it.

Win or lose, there was always great food and, of course, we were starving, although there were plenty of protein bars and protein drinks available during the game. If it was a day game, most guys would head out to a restaurant after the game, unless the clubby brought in something really good. Usually three times a week I would lift weights after the game.

**11:00 p.m. or later** You never knew how long a game would go. There might be a pitchers' duel and it's a two-hour game, or an extra innings marathon. But the earliest I would leave was around 11. It was always at least a ten-hour workday. I was usually a good sleeper, but occasionally I would have trouble nodding off, especially if I wasn't performing well; maybe I went 0-4 or made a big error. I'm the type of guy who keeps thinking about what I could have done differently. Before bed, I would go over my book, my scouting report, everything I would have written about my experiences with the pitcher we would face the next day. I also might have notes on some of the position players, like, "so-and-so likes to steal second base in a 2-1 count" or, "this catcher likes to throw behind runners". I would go over everything I could about the opposition. Usually, I would be in bed by 1:30 a.m.

*Not only is he one of the most gifted athletes in MLB history,*
*Alex Rodriguez is one of the most prepared and was a great teammate.*

# PREPARATION

*"There are no secrets to success. It is the result of preparation, hard work and learning from failure."* ~ Colin Powell

Baseball scouts often talk about "Five Tool Players". These are baseball's best; guys who run, throw, hit for average, hit for power and field better than the average major league player. However, if you ask me, it should not end there. The sixth tool, should be preparation. And, if you want a seventh, it should be self-confidence; belief in yourself.

Every club has at least one "freak" on the roster; players so physically gifted that all they need to do is show up. Even on their off days, they're better than most other players having their best days. Guys like Ken Griffey, Jr. or Josh Hamilton. That's not to say that these guys had no baseball IQ or didn't prepare, but they were so naturally talented that they could get away with being fundamentally less than perfect. They could make up for mistakes with their physical tools.

I was not that guy. I knew I had average skills and if I wanted to stick around very long in this cut-throat game, I had to be better prepared than everyone else. Not only did I need to make sure I was the most-prepared I could be physically, I had to be prepared mentally.

For me, that meant asking questions; surrounding myself with smart baseball guys and picking their brains. The cerebral players, like Bill Haselman and Rusty Greer. They knew how to play the game and always liked talking baseball. They saw the game within the game. They talked strategy. What to do in this situation or in that count. Talking strategy with those types of guys was beneficial to my career. And, I made sure it wasn't only the hitters with whom I talked baseball. I had to try to understand "the enemy", the pitchers. I listened to what pitchers were saying about their approach to hitters and put it in my memory bank for later.

As I stated before, I credit Larry Parrish with being the main reason I got to the major leagues. But, I'll take credit for staying there as long as I did. That was due to my preparation. And I'll give credit for my preparation to my mom. She was a great example. Early on, she instilled in me the need to be prepared. Not just for baseball, but for everything in life.

*SHARON: Yes, he got that from me. It just makes life easier when you're prepared. I've always believed that if your life is cluttered, your thought process was also cluttered. You couldn't give it your best. His preparedness is one of his best qualities. We're both list makers and we both make it a point to accomplish the task. Even as a young boy, he was very prepared and organized. If you saw his closet back then, you would've seen labeled shelves designating where to put the laundry back! Neat, so very neat.*

You've probably been in a situation where you weren't prepared; maybe a test in school for which you didn't study. Remember how awful that feels, that sick feeling in the pit of your stomach? You have probably also experienced how great it feels when you ace a test that you prepared for. Which feeling do you like better? Whatever you do in life, whether it is baseball, the business world or driving a bus, if you are prepared for what might happen you will be able to handle it better.

I take great pride in my preparation. Other players, as well as coaches and managers, would call me the most prepared guy in baseball. I loved that I was getting recognition for something that I never intended on getting recognized for. But, remember that I wasn't a physical freak and I needed to work harder than the next guy. That meant that I had to be aware of what was going on in the game at all times. I didn't want to miss a pitch. I needed to pick up on the pitcher's tendencies and see if he was tipping his pitches. I would collect mental notes from each game and when I went back to my room, I would write down all of my experiences from that day in a book so I could refer to it at any time. (Read more about "The Book" in that chapter.) I wanted to have as much information as possible. I needed to be smarter than the other guys, especially the pitchers that I would be facing. When I stepped on the field and into the batter's box, I needed to exude confidence. I needed to be able to handle the pressure and the failure that comes on an everyday basis. I had seen too many talented players who were unable to hack it at the major league level simply because they couldn't handle failure. I accepted that I would fail some of the time and that success was up to me, so I kept my eyes and ears open and learned something everyday. I had to be dedicated to getting better and continue to have a deep passion for the game. Another piece of that recipe is trust; I needed to trust myself, what I was seeing, hearing and learning. I felt that if I could be diligent at all of these things I could keep up with the "Joneses" when it came to performance on the field. None of these things have anything to do with raw talent. If you aren't the most physically gifted player, you can still be a great contributor to your team, putting up your best numbers by working hard at being prepared.

One of my favorite coaches, Brian Butterfield with the Blue Jays, said once, "There is no one more prepared in the game than Frank". According to Brian, Curt Schilling commented that he thought he watched more video than anyone else in the major leagues, "but apparently Frankie had me beat".

Share what you have learned with any of your teammates who are interested. Making them better makes you better. Before the games, I would tell guys what the pitchers' tendencies were, what pitches to look for in certain counts, how they might tip pitches. I knew in what situations the pitcher got rattled and what pitcher/catcher combination was a good one to run on. There were some teammates who relied on me to be their scouting report. And I was glad to help. If I was prepared enough to share with others, I felt confident and if I was confident I played better. They loved it, of course. Some of them would say, "Why do we need to look at the scouting report when we have Cat?"

As you prepare, be sure that you're doing so within your abilities. You need to know yourself and what you physically can and cannot do. Again, pay attention to what's going on in the game at all times, whether you're on the field or not. Remind yourself before every pitch what you will do with the ball if it is hit to you. Where do you go with it if it is hit to your left or to your right; if it's a slow roller or a laser shot? How fast are the runners? Know the strength of the fielders' arms. Know the dimensions of the field and all the nooks and crannies of the ballpark. Know how the ball may carom off the wall or kick out on a ball hit down the line. Know the size of the foul territory. Never be surprised. Always be prepared.

My preparation would start the night before the next game. I would take out my book which contained everything I knew about every pitcher I faced. (More about the books in the next chapter.) Everything that a pitcher did during the course of the game was logged in the book. I would keep track of pitches he would most often throw in every combination of counts. I would gather as much information from my past experiences against that night's starter and potential relievers. I kept notes on umpires as well. That way, I would have a good idea of where the strike zone might be on that particular night. I would call or text my friends on other teams that may have just faced the team we were going up against to pick their brains and get an idea of what I might see. And once my studying was done, before I fell asleep, I would close my eyes and visualize. I would see the pitcher that I was scheduled to face the next day and see the different pitches that he might throw. I would see the ball coming toward me at the plate. I would see myself having success over and over again. Base hit up the middle! Double to left centerfield! Home run to right! This helped keep me calm and confident and I slept like a log.

The next morning, I would do some visualization drills that I learned from an eye doctor who I saw during the off-season. He made sure my eyes were strong and functioning as well as they could. Your eye doctor can probably suggest similar exercises, the basics of which are working your eyes to focus on something near, then far and back and forth. There are also exercises which help with depth perception. Eye muscles need to be kept in top shape, too. There is more about eye exercises in the Conditioning chapter.

## THE PAYOFF

My biggest sense of accomplishment was when the preparation paid off. My first memory of that was when I started feeling confident enough in my research and in my plan that I began sitting on pitches – waiting for the pitcher to throw what I wanted. In 2000, we were in Seattle playing the Mariners and facing Paul Abbott. In all of my preparation with the video work and the scouting reports I noticed that he threw 0-1 change-ups almost fifty percent of the time to left-handed hitters like myself. Usually in an 0-1 count, hitters don't like to give up on the fastball. So, it took a lot for me to trust myself and trust what I believed he would throw. I didn't want to be in an 0-2 hole but I said to myself before the game, if I get into an 0-1 count I'm going to sit on a change-up. Sure enough, in the sixth inning I got into that 0-1 count. It was time. I was going to let the fastball right down the middle of the plate go and instead sell out to this change-up that I was sure was coming. When the change-up left his hand, it looked as big as a beach ball the whole way in. My eyes got wide in anticipation and I crushed a home run into the rightfield seats. The preparation had paid off. Seeing the results of preparing is very rewarding. Believing in yourself so completely makes a difference in being a confident hitter. If you have a plan and believe in it, you're going to be aggressive and confident. Sometimes, your plan or approach might be the wrong one but at least you can be confident in it and know, at the end of the day, that there was a reason why you did what you did. I felt that if I had enough information and prepared the way I was supposed to, then there was a better chance that my approach would be the right one.

In 2004, I noticed that Curt Schilling was tipping his splitter. I called Vernon Wells over and we watched the video repeatedly and we kept seeing the same thing. His glove would get wider when he took his glove over his head. For the fastball, it would be tight. I trusted in what I saw and wound up having success against him throughout my career. Statistics show that the pitcher wins the battle 70% of the time. If you can lessen those odds by eliminating a pitch or by having a good idea of what might be coming, it makes hitting a lot easier. It makes you more of a confident hitter. Getting every edge possible is important. It isn't cheating. It is watching, studying and preparing. The game is hard. Hitting is hard.

One of the reasons I had such a long career was my ability to spot and exploit those weaknesses. I had to. The guys I respected the most were the naturally gifted players who worked hard preparing for each game. Alex Rodriguez was like that. I am sure he would have been an All-Star just because of his off-the-charts talent, but he spent hours preparing for each opponent. I had the pleasure of playing with Alex for two years in 2001 and 2002 with the Rangers. Not only did the combination of his God-given talent and his preparation make him arguably the best player ever, it made him a great teammate. Alex set the bar high and being able to play with him and see how hard he worked and prepared only helped me improve my game.

If baseball – or any sport or activity – comes easy to you, I hope you'll take that as a sign that you need to work harder.

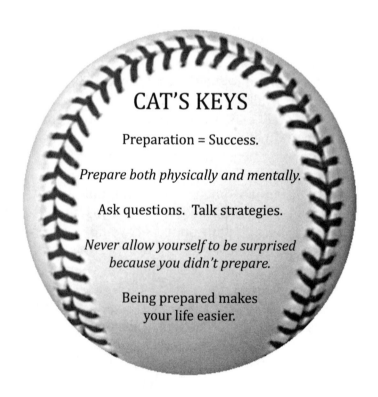

## CAT'S KEYS

Preparation = Success.

*Prepare both physically and mentally.*

Ask questions. Talk strategies.

*Never allow yourself to be surprised
because you didn't prepare.*

Being prepared makes
your life easier.

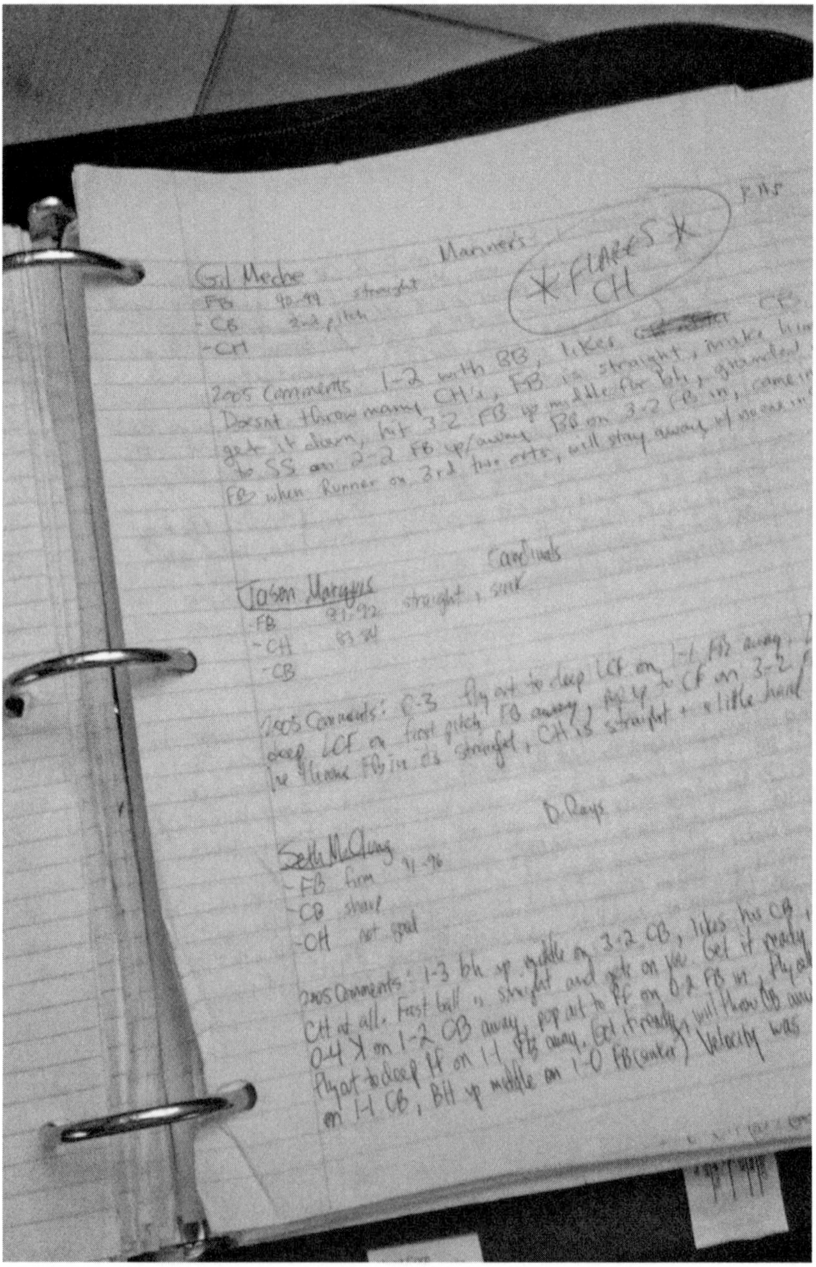

Mariners                    FB5

*FLARES*
CH

**Gil Meche**
FB    90-99    straight
- CB    3rd pitch
- CH

2005 Comments  1-2 with BB   likes ~~CB~~    CB
Doesn't throw many CH's, FB is straight, make him
get it down, hit 3-2 FB up middle for hit, grounded
to SS on 2-2 FB up/away, BB on 3-2 FB in, came in
FB when Runner on 3rd two outs, will stay away if man in

Cardinals

**Jason Marquis**
FB    91-92    straight, sink
- CH    83-84
- CB

2005 Comments: 0-3  fly out to deep LCF on 1-6 FB away,
deep LCF on first pitch FB away, HBP to CF on 3-2 f
line drive FB in 0-3 straight, CH is straight + a little hard

D-Rays

**Seth McClung**  91-96
- FB  firm
- CB  sharp
- CH  not good

2005 Comments: 1-3  hit up middle on 3-2 CB, likes his CB
CH at all, Fast ball is straight and gets on you, Get it ready
0-4 K on 1-2 CB away, pop up to CF on 0-2 FB in, Fly out
Fly out to deep CF on 1-1 FB away, Get it ready will throw CB away
on 1-1 CB, BH up middle on 1-0 FB(sinker) Velocity was

# THE BOOK

*"Ideas can come from anywhere and at any time. The problem with making mental notes is that the ink fades very rapidly."*
*~ Rolf Smith, thinker and author*

Actually there were two books. One where I wrote about pitchers' tendencies and a second book, which I carried with me all of the time and wrote anything that I learned from a coach, player or just from observing. In both books, I found that when I wrote things down, I was able to remember them more easily. I could go back now and then, read my notes and keep things fresh in my mind. Similar to how I would go back and examine the videos of my successful at-bats, I would use the books to go back and read what I had written when I was doing well. This would help me get back on track.

In 1992, I started writing down what I learned in the minor leagues, but I never concentrated on the pitchers. It was always things like where to be on the cut-offs and relays, the proper fielding or hitting techniques and what the signs from the catcher or third base coach were. At AA Jacksonville in 1995, Larry Parrish urged me to keep a separate book on pitchers. He knew that however long I played I would be seeing a lot of the same pitchers. Larry suggested I keep notes on each one I faced. I wrote everything I felt was important that happened during my at-bat or even something I may have noticed during my teammates' at-bats. Anything that might give me an edge, either physically or mentally, I jotted down. The kind of pitches, the velocity of each pitch, what each pitch looked like and how I felt in the batter's box are just a few things I would document. I looked to see if the pitchers fell into patterns or if they tipped their pitches. All pitchers had certain tendencies and I was determined to find them. Also, I wrote the result of each at-bat and what I thought I should look for the next time I faced that pitcher. If I thought I saw a pitcher do something on a particular pitch but wasn't positive about it, I would make a note in the book to take another look the next time I faced him. I would talk to the other guys on the team and ask them what pitches they saw and what their experiences were like. Anything I could write in that book on a pitcher was information that I thought could give me an edge. The more I knew about a guy, the more confident I was heading into my next at-bat against him. I never wanted to be caught off guard or, at least, I wanted to limit the amount of times I was caught off guard.

Since there was so much movement in the league with players changing teams, I listed the pitchers by last name in alphabetical order. Once I got to the major leagues, it became much easier to keep my book because there was so much more information available on the pitchers, without even having to face them. I had access to scouting reports on every team and every pitcher. There were videos on every starter and reliever, so I spent hours at the TV monitors, slowing down the tapes, pausing and rewinding them at the touch of a button. Being able to see a clip over and over helped me discover whether a pitcher was tipping his pitches. I could pick up on his tendencies and really get an idea of what he was comfortable throwing in particular counts or situations.

My book was growing! It started in a six-inch black binder but grew to a fat, loose-leaf binder as I got to the big leagues. After my September call-up to the big leagues in 1997, I went home and knew that if I made the team the next year out of spring training I would be going against a lot of pitchers I had never faced. I was craving information on them, but back home on Long Island, I didn't have access to the video and scouting reports. I wanted to get some kind of info on the veteran pitchers before going to spring training. Our local bookstore had a book

Carlos Silva                    Twins                    RHP
- FB   run 89-93 sink
- SL
- CH

2006 Comments: 0-3, line out to CF on 1-2 FB in, likes
to come in with 2 strikes. FB runs, sinks a little.
Throws a lot of FB's. Comfortable AB. Ground out
to 3B on 3-2 FB away. Ground out to 2B on
2-2 CH. CH is OK. / 1-3, fly out to CF on
2-2 FB middle, ground out to SS on CH down/away
2B to LF on 2-1 CH, CH isn't much slower than FB
but enough to get you to feel for it.
2007 Comments: 1-2 HR on 3-2 CH, ground out to
2B on 2-0 sinker away/down w/ runner at 2B, 0 out.
Tips pitches from wind up, Top of glove is pointed
for FB, rounded for CH.

FB   CH

2-3 basehit over SS on 2-2 CH, threw 1-2 CH for
ball, basehit up middle on 2-2 sinker away, K on 0-2
SL down and in after. CH for K then CH swinging K
I did see him tip again.

Jorge Sosa            ~~TB~~  TB                    RHP
- FB
- SL
- CH                                    * Tips *

2009 Comments: BH to RF on 2-0 SL, Loves SL, Look for it

When he gets set slow and wiggles glove its a FB
Get set faster and doesn't wiggle glove its a SL
He starts with a Breaking ball grip

called "The Scouting Notebook". It gave details on every major league player's strengths and weaknesses. It had the velocities of all pitchers in the major leagues as well as AAA prospects that were projected to be there soon. It detailed every pitch that they threw and even gave statistics about where each pitcher ranked in regards to strikeouts and walks compared to the league averages. It listed situational pitching statistics including "home/road" splits, "vs. left-handed batter/right-handed batter" splits, "with runners in scoring position", "in the clutch" numbers and many others.

I realized I was probably the only guy doing this during the off-season, but as I wrote elsewhere in this book, I found out early that I wasn't the most talented on any of my teams. If I was going to reach my goal of being a big leaguer, I needed to, like my dad told me in high school, out hustle, out work and out study everybody else. Day after day, I diligently sifted through the player stats and wrote in my book everything that I thought would be helpful. Even in the dreary New York winter, months away from my next at-bat, it was a way for me to keep my head in the game. Going into the season, I had a sense of confidence that I carried with me to the plate against pitchers I hadn't faced before.

Odd as it sounds, the one place I never kept the book was in the clubhouse. I guess I was a little paranoid. Not that I really thought someone would go into my locker and steal it, or even look at it, but I didn't want to take a chance that teammates who might be on another team someday would read what I had on them. That would ruin any edge I had. I didn't want to have to worry that someone would take a peek while I was on the field during the game. I didn't need that in the back of my head, so I kept the book at home or in my hotel room when we were on the road and I would refer to it every day before I left for the ballpark. Many times, I panicked while on the plane heading to our next destination because I couldn't remember if I had packed the book or if it was still sitting on the nightstand in the hotel! To my great relief, it was always there when I opened my bag.

Carlos Delgado also kept a book, but he didn't have any of my privacy concerns. Not only would he take it into the clubhouse, he would take it into the dugout and write in it and study it between at-bats. We were teammates from 2003-2006 in Toronto.

After road games, many guys couldn't wait to get back to the hotel and sleep, play video games or go out to a bar. On the road or at home, I couldn't wait to get back to my room to write in my book, especially if I noticed something about the pitcher that potentially could give me a big edge. A mental game I played with myself during each game was to go back to my room with something of substance to write in the book, not just the results of the at-bat. I needed to write something that would help me the next time I faced that particular pitcher.

As shown below, I also drew pictures or symbols in the book. If a pitcher's glove was shaped differently on different pitches I would draw how each looked. Was it flared? Was it tight? Facing different directions? Held tight to the face or chest? When I picked up the book the next time to study that pitcher, the drawings allowed me to get a good visual. Written words alone weren't enough. If I didn't illustrate it, there was no way that I would remember two months later how the glove appeared on each pitch.

Tips pitches from wind' up, Top of glove is pointed for FB, rounded for CH. (FB | CH)

2-3 basehit over SS on 2-2 CH, threw 1-2 CH for ball, basehit up middle on 2-2 sinker away, K on 0-2 SL down and in after CH for K then CH swinging K. I did see him tip again.

I would flag the very important notes with a yellow highlighter. If a guy tipped his pitches or if I knew what signs he liked to use when there was a runner on second base, I would highlight it. It was very gratifying when my work paid off. If some note or drawing in my book helped me get a hit or have a good game, it was a great feeling.

The book wasn't just about pitchers. I had an "Umpire" section featuring every ump and their tendencies. Not only did they have their own personalities and styles, they had their own strike zones. If keeping notes helped me have an idea of how big theirs was, that was another edge. I didn't want to waste an at-bat early in the game because I didn't know that the umpire liked calling the high strike, or was notorious for calling one side of the plate. Knowing that ahead of time kept me from being surprised by an umpire's zone and made me a better hitter. If I had two strikes on me and a particular umpire called a lot of pitches away from left-handed hitters, I had to protect the plate even if it meant just fouling the ball into the seats until the pitcher made a mistake and gave me something I could hit. I wrote reminders in the book about the ump's personality. Some were quiet, some were chatty. Some liked confrontations, some were grumps. I always wanted to know how far I could push an umpire to get my point across. Some would get stern immediately and others would take some abuse. I never got too mouthy, but it was nice to know just how far I could go.

Tim Welke 9/04 called a couple of high strikes but had a pretty good game. 9/05 Was real consistent and didn't miss many pitches. Some lefties were saying that he was calling the comeback from the RHP in off the plate but didn't seem to miss with me.

Mike Everritt - 9/03 Expanded zone away *(off plate)* twice on me, once on 3-1 two seamer away, once on first pitch FB from lefty. Other than that was pretty fair / 4/04 vs CHi Missed all night long on pitch away has a tough time seeing the outside of plate. 5/04 tended to miss down, but won't call high strike.

Gary Darling 8/05 had real bad game missing away alot, called one pitch up and in for strike, later on in game called two strikes away that missed. Can have a short fuse at times 6/7 Continues to favor the outside part of the plate so don't let him get you with 2 strikes out there, foul it off

Along with the three-ring binder I kept on pitchers and umpires, this was my spiral notebook full of years of observations about the game, hitting, fielding, etc. that I hoped would help me improve.

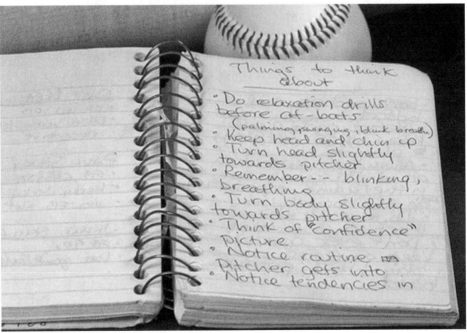

The books, and my diligence in using them, played a big role in not only my success, but also my ability to sustain a long career in the big leagues.

I also recommend that pitchers keep the same kind of book on hitters, but whether you're a pitcher or hitter, the amount of information compiled can really make a difference.

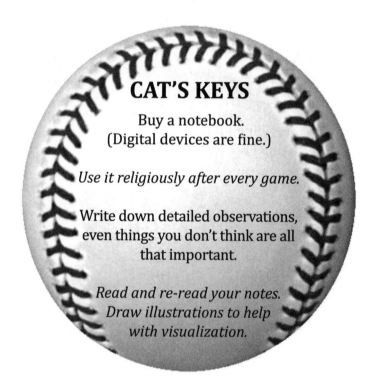

## CAT'S KEYS

Buy a notebook.
(Digital devices are fine.)

*Use it religiously after every game.*

Write down detailed observations, even things you don't think are all that important.

*Read and re-read your notes. Draw illustrations to help with visualization.*

# Jays' bats light up Chicago night

## Catalanotto's 6-for-6 special sparks offensive barage

■ BLUE JAYS 10, WHITE SOX 6

### BY SPENCER FORDIN
MLB.COM

STEPHEN J. CARRERA / AP PHOTO

*Frank Catalanotto's 6-for-6 performance raised his average 53 points from .276 to .329.*

Carlos Tosca wanted a crooked number, and that's exactly what he got. Toronto's manager watched his bats wake up in the second game of a doubleheader against Chicago at U.S. Cellular Field, propelling the Blue Jays to a 10-6 win in Saturday night's finale.

That helped make up for a 4-3 loss earlier in the day, a winnable game that slipped away in 10 innings. In between games, Tosca found himself hoping for some runs, and his team responded with its fourth 10-run game of the season.

"That looked more like our ballclub, in that second game," Tosca said. "Hopefully, a new month, we can get on track and start throwing those numbers around all the time."

Everyone got into the act: the Blue Jays (8-16) racked up 18 hits and seven of the nine starters knocked in at least one run. Eight of the nine scored at least one time. Even with the team theme, **Frank Catalanotto** stood out. Toronto's left fielder went 6-for-6, setting a new career high in hits.

The Jays notched three three-run innings on Saturday night. The first one came early, when Toronto smashed two homers in the third inning. The second came in the fifth, when the Blue Jays used three hits and two walks to do their damage. Finally, with a 7-5 score, the road team scored three times in the seventh to put the game on ice.

"It was a huge win. Obviously, we hadn't been playing well lately," Catalanotto said. "Ted pitched a good game and all of us — not just myself — we all swung the bats really well and scored a lot of runs. Hopefully this will boost our offense and we'll start scoring a lot more runs."

# CONFIDENCE

*"Show me a guy who's afraid to look bad, and I'll show you a guy you can beat every time."* ~ Lou Brock

In 1998, we were in extra innings at Tiger Stadium. I was twenty-four, it was my rookie season in the big leagues. Runners were on first and third with one out and it was my turn to bat. As I walked toward the plate gripping my bat, I was thinking that this was my chance to be a hero.

I had practiced for this moment in my mind countless times when I was a little kid—haven't we all? In my backyard, I would pretend that I was walking up to bat before a screaming crowd in the House that Ruth Built. I would rearrange the dirt in the batter's box as I alternately glared at the pitcher and kicked a hole to make sure my back foot wouldn't slip. With my bat held tight under my left armpit, I would rub my hands together and spit into them, knock the dirt off my spikes with my bat, spit on the ground, settle into the batter's box, resume my glare at the pitcher and then, after working the count to 3-2 and the crowd into a frenzy, I would crush the ball over the left centerfield fence, sailing over Monument Park where plaques honoring Ruth, Gehrig, DiMaggio and Mantle stood in silent approval as my hit would win the World Series, the crowd erupted with deafening screams of joy and I would be immortalized as a Yankee hero!

Of course, I wasn't playing for the Yankees and we weren't in the World Series, but all I had to do to be a hero was hit a fly ball to the outfield and we could go home winners. Everyone on both teams wanted the game to be over and I stood at the plate, confident that I would get the job done. I got the pitch I wanted and as I made contact, I could feel in my hands that there'd be no hero celebration at home plate for me. I didn't get all of it. I popped it up. Two outs. We wound up not scoring and a few innings later, the opposing team scored the winning run. I felt terrible because I would let my team down. Bobby Higginson was one of my Tiger teammates and was a few years older than me. He could see I was struggling with my blown hero opportunity and took me out for a couple of beers. He told me to stop beating myself up over it, that it happens to everyone and no one on the team was mad at me. Learn from it. Let it go, forget it. And he told me (this was great advice) to never stop thinking that I *would* be the hero of the next game or the next chance I got. Be *confident* that the next time I would get it done, because if I kept doing the "coulda-shoulda-woulda" routine, rehashing how I failed, I would start believing that I couldn't get it done. That helped me put it in the proper perspective and was another illustration of the importance of confidence.

Without confidence, getting to the major leagues and staying there is impossible. Successful players are confident players. No confidence? No success. I played in the minor leagues with many players who had much more talent, but they washed out because they didn't have confidence. So, what made me so confident? It might have been preparation or previous success against a pitcher. Success breeds success, but it doesn't matter where it comes from. When I was confident, I saw the ball much better out of the pitcher's hand. When I wasn't feeling confident, it was a battle for me.

Preparation was one key to making me a confident player. If I went to the plate against a pitcher I had never faced or had not seen on video, I was not as confident. In 1998, early enough in my career with the Tigers that I was still afraid nearly every day of being sent down, we were playing the Blue Jays. Roger Clemens was starting. He had won four Cy Young Awards and was working on his fifth, one of the best pitchers to ever put on a uniform. I remember waking up the day of the game feeling bummed out, a sense of dread. Not so much because I was nervous about Clemens, I was just trying to stay in the big leagues and I felt I had no chance against him. Sometimes you'll get your confidence from something someone says or from looking at a situation from a different perspective. I called my dad before the game and was lamenting about having to go up against the Rocket. Dad said, nonchalantly, "He puts his pants on one leg at a time, just like you, right? He has to throw the ball over the plate in order to get you out, doesn't he?" Hearing it from that perspective calmed me down and started me thinking from a position of strength, not weakness. Why should I give Clemens so much credit? Yeah, he's one of the best pitchers ever, but my dad reminded me that no one is so good that they can't be beaten. I wound up getting a hit off Clemens that night. The lesson was that I couldn't let my fear of failure tear down my confidence. After that, whenever I would feel the dread of having to face a tough pitcher, I would just simplify it, breaking it down to the fact that until proven otherwise, I had just as good a chance of winning the battle at the plate as he did.

Although, that isn't quite true. Pitchers have a better chance of winning the battle. That's the way baseball works: it's a game of failure for the batter. If he fails seven out of ten times he's batting .300 and is considered a great hitter. Don't be afraid of failure, but don't accept it either.

## THE PHYSICS OF CONFIDENCE

When we're afraid or anxious our muscles tighten. We can't perform at our best when we're tense. You can see it, just as you can see confidence. Next time you watch a ballgame, watch the body language of the pitcher and the hitters. You'll see a variety of looks, or vibes. Nolan Ryan said it helped him if the hitters thought he was a little crazy, so that's the vibe he put out. That intimidation usually only works if there's confidence to back it up. Swagger doesn't get hits, but it helps. I wrote about this in my chapter on hitting, but it's worth repeating. When I was teammates with Alex Rodriguez in Texas, he taught me something about body language and confidence that helped a lot. He said whether or not you *feel* confident, *act* like you are. When you step out of the dugout to walk to the on-deck circle, keep your head high, chest out and have a swagger about you. Walk like you *own* the diamond. While you're taking your practice swings, keep your eyes locked on the pitcher. Eventually he'll look over to see who's up next. Stare him in the eyes and make him look away first. (You'll always win that stare down. He has to look away because he has to pitch!) But, he may give it back as well as you're giving it. Bob Gibson, one of the most feared pitchers in major league history, had the right attitude: "I was never much in awe of anybody. I think you have to have that attitude if you're going to go far in this game."

When it is your turn to hit, walk to the plate with a strut or swagger that tells the pitcher and anyone watching that you are going to rip the cover off the ball if he makes a mistake. Even if you strike out, keep that attitude. Keep your head held high and walk back to the dugout as if you owned the place. It's not arrogance or cockiness. It's confidence. And even if you don't feel it on a particular day, you can still trick the pitcher, and yourself, into believing otherwise.

## THE WORLD WILL NOT STOP SPINNING

A lot of times when I wasn't feeling confident going into a game, I asked myself, "What's the absolute worst that could happen?" Maybe I go 0-4 with four strikeouts. Even worse, maybe I make an error to lose the game. Is it the end of the world? No. Will my family still love me? Of course. That would calm me down a little bit and help me regain some confidence. Realizing that the weight of the world is not on your shoulders and putting things in perspective can change the way you look at things. One of my favorite Bible verses, "I can do all things through Christ who strengthens me", often helped me when I felt less confident. Another thing that worked for me was a "confidence picture". I would recall a time in my career when I had all the confidence in the world; a time when I was on a hot streak. Often, I would recall a series in Boston in 2005 where they couldn't get me out. When I needed a little boost, I would pull every sense in my memory from that moment—how it looked, felt, sounded and smelled—into a picture in my head that would put me in the right frame of mind: positive, calm and confident.

Another time that I was playing with confidence over an extended period of time was in 1997 when I was at AAA. I was a Toledo Mud Hen and was having a good year. In five hundred at-bats, I hit .300, with a .368 slugging percentage and a .472 on base percentage. I was seeing the ball well at the plate, fielding it cleanly and brimming with confidence. As we got into August and the end of the season was near, there was some talk about me being called up to the major league team. I felt ready and couldn't wait to get the news. It came on September 1st and I joined the Tigers the next day. Five days later, my name was on the lineup card. The night before the game, my manager Buddy Bell told me to be ready tomorrow because I would be starting at second base. Needless to say, I was nervous and didn't have a great night's sleep, as I was praying that I wouldn't embarrass myself. I was making my first start in the big leagues at second base in place of Damion Easley and couldn't wait to get on the field at Tiger Stadium. I was so excited. But then panic set in! After all that confidence I'd had just down the road in Toledo, I was standing at second base in the first inning, shaking like a leaf! A position I had played thousands of times, fielding a million ground balls and there I was repeating to myself, "Don't hit it to me, don't hit it to me!" I was scared stiff, afraid of failing, afraid of embarrassing myself and everybody who had ever known me.

So there I was, twenty-three years old, standing at second as the double-decked stadium loomed over me, filled with people who were expecting me to catch the ball, throw the ball and hit the ball. I was one of the lucky few to realize his childhood dream and make it to the major leagues and all I wanted was to be *off* the field. I might as well have been stark naked out there. I couldn't have felt more exposed. Eventually, the ball was hit to me; a pop fly, which I squeezed into my glove for an out. But I was still nervous about a ground ball being hit at me. A couple of innings later, it happened. A grounder that looked like it was the size of a BB as it sped toward me. I...caught it! I transferred it cleanly to my right hand and threw the runner out at first. If anxiety had a color, you could have seen it draining out of my body, pooling around my spikes on the infield dirt. And with each touch of the ball and swing of the bat, more of it drained away. In thirteen games that September, I hit .308/.379/.385. Not bad for someone who was so crippled by fear that he felt his career was ending. Thankfully, my confidence was back, but I learned that if you let fear in, it can lock you up.

## THE ZONE

Nothing feels better to an athlete than being in "The Zone". The basketball player who knows that it's nothing but net whenever he shoots. The quarterback who knows he'll nimbly sidestep blitzing line-backers and fire a laser shot into the receiver's hands for a touchdown, the tennis player who returns every serve, the golfer whose every club feels like an extension of his arms and the ball goes exactly where he wants it. That's "The Zone".

It isn't like there is a door you walk through and you're there. It just happens. You can't explain how you got in the zone or how to stay there. You certainly welcome it because you are supremely confident. You are in control, the game slows down for you. The ball coming out of the pitcher's hand looks like a beach ball. One of my times in The Zone was in 2005 against the White Sox in Chicago. I didn't feel any different when I woke up that day. My batting practice was routine. There was no warning, it just snuck up on me. I knew during my first at-bat that I was going to have a good game, I just didn't know how good. I was see-ing the ball so well. I was relaxed, focused and so locked in that I don't remember seeing anything else around me. It was just me versus the pitcher. In my first trip, I got a base hit. I doubled in my second at-bat. With each at-bat, my confidence grew. I knew I was going to hit the ball hard. I knew I was going to get a hit. When I stood in the on-deck circle, I could envision myself being successful. Third at-bat, another base hit. Fourth at-bat, another double. Reed Johnson, one of my fa-vorite teammates of all time, came up to me after that and said, "Hey Cat, we're only in the fifth inning. You might get a chance to get six hits tonight." I replied, "Well, there is no one on the planet that can get me out right now so however many at-bats I get, that's how many hits I'll get." He probably thought I was joking and it was kind of a bold state-ment since I consider myself a very modest guy, but I really believed it. I wasn't being cocky or a jerk. I just knew that no one could beat me on this particular night. In my fifth at-bat, I smoked a lined shot into cen-terfield. When I was leaving the dugout for my sixth at-bat in the ninth inning, my teammates were rooting me on, encouraging me and excited about the opportunity for me to become the first Blue Jay in history to get six hits in a nine-inning game. As I stepped into the batter's box, I noticed it was a different pitcher. In fact, the fifth one of the night. He was a guy that I hadn't faced before, but it didn't matter. It could have been Cy Young and it wouldn't have made a difference. It was my night and when I got a change-up down and away, I flicked my wrists and hit a liner over the shortstop's head. Six for six. On that evening, I really be-lieved that I was the best player on the field, all thanks to the confidence

I felt at the beginning and which grew with each at-bat. The Zone!

## HITTING COACHES AND CONFIDENCE

The best hitting coaches are the ones who make sure their hitters are confident. Sure, they needed to know the mechanics, but they needed to be part psychologist, too. Some coaches only worried about teaching swing mechanics. To me, they were useless. Every hitter at the major league level has a swing that was good enough to get them there. Up until that point, I thought it was great to have a coach who focused on mechanics. In Little League, high school and in the minors we learn how to physically hit the ball and figure out the best ways to get the bat head to the ball as quickly and efficiently as possible. In the big leagues, I believe a hitting coach should be there to help with minor adjustments in the swing. When a guy is scuffling, just get him back on track. Major league hitters mostly need someone to help them with their approach, the mental part of hitting and most importantly with confidence. Larry Parrish was the best when it came to that. He played fifteen seasons in the major leagues and knew how to pass his experience and wisdom along to others. He taught me how to sit on pitches. He showed me what to look for when trying to see if a pitcher was tipping his pitches. He made me pay attention while in the dugout so I could pick up on a pitcher's patterns and tendencies. And, just as important as all of that, he would always tell me, "As long as you have a bat in your hands, you're deadly. Even if you're in a slump or don't feel good at the plate, you're deadly." He made me believe in myself and gave me confidence by giving me a game plan for every game and at-bat.

Texas Rangers hitting coach Rudy Jaramillo kept his hitters confident in other ways. He would come to each of us before the game and go over the pitcher's scouting report that had been sent from the advance scout. Rudy would give his opinions on how he thought the pitcher might pitch to me. He was also big on relaxation and breathing techniques. He stressed that if you could control your breathing, it would help you relax and be in better control of yourself and the situation. Rudy knew that the more relaxed he could get his hitters, the more confident we'd be and more success would follow.

Of course, each coach's method and success was driven by his personality and Mike Barnett of the Blue Jays had one of the best. He was the most positive coach I'd ever been around. He had ways of making hitters feel good about themselves. If you weren't feeling confident you could just go stand by Barney and you were sure to hear something positive about yourself come out of his mouth. I believe that the more positive things that go into your head, the better. Whether you were in a slump or on a hot streak, Barney would tell you your swing was great. If you were slumping, he would say how you just weren't getting any luck or that every ball you hit was going right at someone. He never made negative comments or made you feel like you were struggling. He never acknowledged that you were totally in a funk or mechanically off. He'd just make minor adjustments with your swing and tell you how good you were. That was a gift. He gave me such confidence day in and day out. Even if I was going through a rough patch with my swing, as long as I had confidence, I had a chance. And Barney always made me feel like I had a chance.

They say if you're a baseball player, it is good to have amnesia or at least a short memory. Again, it is a game where if you fail seven out of ten times, you are a star. There is no time for pouting because the next day you are right back on the field. You can't keep your failures with you. Learn from them and then let them go. Remembering every time you fail will only make you unsure of yourself. No confidence, no success.

**CAT'S KEYS**

Believe you'll be successful.

*Display a successful attitude.*

Be prepared. Preparation
breeds success.

*Remember your successes.*

Learn from failures, then
forget them.

*Studying a pitcher during a spring training game in 2001. One key to breaking out of a slump is looking for any edge that will help you succeed.*

# SLUMPS

*"Slumps are like a soft bed. They're easy to get into and hard to get out of."*
*~ Johnny Bench*

In my nineteen years of professional baseball I learned a lot about slumps, sometimes the hard way. As I look back, it is probably more beneficial to you if I write about what I should have done, versus what I sometimes did.

Before you get stressed out about being in a slump, make sure you're really in one. Hitting a baseball is one of the few things in life where you can fail seventy percent of the time and still be considered a success. The sooner you realize that you are not going to get a hit every trip to the plate, the better you will deal with the inevitable rough patches. 0 for 4 is not a slump. 0 for 20 might not be a slump. Don't be too eager to get back on track when you may never have gotten off track. Tinkering with your mechanics after you go 0-4 will probably cause more problems than it solves. What's important is how you're dealing with being 0 for 4 or 0 for 20. That determines what happens next.

You'll know when you're in a slump. It consumes you. It's all you think about. Day and night. You can't sleep because you keep seeing those numbers flashing in your head: 0 for your last 21, a .208 batting average. Whatever the stat is that reveals your slump, that is all you see. It seens as if everywhere you go, you're wearing a big sign showing your slump stats. You know people are staring at you, appalled that you call yourself a professional. You think you see them whispering about you and stealing glances at what a repulsive excuse for a baseball player you've become. Slumps make you paranoid. They make you jealous of teammates who aren't in them. If you give in to the slump, you press harder and harder at the plate with each hopeless swing pulling you deeper into your misery. It feels as if there's no relief, no way out.

Slumps happen to every player, no matter how gifted. It is a natural part of being involved in a sport where success is so elusive and so dependent on both physical and mental agility.

There were slump nights where I took a sleeping pill just to get some much-needed rest. If I woke up in the middle of the night, the "slump bugs" immediately took control of my thoughts again and all I could do was toss, turn and wonder, "When will my slump end? When will I get that ground ball with eyes or that broken bat blooper to take the pressure off?" Game after game, I would see guys get cheap hits and wonder why the heck couldn't that be me! You begin to feel sorry for yourself and you get in a rut, even depressed. Sometimes I think the fans believe the player doesn't care or isn't working hard enough to fix the problem. It is the opposite. We care too much and work too hard and put too much pressure on ourselves. We try to get a hit on every pitch and start chasing bad pitches that are out of the strike zone.

One reason I would wind up trying too hard and putting too much pressure on myself is that I always expected to contribute to my team. Of course, I knew that it wasn't possible to get a hit every at-bat, but I had a tough time accepting failure. Extended slumps can get guys sent to the bench, or worse, to the minor leagues. There was always someone waiting to take my job. That's why I tried to keep my slumps short and my hot streaks long. That's easier said than done, but I felt that if I could recognize that a slump was coming, or starting, I could address it right away. I didn't want to let it run its course and end whenever it ended. I wanted to be, I had to be, proactive.

You would never know when a slump would start, but there are many reasons that they do. Fatigue (mental or physical), a bad mental approach, lack of confidence and mechanical flaws are just a few. As you try to analyze your slump, it's important to eliminate possible causes.

- *Is it physical? It is natural to assume that your slump is caused by something going on between your ears, but let's rule out physical causes.*

  - If you aren't hitting, is your grip, stance or swing off? That's where watching video of your at-bats can be valuable. Studying video can also help you spot problems if your fielding is sloppy or you're prone to errors. Is there something going on with your footwork or other techniques?

- *If it isn't physical, is it emotional?*

  - Are there things going on outside the lines that are causing problems? For young players, maybe there's a problem at school or with your girlfriend or family causing you to lose focus during games. For older players, it could be financial stress or any number of issues.

  - For players of any age, but especially younger ones who are still finding what techniques work best for them, coaches can have a significant impact, which may not always be positive. Make sure that there is adequate communication between the player and the coach, or, between the parents and the coach to make sure there isn't unnecessary pressure being put on the player.

You can't do well at the plate if your head is full of thoughts about things other than the job at hand. Quoting Yogi Berra again, "How can you hit and think at the same time?"

Sometimes fans don't help the situation. When you're in a slump, you want to hide under a rock, but then there's a loudmouth in the stands screaming at you, "Hey, you no-talent bum, you're 0 for 4... pack your bags and go back to the minors where you belong." Some fans feel the price of admission includes the right to be as rude and obnoxious as they want. Add a few beers, and they get ruder and more obnoxious. It is impossible to tune it all out and you'll have some kind of emotion inside, but you have to keep it there. It makes you feel terrible and you realize that whatever you do, you are under a microscope. Your ego has already taken a big hit and when they yell about it at the park, it can really rattle you. Your voice inside your head has to be louder and more persistent than the hecklers. Keep telling yourself, "I'll get 'em next time, the odds are with me, I am a good hitter." I have been there many times when it's been very difficult to be positive, but the more good things you can say to yourself the better off you will be.

When you are slumping you need to manage your moods around your teammates. Some guys wear their emotions on their sleeves, meaning they want you to know how bad they feel about being in a slump. What bothered me about guys like that was when we won a game and they were 0 for 4, they were so focused on themselves that they didn't share in the team's success. Even when you're slumping, you have to be able to go into the clubhouse with a smile on your face, shake hands with your teammates and at least pretend to be happy. You have to respect the win. On the flip side, if you have a great game and the team loses, you have to respect the loss. If you are joking around with a big smile on your face because you had a great game, that is disrespectful. I was proud that I was pretty even-keeled because some guys could bring other players down when they were in a slump. When they were playing well, they were in great moods but could be terrible to be around when they weren't. It can rub off. Michael Young was awesome at staying even tempered. Unless you looked at the box scores, you never knew if he was slumping or on a hot streak. He was the same guy every day. You like to have that consistency from a teammate.

As for dealing with slumps, there are as many ways of trying to get back on track as there are players. You have probably heard of some of the more unusual slump busters, like Jason Giambi's choice of underwear: a gold-colored thong. It worked for him. I'm assuming the presence of the thong and the discomfort it provided gave Jason a constant reminder that he needed to focus on doing the things that made him successful before the slump. I preferred a different approach.

Early in my career, I tried to figure out how to be proactive and keep a slump from snowballing. Here's a checklist of things that I did when I wasn't feeling good at the plate or if I was slumping. If nothing else, they would trick me into feeling confident.

- SLOW IT DOWN I felt that when I wasn't hitting, it was

because I wasn't seeing the ball well. Maybe it was because of a lack of confidence or because I wasn't focusing enough on the area where the pitcher was going to release the ball. In either event, what I would do to correct that was to stand in at the plate, as if I was at bat, on a pitcher's session in the bullpen. Some pitchers didn't like having a guy stand in, but there would always be a couple who didn't mind. While waiting for his pitches, I would focus on an imaginary box by his ear where his release point would be. I would make sure my head was turned all the way toward the pitcher so I was seeing him clearly with both eyes. I would track the ball all the way to the catcher's mitt. I didn't have to worry about my mechanics, my swing or my approach. I didn't swing. All I was focused on was seeing the ball, picking up the spin and relaxing. I wanted to slow everything down because when I was slumping it was natural to speed things up in desperation to succeed. The more I pressed to do better, the faster the pitch seemed to travel. Slowing it down really helped me out. I liked to do it just before batting practice so that I could immediately swing at pitches and have a confident feeling going into the game.

- VISION TRAINING You can't hit what you can't see. As mentioned above, slumps can happen because we aren't seeing the ball well. Never take your eyes for granted. I went to vision-training specialists who provided me with training tools I could use at home, in hotel rooms while on the road or at the ballpark. These training techniques would help me strengthen and relax my eyes. Maybe some of it was psychological, but it worked. I was more confident about seeing the ball.

- SLEEP AND REST As I looked back on what was going on with me when slumps started, I noticed that if I wasn't getting enough sleep or if I felt run down, my eyes would be a little dry and blurry. Taking care of your whole body, including your eyes, and getting enough sleep is critical to being successful in any sport. You can't always work your way out of a slump. Overworking can prolong it. Practicing harder or longer would often work against me. I would get tired and create bad habits. Find the happy medium. When you feel yourself getting too tired, stop. Rest and go back to it later on. Quality over quantity. Listen to your body. It will tell you when it is time to back off. There is a fine line, though; you don't want your manager, coaches or teammates to think that you don't care or aren't working hard to get out of your slump. Be careful how you approach it. Make sure you let your coach know that when you overdo it you start creating bad habits. He'll understand.

- THE HANDS For me, when I was concentrating on my hands, I would practice my swing with no stride. I wanted to simplify it and make sure that I got the bat head to the ball. Instead of worrying about ten different things mechanically, think about one or two. Otherwise, you'll make yourself crazy. Take your body out of your swing and get back to the most important part: seeing the bat hit the ball. The hands are always a good place to start because, in my mind, they're the most important. If your hands are working right you give yourself a chance to be successful.

- BE IN THE MOMENT If you are walking to the plate and are 0-20, there is nothing you can do about those twenty at-bats now. They're over. Focus on the next pitch. *Be in the moment.*

- NEVER LET 'EM SEE YOU SWEAT Maybe you're too young to remember that iconic sell line from an antiperspirant commercial, but the concept is that while you may be dying inside, don't let it show on the outside. When you're struggling, act as if you're hitting a thousand. Show it in your posture, the way you walk, the way you stare down the pitcher as you approach the plate, the way you walk back to the dugout after a failed at-bat—never let 'em see that you're discouraged. If a pitcher sees you pouting or acting like you're defeated, that only makes him feel stronger and more confident. Don't throw your batting helmet or bat in the dugout. Don't stomp off to sit at the end of the bench with your head in your hands. You are part of a team. Be enthusiastic for your teammates. Your misfortunes will turn around.

- FEAR When you're in a slump it is easy to get pulled down by all of the pressures of the game. There is the fear of getting sent down, the fear of failing and the fear of humiliating or embarrassing yourself in front of all those people watching you play. Letting down your teammates or your family and friends is a very unpleasant emotion. Signing a big contract or getting a college scholarship may cause unnecessary pressure if you try to prove you are worthy. Combine all of these with a slump and it is a recipe for disaster. Remember: you cannot worry about what you cannot control. Relax and breathe. Slow everything down. When the game seems like it is getting too fast for you it is time to take a step back and evaluate your thought process.

- GARBAGE IN, GARBAGE OUT When you are in the batting cage, the on-deck circle or at the plate, make sure you're telling yourself the right things. Talk to yourself in positives, not negatives. Tell yourself what you are going to do, not what you're *not* going to do. Visualize what you want to have happen, not what you're afraid is going to happen. Believe in yourself. Believe that with the right mental and physical approach, you'll be successful. Even when you fail, talk to yourself about the good things that happened during that at-bat. Remember your successes. Don't look for pitches you can't hit. Look for pitches you can hit. Your slump could be caused, in part, by what you say to yourself about your failures. Garbage in, garbage out.

- BREATH CONTROL One key to stress control and muscle control is proper breathing. Learn how to control your breathing by using your diaphragm. A quick way to tell if you are using your diaphragm is by putting your palm on your belly, just below your breastbone. As you breathe in, your hand should move out. If it doesn't, you are breathing improperly through your chest.

Finally, and perhaps most importantly:

- ATTITUDE  You are not someone who *tries* to hit. You *hit*. Be crystal clear on this:  you are a hitter. Don't lose sight of that.

**CAT'S KEYS**

Get back to basics.

*Remember times when you were doing well.*

Is there a physical cause?

*Is there an emotional cause?*

Everything about a slump is in your control.

*We are a super-competitive family and here I am, as a
Toronto Blue Jay, with the leader of our pack.*

# 11

# COMPETITIVENESS

*com-pet-i-tive  adj.  1: Having or displaying a strong desire to be more successful than others*

Who likes to lose? I don't. Whether it is a board game at home with my family, soccer in the backyard with my daughters, a pick-up basketball game or playing a Major League Baseball game, I hate losing. Of course it happens, and when it does I feel as though I should have found a way to win. I think of what I could have done differently to change the outcome. I try to make sure I don't have to taste that losing feeling again. Or, at least I try to limit the number of times I'm on the losing side. Family and friends sometimes say I'm TOO competitive. I don't think there's such a thing. If you aren't trying to win, why are you playing?

Having that burning fire within, that desire to win, a passion to be the best and a refuse-to-lose attitude will only make you physically and mentally stronger. You can't be the best you can be if you aren't competitive.

I suppose part of it is genetic. I learned to be competitive at a young age. My family was always making everything into a game. Dad had a way of putting a spin on something and making it fun.

*CHRISTA: It's the whole family! I think our competiveness is innate. We are so competitive and will make a game out of anything, like let's see who could roll a quarter closest to the edge of the carpet or who can clean up the fastest. We love card games, board games and making up our own games. After dinner, we would often go downstairs and play soccer on our knees, hitting the ball with our hands (a game we had made up) or challenge each other in foosball, ping-pong, or pool. Many times, if we were sitting on the couch watching a show, during the commercials we would be throwing a ball back and forth to each other trying to fake out the person we were throwing it to just to see if they can still catch it. Friends knew if they came by, they would likely be involved in our antics. We loved being together, and still do. Now, during football season, we are together every Sunday at somebody's house. We watch football, eat and have a great time. A lot of people ask, "Do you really want to be with your family all the time?" Yes, we do. We really enjoy being together.*

*MICHAEL: We had Game Night, which was so much fun and so important to all of us, we made sure we didn't miss it. My friends would call up to ask me to go someplace and when I'd tell them, "Oh no, I can't, we're playing Scrabble tonight," they thought it was hysterical. When we played ping-pong, we wore a hole in the carpet, diving all over the place, getting injuries because we were so competitive with each other. Every single thing we do, even today, turns into a game. Washing dishes would turn into a game...it made it fun. We do that all the time. We were throwing a football around the other day and it accidentally landed in a large vase. So the game became who could get it into the vase. My parents play with us...my dad is usually the one setting up the games. You could be sitting on the couch doing nothing and you would get a ball on the side of the head. Suddenly, the game's on!*

Now, I understand that there is a fine line between being competitive and being a sore loser. There was no pouting or cheating allowed in our family games. Our parents did a great job of not only showing us how to enjoy each other, but that there's a right way to win and a right way to lose. No pouting, but I'm just saying that losing shouldn't feel good. It should bother you. On my teams growing up, even in the pros, I'd get angry if I saw a guy on my team smiling, laughing or fooling around right after a loss. Being competitive gives you an edge. It made me work harder in practice and in the gym lifting weights. Without that will to win, I wouldn't have been as successful. Competitiveness kept that fire inside burning and made me feel that I could compete with anybody. I believed in my ability to win the battle no matter what the situation. That will to win can't be underestimated. It's often the difference between success and failure, whether it's in baseball or whatever you do in life.

There's an old saying attributed to many people, including legendary NFL coach Vince Lombardi: "Show me a good loser, and I'll show you a loser".

*The adjustments I made in the minor
leagues helped me get to the big leagues.
Above, I am adjusting to playing third base
as a Toledo Mud Hen.*

# 12

# MAKING ADJUSTMENTS

*"The baseball fields of America are littered with the shattered dreams of young men who would have been big leaguers except for one thing: they couldn't—or wouldn't—learn to hit a breaking ball." ~ Unknown*

You can't succeed in baseball unless you know how to make adjustments and having an open mind is key to being able to make adjustments. Be aware that there is room for improvement and be willing to make changes. Many people think they know it all or can figure it out on their own. Some people just don't want help or can't take criticism.

*LARRY PARRISH: AA ball is the level when you can see if a guy can make the adjustments and go on. AA separates the guys. I remember many hitters who had all the talent in the world and were setting A ball on fire, but they couldn't hit the breaking ball. That's the difference. One guy makes the adjustments and goes on to have a great big league career and the guy with the great talent couldn't make it out of AA.*

I had seen guys with a lot of talent get left behind because of their inability to make both physical and mental adjustments. I didn't want to be one of those guys. Ruben Rivera was an example of a guy who had such sick natural talent that even AA didn't slow him down. We played against each other in the minor leagues. He was in the Yankees' organization and was being touted as the next Mickey Mantle. He had all the physical tools. He could run, hit and throw better than everyone else. Ruben was simply a stud who was feasting on minor league pitching and rocketing through the system, a couldn't-miss prospect destined for greatness. I made sure that I got his autograph when we played on an all-star team together. I didn't want to miss out on getting the next Mickey Mantle's autograph. The game seemed to come easy to him, and my teammates and I were always excited to get to play against him because we knew we would see something cool from Ruben during the game. Only thing was, when he got to the major leagues, pitchers found his weakness. He couldn't hit the inside pitch. Ruben couldn't make the adjustments. He couldn't get his swing to hit that inside pitch that they kept throwing him. If a pitcher made a mistake and threw the ball into his wheelhouse, he would hit it a mile. But at the big league level, pitchers don't make mistakes very often. He wasn't getting that pitch in his comfort zone and, mentally, he had a tough time dealing with it. All of a sudden he'd gone from this player who was drawing comparisons to Mickey Mantle to one who couldn't figure out why he wasn't successful. Maybe the fact that he didn't have to make many adjustments as a kid hurt him. He didn't know how to do it when he got to the major league level. Making adjustments is not a bad thing and doing it at a young age is great. It'll make you realize that there are different ways to do things and you'll be less afraid of change.

I was flying high when I got shot down. I was enjoying a great start to my AA season in Jacksonville, Florida, hitting over .350 through the first month and a half of the season when Larry Parrish, the roving minor league hitting instructor, came to town. L.P. would stop in for a week at every Detroit Tiger minor league affiliate to help with the hitters. While we were out for early batting practice, he told me we needed to totally revamp my swing. I thought he was joking. Here I was having a great start to my season. Why would I change my swing now and risk blowing such a good start?

*LARRY PARRISH: At the time, he had a flat bat and stayed on the plane really well. He never swung and missed, his average was high, but his defense was so-so. One day I asked him to come out early to the ballpark. He showed up early and we planned to do some extra hitting. Most of all, I just wanted to talk a little bit. We sat on the bench and talked about his defense. I said there's always going to be another second baseman that was going to be slicker, more skilled than he was. They may be able to steal bases.*

Larry told me, "So what that you're hitting .350? All you are is a slap hitter who plays average defense and can't run. We could find hundreds of Latin players who can slap the ball like you, play better defense and run faster. You need to separate yourself from them. You need to start driving the ball". I was crushed at first, but then I realized he was right.

*LARRY PARRISH: I asked him what he thought his best tool was. He said, "Oh, it's my bat." Well I agreed with him and said I wanted to try something a little different with him that day. I didn't know what would work, but I had been thinking about what we could do to take him to another level. I said, "You have great hand-eye coordination and we're going to tilt your bat forward instead of laying it backwards. We're going to give your swing a little loop and see if we can create a little more power. We want to separate you from the slick fielders and you'll be able to hit for average and have some pop".*

We got right to work. L.P.'s first order of business was to get my hands up. I had been a groundball/line drive hitter. I had always hit the ball to the opposite field and rarely hit for extra bases, especially home runs. My bat had been laid flat back with my hands close to my body. Larry wanted me to start to create more of a loop in my swing and get more momentum, leverage and length as well. Instead of tapping the ball or trying to meet it with a real short stroke, he wanted me to have a pendulum-type swing to create more power. He had me get off my back side and really explode into the ball, making a positive, aggressive move to the ball instead of sitting on my back leg and just spinning on it. This would create more torque and more violence throughout the swing. All of this was totally different to me, but I trusted him. I had been lifting weights and getting bigger, so maybe L.P. felt like it was time to put his plan into action. Besides, at the big league level, even the middle infielders were putting up gaudy power numbers.

*LARRY PARRISH: A lot of guys who hit .300 coming up through the system wouldn't have been willing to make some changes. They would feel, "Hey, I've been hitting well, it's not like I've been hitting .220". Cat didn't have that attitude. He said, "Okay, if you think that will make me better". I didn't know if it would make him better, I just wanted to try it and see if we could get more juice out of him. We went on the field, made the change and he started hitting the ball with more pop right away. A lot of credit went to Frank because he wasn't afraid to change his swing to try to be better. Then he went on to a great big league career.*

Whatever L.P. told me to do, I did. If he told me to move my hands or lengthen my stride, I did it, even if it didn't feel comfortable. He warned me it may feel awkward, but sometimes in order to get on the right track, you have to endure some awkwardness until the body and muscles get used to the new way. At night, I would go home and stand in front of a mirror and practice what he taught me so I could see exactly what I should be doing and exactly how it should look and feel.

It was very frustrating, but I knew that in order for me to make the adjustments successfully I had to be open to it. Sometimes you need to take one step back in order to take two steps forward. I bought in. I learned that sometimes to make change you need to totally break down the old ways and start over. The great reward was seeing my hard work pay off during games, but that didn't always happen right away. I struggled and it got a little discouraging, but I stuck with it and wound up driving the ball the rest of the year. I finished with seventeen home runs, the most I ever had in a season. My all-around numbers were great and although I had never been much of a power threat at the plate, I was now more than just a slap hitter. For the first time, I felt that I had a chance to make it to the major leagues.

There were many lessons learned in that process. Being open-minded and accepting the change allowed me to learn quickly. You must believe in yourself and trust that you can make change work. You have to be able to commit to the change or adjustment. Embrace it and be positive about it. Too often, players make excuses and blame others. It's your responsibility to pick and choose what adjustments feel right for you and which ones you want to discard. You know yourself, your strengths and weaknesses and what may help your game. There is no one, perfect way, no one size fits all. We are not robots. No two swings are the same. Not everyone throws or fields ground balls the same. Of course, there are certain fundamental things that all good hitters, pitchers and fielders do. Aside from those things, be yourself. What might work for me may not work for you. That's why you have to take a little bit from everyone and apply it to yourself. Try different things and find out what works best for you. And as I mentioned, sometimes you have to take that one step back in order to go forward. It's okay for change to feel uncomfortable or weird; it's supposed to. It is also okay for you to abandon tweaks in your swing after you give them a fair chance to work and they don't.

## TOO MUCH OF A GOOD THING

Justin Mashore had tools. He could run, had some power, had a real good arm, could play a great centerfield and had a deep passion for the game. Probably too deep. He had such a passion for being perfect that I feel it hurt him and may have cost him a chance to play in the big leagues. Justin was drafted out of high school by the Tigers in 1991. After almost every game, he'd go to the batting cages to try and figure things out. He was obsessed with getting it right, but he never gave himself a chance. He wasn't patient enough to breathe and take a step back. He hated to fail. If he didn't get a hit or didn't have a good game, he would come out with a new swing the next day. You could drive yourself crazy, not to mention run your body down by overworking. Whenever I did too much and was fatigued, I created bad habits. I always admired Justin's work ethic and his desire to get better but sometimes you can be your own worst enemy. Justin made it briefly to AAA with the Tigers. He bounced around as a minor league free agent with five other clubs, as well as a couple of Independent League clubs, before retiring after eleven seasons.

Find your happy medium. The game of baseball is one of constant change and adjustment. Once a pitcher figures out where the holes in your swing are or how to get you out, you need to adjust. If he's pounding you in with the fastball and you can't catch up, you need to figure out how to get to that pitch. Maybe you need to back off the plate or choke up on the bat. Be willing to change or the pitcher will continue to exploit that hole.

## MENTAL ADJUSTMENTS

Your thought process at the plate can change from game to game, at-bat to at-bat. We are constantly making mental adjustments and altering our plan depending on the situation. Considerations include who's pitching, how well or poorly you've been swinging the bat, who's behind the plate and many other factors. You always need to be thinking and trying to stay ahead of your opponent. When he adjusts, you need to adjust. Recognize the changes in the approach and what the pitcher or hitter may be thinking.

Before every game I'd plan my mental approach at the plate. I'd ask all the left-handed hitters what their approach was against that day's starter. Mine might change depending on what I heard. There may have been a bit of information that I didn't know about. Concentrating during the game will help you come up with a good approach for every at-bat or every pitch. Whatever mental approach you take, believe in it. Don't waver. Players wear their emotions on their sleeves. If you are unsure of yourself or your approach, your opponent will surely notice.

*LARRY PARRISH: Frank was really great for a young guy like me starting out coaching because he had a good mind and the willingness to work hard. You can see how far a young kid can come. Here they wanted to release him out of Instructional League and he went on to play nearly fifteen years at the major league level! That is quite a tribute to Frank.*

I always knew there was more to learn. Each day I wanted to go home and be able to write something down in my book that I had learned. My eyes and ears were always open, waiting to learn from a coach or player.

*LARRY PARRISH: After Frank had been in the big leagues for several years, a couple of Tigers' coaches and I would talk about Frank and say...this kid made himself a great big league career. It wasn't all on raw talent. He worked himself into a big league player. Near the end of his career, Frank and I laughed about when you're young, you hit the fastball and you live off the fastball. As your career goes along it sometimes get easier to hit the breaking ball because you don't have to be as quick. I'd tell him, "Cat, you need to jump on that breaking ball. Go ahead and drive that run in". He'd say, "No way. I want that fastball". We laughed about the memory and, how, in the latter years of his career he wanted the breaking ball. "That's the one I want to hit."*

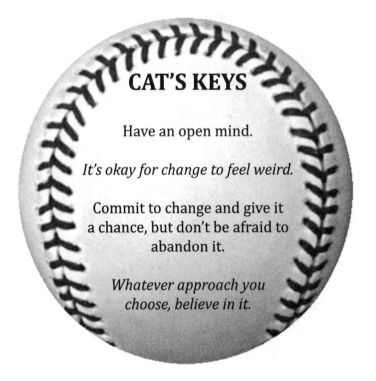

**CAT'S KEYS**

Have an open mind.

*It's okay for change to feel weird.*

Commit to change and give it
a chance, but don't be afraid to
abandon it.

*Whatever approach you
choose, believe in it.*

*One of my routines was getting dressed the
same way before each game.*

## 13

# ROUTINES

*"I had only one superstition. I made sure to touch all the bases when I hit a home run."* ~ *Babe Ruth*

Baseball Hall of Fame third baseman Wade Boggs ate chicken before every game, always took batting practice at 5:17 p.m. and ran sprints at 7:17 p.m. He drew the word "Chai" (Hebrew for life) in the dirt before every at-bat. Boggs admits to being superstitious, but you can't argue with the results.

Wade had chicken. I had Red Bull and bananas. I never felt like I was superstitious, but I definitely had my routines and *needed* them to make me feel comfortable. If I didn't do those things on a daily basis, I would be out of sync and feel "odd". I got to the ballpark at the same time every day; I did my treatments with the trainers, core exercises and stretching in the same order each day. Then, just before batting practice, I had a Red Bull and a banana. I needed them or I felt "off". There was a routine to my batting practice, too. During my first two rounds, I would hit everything the other way. (I bat left, so the natural swing is to hit to right field. Hitting the other way meant trying to hit to left.) Then, I would hit up the middle for the next round. In the next to last round, I would try to drive the ball into right centerfield and pull the ball down the right field line. The last round, I would just hit it where it was pitched. The important thing about batting practice is to do it with a purpose, not just go through the motions.

For a 7:05 game, the usual start for night games, I would go to the trainer's room at 6 p.m. and have my ankles taped. At 6:15, I would start drinking my energy drink. At 6:25 on the dot, I went to the bathroom to get away from the craziness in the main part of the clubhouse. There, I would unwind and think about my game plan. At 6:35, I started to put on my uniform. There was even a certain way I would get dressed.

At 6:40, I sat at my locker and did some visualizing and at 6:46, I went out to the field. During warm-ups, I always did the same number of each exercise movement: same number of sprints, shuffles, high knees and stretches. I made sure I was back in the dugout in time for the national anthem. Then, I did some calf stretches and wished each of my teammates good luck. If I didn't do all of these things, I would not feel right. I wouldn't have been in my comfort zone. You may have called it superstition. I called it routine. It was an important part of keeping me relaxed and focused. The consistency created a calming effect and helped take away some of the nervousness.

Roy "Doc" Halladay, my teammate in Toronto and one of the most dominating right-handers in major league history, is great for many reasons, including his routine. On days he pitches, his focus is remarkable. Our first season together, I thought that he was ignoring me. When I would pass him in the clubhouse, I said, "Hi", but he didn't respond. Five days later, his next start, I saw him looking right at me. Again, I said, "Hi", but there was nothing. No response. Not a head nod or anything. It was starting to annoy me, but a teammate who saw me trying to get a response from Doc said, "Hey man, don't talk to him. He's pitching today". On Roy's pitching days, he was so locked in with his mental preparation that he tuned out most of what was going on in the clubhouse. The rest of us didn't tiptoe around him, but we respected him and his routine. When it was his turn to get on the training room table, you got up. When it was his time to go over the scouting report with the pitching coach, you shut up.

Still, I thought that Doc's refusing to say a simple "hi" back to me was a bit much and on one of his off-days, I asked him about it. He said he hadn't even realized that I had spoken to him! He told me how his visualization techniques caused him to have tunnel vision, where he blocked out everything and everyone not involved in his preparation. With Doc, it wasn't just a pitching day routine. On the four days in between starts he would talk to me, but kept busy with his routine, always doing something to get himself ready for his next start. You would never find him playing cards or just sitting around passing the time. He would be running, throwing side sessions in the bullpen, lying in the hyperbaric chamber that he bought for the clubhouse, doing his shoulder exercises, lifting weights, watching videos, studying scouting reports and more. He was a machine, sticking to his routine religiously. That is part of his greatness and I admired his focus and determination. (A hyperbaric chamber, which looks kind of like a see-through plastic coffin, is a pressure chamber that raises the level of oxygen to one hundred percent. They are most commonly used to treat victims of carbon monoxide poisoning. I used it occasionally when I wasn't feeling well or was injured. It seemed to speed up the healing process.)

Once the game started, I had more routines. In the batter's box, I went through the same routine, whether it be stepping out after every pitch, re-strapping my batting gloves or tapping my spikes with my bat, taking the same number of practice swings between pitches and reiterating my plan for the next pitch in my head. Getting into the habit of performing routines helps get your mind focused on the task at hand and when your mind's prepared, your body will follow.

Then there was the walk-up music. Hearing the songs I chose blasting over the P.A. system as I walked toward the plate helped get me pumped up and locked in. Some of my favorites over the years:

1. "Down With the Sickness", by Disturbed

2. "Let the Bodies Hit the Floor", by Drowning Pool

3. "Higher", by Creed

4. "Kick Start My Heart", by Motley Crue

5. "Your Love", by The Outfield

Although not typical at-bat music, "Your Love" was a fan favorite. I started using it in Milwaukee in 2009 after I heard Kelly Johnson come out to it in Atlanta. I told some of the guys on the bench that I was going to start using it when we got back to Miller Park. They didn't really believe me because it was so unlike most music players chose. But, every time I came to bat in Milwaukee, the fans would stand and sing along. It was great that they got involved. I answered more questions about my walk-up music than I did about baseball that summer. I used a couple other songs along the way but not for too long.

When I was in the field on defense, I had a mental routine between every pitch where I would remind myself of how many outs there were, how many runners were on base and how fast they were. I focused on what I was going to do with the ball if it was hit to me, in front of me, to my left, to my right, over my head or, if the batter hit a soft bloop, or really smoked it. I tried to visualize making all different types of plays before they happened. It's important to constantly stay focused. There aren't many things worse in life than being embarrassed in front of your teammates, coaches, manager and, not to mention, thousands of fans, because you aren't paying attention. You have to remain focused between pitches and batters and not let yourself become distracted by something off the field. If you do, you may make a boneheaded play or misplay that might also get on *SportsCenter's* "Worst Plays of the Day". Pay attention. Respect the game.

Even during the off-season, I'd get into a routine by working out at the same time each day, doing the same active warm-up and the same batting drills in the same order each time. When you get used to the structure of having a routine, you feel a little lost without it.

Most major leaguers have some kind of routine. Find routines that work for you. They'll calm you down and help you focus.

One other major leaguer notorious for his routine, or superstitions, was Turk Wendell, a reliever for the New York Mets, as well as other teams. He'd leap over the baselines when walking to the mound, chewed black licorice while pitching and between innings, he brushed his teeth. Turk also wore a necklace decorated with teeth from the wild animals he hunted. His lucky number was nine, so he chose uniform number 99 and when he agreed to a contract with the Mets in 2000, he asked that it be for $9,999,999.99.

Rob Cuni

*Focusing on the pitcher to see if he was tipping his pitches. I was always trying to find an edge.*

# 14

# GETTING AN EDGE

*"Cheating is baseball's oldest profession. No other game is so rich in skullduggery, so suited to it or so proud of it."*
~ *Thomas Boswell, sports columnist*

Whether it's baseball, a backyard game of tag or a hand of poker, players are always looking for ways to get a competitive edge. It has always been that way and will continue to be forever. It is a by-product of humans playing a game. In professional baseball, you are talking about some of the most competitive people on Earth. Any hitter, given the chance to know what a pitcher was going to throw, would do whatever he could to find out. Similarly, the pitcher would do whatever he could to know what the batter was expecting. He might even alter the flight of the ball with sandpaper or hair gel so that it would be harder to hit.

Managers and coaches want to win and will steal signs or have their base runners do so if necessary. Hitters put on Academy Award-worthy performances as they fake getting hit by pitches. Fielders may use gloves that are longer than are permitted. Players want their team to win and strive to do well personally in order to receive the biggest contract possible. Cheating in baseball is part of the game. Players will attempt to get any edge possible, even though they know there is a penalty if they are caught.

I would argue that there are different levels of cheating in baseball. In my opinion, much of it shouldn't even be called cheating. It's more like being sneaky. A lot of it is relatively harmless, for example trying to sneak a peak at the catcher's signs. If a pitcher holds his glove differently when he's throwing a change-up, that's his problem, not the batter who notices. Cheating becomes a problem when it creates an un-level playing field. For instance, the altered ball, the corked bat and the use of performance enhancing drugs. The spitters and corkers seem to always get caught and the game has done a great job of cleaning up its performance enhancing drug issue through frequent and random testing. (I have some thoughts about steroids in a later chapter.) It is human nature to want to gain a clear advantage over the competition.

## THE BIGGEST CHEATERS[1]

Cheating goes back to the early years of baseball. In Ken Burns' "Baseball: An Illustrated History," he wrote that around 1900, third baseman John McGraw "held far bigger base runners back by the belt, blocked them, tripped them, spiked them—and rarely complained when they did the same to him." He was known to grab onto runners' belts as they rounded third and to hold their belt loops while they were attempting to tag up. A reporter at the time wrote that McGraw "uses every low and contemptible method that his erratic brain can conceive to win a play by a dirty trick."

*ESPN The Magazine* wrote about Gaylord Perry, a Hall-of-Famer who, "compiled his 314-265 record on the wings of a Vaseline ball. He'd stand on the mound, touching his cap or his sleeve, either loading up the ball or trying to convince batters he was doing so. In 1982, he became one of the very few pitchers to be suspended for doctoring the ball. Gene Tenace, who was Perry's catcher with the Padres, said the ball was sometimes so loaded he couldn't throw it back to the mound. Indians president Gabe Paul defended Perry: 'Gaylord is a very honorable man,' he said. 'He only calls for the spitter when he needs it.'"

In 1987, Twins pitcher Joe Niekro's slider was defying the laws of physics, so the umpire headed toward the mound for a look. As he approached, Niekro flipped an emery board out of his pocket onto the

---

1) *Excerpts on pages 134, 135 and 137 courtesy of ESPN.com*

ground behind him. He denied doing anything wrong, saying he needed it to file his fingernails so he could throw the knuckleball. And the small piece of sandpaper contoured to fit his finger that the ump also found? Niekro said that sometimes he would sweat a lot and the emery board got wet, so he would use the sandpaper. He said he also used it for small blisters.

Yankees' great Whitey Ford admitted using his wedding ring to cut the ball or had catcher Elston Howard use a buckle on his shin guards to do it.

Norm Cash, a White Sox and Tigers outfielder, told *Sports Illustrated* that he used a corked bat during the 1961 season when he led the AL in batting with a .361 average, hit forty-one homers and drove in one hundred thirty-two runs. He never came close to that with his un-corked bats.

In 1980, Rick Honeycutt was pitching for the Mariners. He recalls that he was struggling and as he passed a bulletin board in the clubhouse, he grabbed a thumbtack and taped it to his thumb so he could cut the ball. Not only was he caught, suspended and fined, but also during the game he had forgotten about the tack and absentmindedly rubbed his forehead, leaving a gash.

In 1999, my Tigers' teammate Brian Moehler was caught on the mound with sandpaper on his finger. Our manager, my mentor, Larry Parrish told reporters later, "There's not a pitching staff in baseball that doesn't have a guy who defaces the ball ... If the umpires want to check things like that, I think half to three-quarters of the league would be suspended."

Even groundskeepers got in on the cheating. In Seattle, manager Maury Wills had the groundskeepers enlarge the batting box, making it possible for the batter to stand a foot closer to the pitcher. In Chicago, longtime White Sox groundskeeper Gene Bossard would raise the foul line so Nellie Fox's bunts would stay in; he watered down the infield grass so Chicago's groundball pitchers would be more successful and soaked the dirt around first base so opponents would spin out while trying to steal. To give pitchers an edge, he tried freezing baseballs. In later years, he put them in a humidifier so they would weigh more.

## PITCHERS

Over my career, I saw pitchers doctor balls in a variety of ways but all with the same goal, to make the ball's flight less true. Sometimes, they would have the catcher or the third baseman do it for them. There were times when our catcher had glued a small piece of sandpaper on the outside of his right shin guard. He would use a marker and color it the same as his shin guard so no one could tell it was there. When he would take his hand back to throw the ball to the pitcher he would rub it up against the sandpaper and scuff the ball. There were times when our third baseman did the same thing, but he would have the sandpaper glued to the inside of his glove. After each out when the infielders would throw the ball around, the third baseman would get it last and scuff the ball before flipping it to the pitcher. What I never understood is why umpires never questioned the third baseman. They checked the pitcher or the catcher but not the third baseman.

Pitchers could really make the ball dip and dive with a scuff on it. Hair gel and pine tar also allowed them to modify the ball's path to the plate. Sometimes, I would see the starting pitcher doing his hair with his favorite hair gel in front of the bathroom mirror minutes before he was to take the mound. Then, during the game he would run his fingers through his hair so he could make the ball do tricks. Pine tar, thick and sticky, really helped the pitcher's grip on the ball so he could give it extra spin on the curveball and slider.

A pitcher who I played with in Texas would rub a bar of soap into his white uniform pants so it was imbedded into the fibers. On the mound, he would rub his hands down his leg across the soap so his fingers were slick. Then, when he rubbed up the ball, the soapy film made it act like a spitball. It would dart down like a super sinker, which was almost impossible to hit. It moved so much that the pitcher had a tough time controlling it. As teammates, we knew these guys were doctoring the ball but we also knew that opposing pitchers were probably doing it as well. We wanted to beat the other team so no one on the team (even hitters) really had a problem with it.

Batters had the option of asking for a new ball if they suspected it had been cut up or gooped up. I would ask the umpire for a new ball if

I thought it looked too dark or if the pitcher had just skipped one in the dirt to the catcher for fear it might be scuffed. Certainly, if I suspected it might have been doctored, I'd ask for a new one. Sometimes a team-mate might have suggested I ask for a new one because during his at-bat he felt like the ball was moving in a way it shouldn't have. However, I made sure that I didn't ask for a new ball too often because pitchers sometimes would take offense and plunk you with that brand new ball.

## HITTERS

Corked bats were not around much when I played. There were a couple of times when I knew a guy was using one. I tried one in batting practice a couple of times and, wow, it made quite a difference! I was hitting bombs. The ball just seemed to jump off the bat. I've been told that corked bats were used a lot in the seventies and eighties. I recall the story of Graig Nettles, of the Yankees, breaking a bat and six superballs went bouncing around the infield. Nettles said a fan gave it to him for good luck. The fan had apparently drilled a hole down through the barrel of the bat, stuck the superballs and cork inside. Then he put some sawdust back into the hole, sandpapered it down and added a little pine tar over the top of it. I don't know of anyone specifically using them now, but it wouldn't surprise me. As great as it was to use one in BP, I was too nervous to use one in a game. I would have been mortified if that bat had broken open.

## STEALING SIGNS

Here's another trick that goes back decades. During the 1951 season at the Polo Grounds in New York, which was highlighted by the Giants' National League pennant win over the Dodgers on Bobby Thomson's "shot heard around the world", the Giants admitted that they were stealing signs. Coach Herman Franks would sit in the Giants clubhouse, conveniently behind the center field fence, and use a telescope to read the catcher's signs. He would then set off a bell or buzzer in the Giants' bullpen that would identify the next pitch, and a relay man would signal it in to the hitter.

Nowadays, stealing signs happens often, but not through tele-scopes in centerfield. Runners at second base can see the catcher flash his signs, then signal to the batter what may be coming. My feeling is that if the pitcher's concerned about it and doesn't want it to happen, he should make his signs more complicated. A lot of pitchers will go with the second sign, or the sign after the two, or the number of outs plus one. Those are the easy ones to pick up. When I played with the Toronto Blue Jays from 2003-2006, we would steal signs, but it had to be a perfect situation. First of all, there were usually only three or four guys on the team who were good enough at figuring out the signs and comfortable enough to relay them to the hitters. And not every pitcher would have easy signs. Roy Halladay and Roger Clemens were among those who had complicated signs. Sometimes it would take five or six innings before we could decipher the signs. That would often be too late, because the starter would come out of the game in the sixth or seventh. Plus, there had to be a runner on second in order to start figuring out the signs. Some games, we may have only had a player reach second base once or twice, or maybe not at all.

As a hitter, it was nice to know what was coming, especially if a pitcher had a really good out pitch like a splitter or change-up, but that's assuming the base runner had the signs right. There were times he didn't. Maybe he messed it up, or maybe the catcher changed the signs, but as the batter, it would totally screw you up. You might take a fastball right down the middle for a called strike three because the base runner signaled to you that it was going to be an off-speed pitch. One year, a rumor was going around the league that we were getting the catcher's signs from second base, which actually worked in our favor at times because the pitcher got so rattled worrying about the guy at second that he wasn't concentrating on executing his pitches. Inevitably he would throw up some fat pitches.

As the base runner relaying signs, you needed to be nonchalant. If you were too obvious the hitter might take one in the ribs. It was important to behave the same way at second as you would when you didn't have the sign, especially once the word was out that we were stealing. Some of our guys became so nervous or anxious, they would be too obvious in their deliver. This resulted in the pitcher waving the catcher out and changing the signs. Maybe he would throw the next pitch at our hitter. It was quite a game within the game. We had many things we would do at second after we got the sign. Looking to the left would indicate a fastball and to the right would be an off-speed pitch. That didn't look obvious because as a runner, you would always check the middle infielders to see how far they were playing off the bag.

This way you wouldn't get picked off. So, the first direction you looked would be the sign to the hitter. Other times, it might be hands on your knees or fixing your helmet. There were many signs we would come up with and we changed them each game.

During one series with the Red Sox, catcher Jason Varitek was convinced we were stealing signs because we were hitting so well. He came up with signs to the pitcher that no one would ever be able to figure out. Instead of putting fingers down, he'd touch different parts of his body over and over again. The signs were so hard that it made it easy on us: we didn't even try. No reason to waste our energy and lose our focus on signs that would take us all game to figure out, if at all. It seemed like a lot of the Red Sox pitchers, especially relievers, didn't understand or like the signs. Varitek was constantly going out to the mound, which can ruin the flow and rhythm that pitchers like to get into.

Smart pitchers would change their signs from start to start. Some would even change their signs from inning to inning. But, most were creatures of habit and liked to stick with the same signs all the time. We feasted on those guys! I would always write in my "book" what signs the pitcher was using so the next time we faced him, I'd have an idea of what he might use.

## COACHES' SIGNS

It's fascinating to watch the signs that coaches and managers use. Third base coaches, especially, can put on quite a show. It looks complicated on purpose because they know the other team is trying to steal, but are usually pretty simple for the batter or runner to read because of how they are set up. Usually, there is an indicator which lets you know that a sign might be on. Let's say the indicator is the hat. If the coach never touches his hat then no sign is on. If he does touch his hat at some point during his "show", then the very next thing that he touches will be the sign. For instance, if his arm is bunt, his chest is hit and run and his belt is steal, then after he touches his hat followed by his chest, it would be a hit and run. Sometimes the indicator could be when he touches the same body part twice in a row. That would let the player know that the very next thing that he touches will be the sign. There are so many variations that can be used and some can be very difficult to learn. When we were on defense, our coaches were constantly trying to figure out what it all meant and it could take several times before they did. Is the hit and run on? A bunt? Will the runner go? Our coaches also kept an eye on the bench coach's signs to the catcher to get an idea of when he might be throwing through to second base, throwing to third or not throwing at all on a double steal. All teams try to steal the signs and no one gets offended. If, for some reason, a team's signs are not difficult enough, or you have a guy smart enough to figure them out, why not take advantage of it?

## STEALING AT HOME

I've heard of hitters peeking at the catcher's signs, but I never understood how they were physically able to do that. My eyes don't stretch like that, but apparently there are some who appear to be looking at the pitcher, but are able to see the catcher's signs out of the corners of their eyes. During day games, these guys would wear sunglasses, which kept others from seeing them peek. But, they did so at their own risk. I've seen guys take one in the ribs just because the other team suspected he was peeking. The same went for peeking at where the catcher was setting up.

I tried to bait catchers and pitchers all the time. It was part of my plan and sometimes it worked. At least it gave me confidence and it allowed me to believe in something one hundred percent. As a hitter, if you're in-between or wishy-washy, you really don't give your plan a good chance to succeed. Let me explain. First, I would always remember what I said to a pitcher or catcher and kept it in my memory bank for later. Often, we would see the opponent in the weight room or on the field during batting practice. Nearly all of my conversations with them had a reason: I was looking for an edge. If I bumped into a pitcher who had owned me, I might say, "Damn, your change-up is really good. I have a real tough time seeing it out of your hand." The next time I faced him—even if it were a couple of months later—he would remember our conversation. That seed I planted in his head had bloomed and he would throw his change-up, which I would be sitting on, ready to pounce.

Other times, while at bat, if I took a bad swing on a pitch, I would say something to the catcher like, "Wow, that was nasty!" Sometimes it was, but a lot of times I just had a bad swing for some other reason. Maybe I was looking for something else and got fooled. But, after my comment, I knew the catcher would be thinking about what I said, call that "nasty" pitch again and I would be all over it. Sometimes, I'd even involve the umpire in my little charade. If there was a pitch on the outside corner that I took for a strike, I'd complain and say, "Let's go, that's off the plate", making the catcher think that I was having a tough time seeing the ball away. Guess what I'd look for the rest of the at-bat? You guessed it. Fastball away. I'd give up the rest of the plate, move closer and hunt for my fastball away.

For the pitcher who had that great out pitch, like a split-fingered fastball or a change-up that he got me to chase in the dirt, I would purposely move way up in the box and dig in intently, making sure the catcher noticed. He would think that I was trying to protect myself from that nasty pitch in the dirt and that I would have no chance on a good hard fastball in. Surprise! I would choke up and look for the inside fastball. My bait worked most of the time. And the worst-case scenario was that if he did throw another one in the dirt, I would be up in the box anyway and have a good shot. Trust me, it didn't work all the time, but it gave me a plan that I trusted one hundred percent. I wasn't wishy-washy or in-between. I had a plan and committed to it, for better or worse. You won't be right all the time, but if you have confidence and a well thought out, educated reason to do it a certain way, you will be more successful. The only thing worse—and not by much—than being at the plate and not trusting your plan, is not having a plan.

Whenever I planted a seed in a pitcher or catcher's head, I would write it down in my book. The next time I would go up against them, I would read what I had written and instantly feel as if I had an edge. In the minor leagues, I surrounded myself with pitchers. Every season, I would rent a house with pitchers. I wanted to pick their brains, try to get in their heads and try to understand how they thought. I did and they told me everything. They told me what the pitching coaches told them, what their game plans were and when they were vulnerable. I wanted to know what made pitchers tick, how they felt in certain situations, what they looked for in a hitter's body language, what pitches they tended to use in specific counts and what got them rattled or off their game. Any of that information was pure gold and I felt I had a better idea of what to expect at the plate against other pitchers.

In the dugout during rookie league our pitching coach, Jim Van

Scoyoc, mumbled more or less to himself after a pitcher gave up a home run, "The first pitch after a home run is always a fastball right down the middle because the pitcher's rattled". I made a mental note of that and the next time I was up right after a home run, I was aggressive and feasted on that fat pitch right down the middle. Maybe it wasn't a fastball every time, but if it happened eighty-five percent of the time, that was enough for me to believe in my plan. It is hard enough to get a hit, so use all the information you can and make it work to your advantage. Getting every edge possible will only make you a better player. Again, have a plan and believe in it until it's proven to be a bad plan. By the way, my first-pitch-fastball plan worked quite often in the minor leagues, but not as much in the major leagues where pitchers—some of whom were my victims in the minors—were wiser.

Be thinking at all times about what might help give you and your teammates an advantage. Like Yogi famously said, "Ninety percent of this game is half mental". There are ways you can get an edge by keeping your eyes open and using your head.

*Waiting for the cutoff throw.*

# BIG LEAGUE MENTALITY

*"A man has to have goals – for a day, for a lifetime – and that was mine,
to have people say, 'There he goes, the greatest hitter who ever lived.'"*
*~ Ted Williams*

I f you want to be a big leaguer, you have to have a big league attitude. Let me explain what I mean by that. The most powerful organ in your body is your brain. I have no doubt that a key reason I became a major league player is because I consistently thought that I would be one. Whether you're on a Little League team, or a minor league team, if you want to make the big leagues, you have to have that big league attitude, convincing yourself that you are good enough, or will be good enough, to be a big leaguer. It's the power of positive thinking.

In Chapter One, I wrote that I dreamed of being a Major League Baseball player. There's no question that dreaming about it and seeing myself on that big league field helped me get there. I believed in myself and believed that my dreams could come true. Having a vision and seeing yourself have success go a long way when it comes to believing in yourself. You should repeatedly see it in your head first so that when you are in a certain situation it won't seem foreign to you. It will seem familiar, even though it may have never actually happened to you before. Draw on your successes and positive experiences, mentally reliving them. Sometimes, no matter where I was, I would stop, close my eyes and see myself getting a hit. Sitting in the dugout or even standing in the on-deck circle were good places to do this. Visualizing can help you create positive expectations.

Never underestimate the power of your mind and especially the power that you have over it. For example, when you're walking to home plate, you should be telling yourself what *to* do, rather than what *not to* do. Before I learned that trick, I'd catch myself finishing a thought with a negative and almost every time, that's how it played out. I failed. Focus on what you want to happen as opposed to what you don't want to happen.

Along with having your mind focused, you have to have heart, which I think is underrated. You've got to want it. It bothers me when I see kids taking lessons who seem uninterested. They're just going through the motions. Sometimes I'll ask them, "How far do you want to go with baseball? Do you want to play in high school? College? Do you want to get drafted? Go to the major leagues?" Depending on the answers, I might suggest they have a heart-to-heart talk with their parents about the reasons for the lessons. Maybe the child's goals and the parents' goals aren't in sync. Or, maybe they all need to understand their individual expectations. Unreasonable expectations can kill a dream.

Certainly, a AAA player is going to have a different mindset than a Little Leaguer or a high school player. However, the essentials are the same: each has to work hard, practice hard and play well to move up. Major leaguers have to do the same things to stay in the big leagues. Regardless, whatever the level, heart – which no scout can accurately measure – is a huge asset in athletics, especially in young athletes, because it can take them a long way.

What I learned in my first year or so in the big leagues shocked me. There I was, living my dream after I had worked extremely hard for fifteen years. But if I wanted to stay there, I had to work harder than I had ever worked in my life! That wasn't easy to swallow because I had always prided myself on my work ethic and how hard I trained and practiced. In that first year or two, I still struggled with feeling like I belonged and feared that I would be sent down. It was a stressful time and whenever I had a bad game or played poorly for a week straight, I would tell myself that I really needed to start working harder or else I would be sent to the minor leagues in no time and may never get back. Then, in my second major league season, I learned that Barbara and I were expecting our first child. I started thinking that if I was sent back to the minor leagues I wouldn't be able to support her and our baby.

*BARBARA: Frank had been up and down between Detroit and Toledo the year before Morgan was born. It was a little nerve-wracking because he wasn't confident he would be on the major league roster. He felt a lot of pressure because he had another mouth to feed and he wasn't sure what was going to happen. Frankie put a lot of extra stress on himself.*

So, I rededicated myself. I had to be all in because I wanted to give my child the best life. If I were to get released, not making that much money, I would have been left in No Man's Land: no career, no skills and mouths to feed. I have seen it happen to other players who never made it out of AAA, or even AA, had a wife and a kid or two and when baseball ended, they had to scramble to put food on the table. I wanted to play like my hair was on fire every time I went out there and really make an impression.

My last years were a little bit different. I had made a lot of money, invested well and no longer had to worry much about bringing home big paychecks. While in the first couple of years, I kept thinking I needed to play well and become a better player, I wasn't able to soak it in. In those last couple of years, my mentality was enjoy every moment because once it's over, it's over. The last year I brought a camera with me everywhere I went. I took pictures of stadiums, locker rooms and all the big league cities.

My attitude toward my performance also changed. While I wanted to play, if I didn't get to play in the game, it didn't bother me like it did when I was younger. If I didn't have great games, I didn't get as upset about it as when I was young. I was getting older and my body wasn't the same. I wasn't as capable as I was in the past. If I wasn't in the line-up, so what? I'm still here in the major leagues, still contribut-ing. However, I never felt that gave me the right to slack off. I always worked hard and wanted to show the younger guys the right way to play the game, the right way to practice, the right way to respect the game. I was a professional. I never wanted anyone to say I was coasting, that I wasn't trying and had stopped working hard. Even times when there was early hitting and maybe only a few guys would go out, I would always join them, letting the rookies know that I expected them to be out there, too.

The big league mentality also includes playing unselfishly, giving information and tips to teammates that might help them succeed. So what if they didn't do the extra video or scouting work that you did? Share it with them. Helping them enhance their skills makes you better. At every game I would speak with the guys who were in the lineup and tell them what to look for in the pitchers. Helping others when they fail, patting them on the back when they are not playing well and recognizing that the ultimate goal is to win is all part of the big league mentality.

For younger kids, I don't care as much about you learning to play a position as I do about you learning to play the game. Be a student of the game so you know what each guy on the team should be thinking. It will make you a more valuable player. You need to know the ins and outs of the game and why the manager is making decisions. It makes you a complete player. Kids can start doing this at an early age. When I ask kids what position they play and they tell me "shortstop", I ask, "Is that it?" Make sure you play all the positions because you will become more athletic and have a better understanding of the entire game.

For players of all ages, be enthusiastic. Being excited and interested in playing the game will shine through and make you a better player. It will show others that you love the game and want to get better. Coaches and scouts will see the enthusiasm and that will help them project whether you will become better in the coming years. You need to want to be there and have fun playing. Enthusiasm can compensate for some shortcomings.

Don't let sports use you; use sports to get what you want out of life. Get the most out of your ability and talents. Use sports to help you in your future endeavors. Sports can help you get a college education. They can help you determine your career and meet future business partners or associates. Sports teach you how to collaborate, how to win, how to lose and how to enjoy competition. After my playing career, many doors were open to me because I always understood that baseball was a path toward other things.

## GOALS

Setting goals is essential. People who have a vision and are goal-oriented are usually successful people. I always had a plan and a desired end result. There's something empowering about writing something down on paper, putting it where you can see it everyday, then crossing it off when you've achieved it. Parents may need to help children set goals to make sure they're realistic.

---

*TYPES OF GOALS*

*1. LONG-TERM: I dream of being* _____
_____ *when I grow up.*

*2. INTERMEDIATE: In the next five years, I want to* _____
_____.

*3. SHORT-TERM: In the next year, I want to* _____
_____.

*4. IMMEDIATE: This week, I want to* _____
_____.

---

Goals should be attainable, and for younger kids, adjustable.

- It is important for parents, coaches and young athletes to be on the same page when it comes to goal setting.

- Make sure they are the child's goals and not the parents' goals.

- Setting specific goals helps the player focus on strengths and weaknesses and ways to improve.

- Set goals that are S.M.A.R.T.: Specific, Measurable, Attainable, Realistic and Timely.

- Be in control of each goal.

- Always write the goals in the positive instead of negative. Stay away from "not striking out" or "not walking hitters" when stating goals.

- Have a combination of short-term and long-term goals.

- Goals are a player's important tool. They help focus your attention and energies.

- Goals must be compatible, prioritized, limited in number <u>and must be in writing.</u>

- Pick a goal or two to work on each week.

- Remove and add goals at regular intervals. Review your goals on a daily/weekly basis to keep them fresh.

- Have some long term or "dream" goals.

---

*SAMPLE GOAL SHEET FOR YOUNG ATHLETE*

*1. Have fun.*

*2. Play with buddies and make new friends.*

*3. Exercise.*

*4. Learn the basics of baseball.*

*5. Play middle school ball.*

*6. Use athletics as a way to spend time with parents.*

*7. Play baseball in high school and college.*

---

You can set goals within goals, specifically identifiying some for games, for practice, for conditioning and nutrition. For example, here's what one of my early goal sheets might have looked like:

Name:  Frank Catalanotto                                    Age:  12

1. Learn the game.

2. Learn every position.

    a. Read books and watch instructional videos.

3. Practice.

    a. Hit ____times off tee each week.

    b. Catch and throw ____times each week.

4. Make the team.

    a. Become a starter.

    b. Lead team in hitting, fielding or pitching.

5. Conditioning

    a. Jump rope 100 times without missing.

    b. Run a 40-yard dash in _____ seconds.

    c. Do ____ push-ups in five minutes.

    d. Do _____sit-ups in five minutes.

6. Nutrition

    a. Replace unhealthy snacks with fruit and veggies.

    b. Replace soda with water and fruit juices.

    c. Replace fried foods with grilled foods.

7. Be a stronger and better player at end of season.

It may make sense to break it up into months or first half/second half of the season.

---

**MINOR LEAGUE PLAYER GOALS**

1. Be a starter.

2. Hit at least .300.

3. Commit no more than ____ errors.

4. Move up a level by the end of the season.

5. Get bigger and stronger going into next season.

---

For major league players, the goals can get much more specific:

---

**MAJOR LEAGUE PLAYER GOALS**

1. Get 400-500 at-bats.

    a. by April 30: 70 AB

    b. by May 31: 150 AB

    c. by June 30: 225 AB

    – etc.

2. Hit at least .300.

    a. Be in the Top 5 for batting average each week

3. End the season with 10-15 home runs.

    a. by April 30: two HR

    b. by May 31: four HR

    – etc.

4. Drive in 50-60 runs.

    a. by April 30: 10 RBI

    – etc.

---

*(Major league goal sheet, continued)*

5. Steal 10-15 bases.

    a. by April 30: 2 SB

    – etc.

6. Score 65-75 runs.

    a. by April 30: 12 runs

    – etc.

7. Fielding percentage of .1000.

    a. Errors

    b. Put-outs

    c. Assists

8. Make All-Star team.

9. Be in contention for the batting title and Gold Glove.

## Or, your goals might be specific to a weakness in your game:

- Work on getting the ball out of your glove quicker.
- Work on pitching inside to lefties (or righties, or both).
- Work on hitting to the opposite field.
  - Do ___ minutes of extra batting practice per day.
  - Do ___ minutes of tee work after each game.
  - Do ___ minutes of hitting curve balls each day.
- Make better contact at the plate.
  - Examine stance, grip and swing.
  - Do ___extra minutes of cage work each day.
  - Do ___extra minutes of video work each day.
- Stay healthy, strong and injury free.
  - Perform ___extra minutes of strength and conditioning workouts per week.

When setting goals within goals you are essentially planning how you will achieve your ultimate goal. Short-term goals help to keep us motivated.

---

1.  String together at least one hit per game for five games. (then ten, then fifteen)
2.  Create competitions with yourself relating to any part of your game.

---

When you only have long-term goals you can get frustrated by not seeing them get closer. Setting short-term goals within goals makes you continually want to push. The baseball season is long so we need to reach some goals along the way to give us that sense of accomplishment. Goals keep you moving in the right direction.

No one else has to know what your goals are. Write them down on a piece of paper before the season. At the top of the list should be your most important goal and work your way down. Reread the list from time to time to keep them fresh in your mind. Make sure you don't set yourself up for disappointment. But, don't set goals that are too easy to attain. We always need to be striving for something. It helps give us that drive we need. No one says that goals can't be changed or adjusted during the season. Sometimes if you reach your goals with a month left in the season you will mentally go on vacation. Or, if you see you have no chance to reach your goals you could be very disappointed and give up.

Sometimes, it helps to have a little push, a reminder of why we set our goals. Big motivators for me were all the people who never thought I'd make it to the major leagues. They drove me. When I thought about the minor league coordinator for the Detroit Tigers who wanted to cut me after my first short season; that motivated me. When I thought about not making the Single A team and having to go back to Rookie Ball, that motivated me. When I thought about the rumors that I heard from back home that some of the kids that I went to high school said that I would never make it; that motivated me. It all helped me work harder to prove them wrong. It drove me in the weight room and kept me in the batting cage longer. In a way, I liked when someone doubted me because I knew that with my work ethic and my passion to be my best, I would prove them wrong. A fire was always burning inside me. That worked for me, but everyone finds motivation in different ways and forms. Yours might not be to prove people wrong, but whatever it is, use it to drive yourself to the next level.

*MICHAEL: Frankie was a confident and driven guy. Very organized, constantly doing something. He would be outside all day, into the dark, throwing the ball against the side of the house. He would spend hours in the basement smacking that Wiffle golf ball with the broomstick. He sawed off a baseball bat and attached weights to the end so he could swing it and strengthen his arms. These are things he would come up with on his own to make himself a better player. He was always working on it. To this day, whatever he does, I always say he will find the right way to do it. His drive to be his best was amazing.*

CAT'S KEYS

Never underestimate the power of your mind.

*Visualize positive outcomes.*

Tell yourself what to do rather than what not to do.

*Set S.M.A.R.T goals: Specific, Measurable, Attainable, Realistic and Timely.*

Goals must be in writing.

Rob Cuni

*In my last couple of seasons, including 2010 with the Mets, my role changed from starter to primarily coming off the bench.*

*One of my first cards.*
*Nine years old*

*My Long Island Little League team when I*
*was thirteen. My dad is in the Yankees jacket.*

*Signing my first professional contract, 1992.*
*L-R: Dad, Christa, me, Michael, Ramon Pena, Mom.*

*With the guy who taught me how to play baseball,
my dad, at the old Detroit Tigers' stadium, 1997.*

*The woman who made it all possible, Mom.
At Rangers' spring training in Surprise, Arizona.*

*Above: My baseball career, illustrated. Below: First MLB hit and HR balls and bat.*

*My mentor, Larry Parrish, and I heading for the bus after a spring training game in 1993.*

*In the cage during 2000 Rangers' spring training in Port Charlotte, FL.*

Rob Cuni

*The Rangers' private plane.*

*Relaxing with a movie.*

*Few things rival the joy of a game winning hit and the traditional postgame beer shower from your teammates as you walk into the clubhouse. This was after I got a walk-off hit at the Ballpark in Arlington.*

Courtesy, Matt Walbeck

*Turning a double play against the A's.*

*Looking for an edge against the next starter, C.C. Sabathia.*

*Running down a fly ball in front of the iconic ivy at Wrigley Field.*

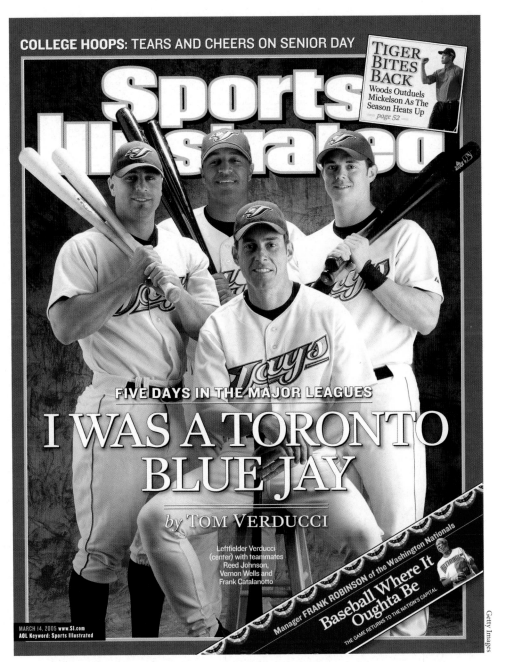

That's quite a group: Reed Johnson,
Vernon Wells, Tom Verducci, Tiger Woods,
Frank Robinson and me.
March 14, 2005

Matt Walbeck

*At my locker in the old Yankee Stadium.*

Above three photos by Rob Cuni

Rob Cuni

*I was grateful to be able to finish
my career in New York.*

*An outfield "high five" after a Milwaukee win.*
*Left to right:  Ryan Braun, Mike Cameron, me.*

*At Miller Park, Milwaukee in 2009.*

*Part of 2006 Team Italia, L-R Me, Frank Menechino, Mike Piazza.*

To Barbara and Frank Catalanotto
With best wishes,

*Family photo day at Miller Park in Milwaukee 2009.*
*Frank, Karson, Camdyn, Barbara, Gracyn, Morgan*

*Team Catalanotto at Miller Park in Milwaukee 2009.*
*Frank, Karson, Camdyn, Morgan, Gracyn, Barbara*

*The Catalanotto Clan, 2010*

# 16

# COMING OFF THE BENCH

*"When you're on the bench, don't let yourself be sucked in to being a spectator of this grand, beautiful game. The moment you do is the moment you jeopardize the chance of helping your team win." ~ Unknown*

In the early days of baseball, pinch hitters were virtually non-existent. Rosters were smaller and every player was expected to take his regular turn at the plate. Only when there was an injury could a pinch hitter go into the game. That changed in the early twentieth century and became a standard piece of the manager's arsenal when rosters were expanded and specialized relief pitchers became routine.

I did a lot of pinch hitting during my career, probably because I was pretty good at coming off the bench. My preparation had a lot to do with that, but I was also well instructed by some former teammates early in my career. Guys who spent the last few years of their careers as bench players, like Pete Incaviglia, Dave Magadan, Greg Jefferies and Billy Ripken, among others. They all told me the same thing: be aggressive. That was hard for me because it went against how I normally was as a hitter. I hardly ever swung at the first pitch. I liked to see a few pitches and get comfortable in the at-bat. But their reasoning was this: usually, you pinch-hit late in the game and the pitcher probably had a good, hard fastball and a real good out pitch. Maybe a good split or a nasty slider. You never wanted to have to hit those pitches. Pitchers, relievers especially, didn't want to fall behind in the count. They liked getting ahead, usually with a first-pitch fastball. If you went up to the plate passively and took a strike you were down 0-1. A lot of times as a pinch hitter it might take you a swing before you are able to put the ball in play, so you may foul off the next strike. Now you had two strikes on you and were faced with having to possibly see this guy's best pitch.

If you approached your at-bat aggressively and came out swinging, your whole mentality changes. You are in attack mode, not back on your heels. You were ready for any strike that crossed the plate. It didn't have to be a fastball, it could be anything that looked good to hit. Many times when a pitcher would throw a first-pitch breaking ball it would not be his best one. It might be a hanger, one that he was just trying to get over the plate for a strike. When you're in attack mode, you could do damage even if you were expecting a fastball away. Even if you were to foul off that first pitch, at least you were able to gauge the pitch and get loose with your swing. When you take a good hard rip at a ball, it allows you to make the adjustment on the next pitch. Maybe you were late or maybe you felt like you over swung a little bit. You'd have some added confidence going into the next pitch.

Being aggressive generally meant better at-bats and I tried to take that frame of mind into my at-bats even if I was starting the game and knew I would be up four or five times. Of course, I worked the count more when I was in the starting lineup, but when it was time to be aggressive I didn't hold anything back. It greatly improved my plate discipline. As the pitch was coming in I would repeat in my head "strike, strike, strike", until I recognized that it was a ball, and then I would say "ball". The reason I did that was so I was aggressive and ready to hit. I expected it to be a strike and only gave up on the pitch once I saw that it was not what I wanted. If I'd expected that the pitch would be a ball, it would be too late to react to that fat pitch right down the middle of the plate. Being at home plate and saying "ball, ball, ball, strike" was being unsure of what you wanted and would ultimately cause you to swing at bad pitches. Over the course of my career I took notice and realized that the aggressive pinch hitters were always the most successful.

Knowing the situation is also so important, which I learned the hard way in 1999. Larry Parrish was managing the Tigers that year and had asked me to pinch-hit in the bottom of the ninth inning of a close game. We were down two runs with a runner on second base and one out.

*LARRY PARRISH: I used to say...the thing about Cat that makes him a great bench guy or everyday player is you can play him against a starter, he can hit breaking balls, change-ups; he can hit everything in the pitcher's repertoire. He can hit but he has the ability to sit on the bench for seven innings and he can hit the fastball late in the game. That's tough to do. A lot of bench guys can hit a fastball or can hit the starting pitcher but when it gets late in the game, they can't catch up.*

I had a great at-bat and wound up drawing a walk. I was excited and felt like I did my job by getting on base. The next hitter grounded into a double play to end the game and when I came into the dugout L.P. was furious.

"What the hell were you thinking out there?"

I didn't understand what he meant.

"The reason I sent you up there to hit, was to hit! The guy behind you can't hit, as we just saw. I wanted you to swing the bat."

I didn't even realize who was hitting behind me. When I got a 2-0 fastball right down the middle, I took it because I was trying to work a walk. Larry wanted me to be aggressive and drive the ball instead of leaving it for the weaker hitter. He put me up there to hit, not to walk, hence the name pinch HITTER. It all made sense after he told me and from then on I always thought about the situation and what my job actually was.

When coming off the bench, preparation is so important. You may get one chance to help the team out. Be thinking ahead while you're on the bench. Play manager in your head and try to figure out what situations could develop and where you might fit in. Know who the manager might want to pinch-hit for. Know who he might want to put into the game as a defensive replacement. Have your body warm by the time you think you may be used. I would always go into the underground tunnel and run sprints, stretch and throw to stay loose. I would go to the batting cage and take some swings so I would be ready for that big at-bat at the end of the game. I would keep an eye on the visitor's bullpen to see who might be coming into the game. If you have video or scouting reports on the relievers, take a look to get an idea of what you might be facing. It's better to be ready than to be caught off guard. There were many times that I would be ready but would not be used. That was fine with me, I just did not want to go into a situation where I felt like I was unprepared both physically and mentally. The book that I kept on the pitchers helped me be a productive pinch hitter and allowed me to be ready in a pinch.

**CAT'S KEYS**

Always be game-ready.

*Keep your body warmed up.*

Pay attention when you're on the bench.

*Be thinking ahead.*

Know the situation.

*Be aggressive.*

## 17

# HITTING

*"Every great batter works on the theory that the pitcher
is more afraid of him than he is of the pitcher."* ~ *Ty Cobb*

Mariano Rivera was one of my toughest matchups until I found the right bat. The Yankees' closer has a great cutter that just eats up left-handed batters. His ball breaks hard in on the hitter's hands and he makes it tough for you to get the good part of the bat on the ball. Nearly every time I faced him, he broke my bat. So, I came up with the idea of using a special bat for Mariano. I figured if I had a short bat that was basically nothing but head, I would give myself a better chance to get the barrel to the ball. I ordered a 30-inch bat that was 30 ounces. It was like a little club, but it actually wound up working. The first time I used it against Mariano I got a single to right field. It was the best contact I ever made against him. I only had a few more at-bats against him after getting "the club", but I did pretty well with it.

Normally, I used a Louisville Slugger C271, ash, 33.5 inches and 31 ounces, black in color. I fell in love with that model in the minor leagues and never changed, other than the special Rivera bat. Other companies would ask me to use their bats, but I would tell them to make it exactly like the Louisville C271. I would give them a try in batting practice, but they never felt the same or had the exact same weight distribution. I was very particular. When an order of bats would come in for me, I would always look through the box for the ones with the least amount of grain in them, which meant the wood was harder. But, some bats just didn't feel right, maybe a little heavy or the handle's taper didn't feel like the others. Those I would use for BP or not use at all. I didn't go through a lot of bats during the year, maybe a couple of dozen from spring training through the end of the season. Some guys would change bats all the time and use over a hundred each season. If I was hitting well with a bat, you better believe I was going to continue to use it. Sometimes even if it got a minor crack in it, I would stick with it. If I went a few games without a hit I would probably put it aside to use in BP and pick out another one for the game. There were a variety of funny sayings about whether the bat or the batter was the problem. Yogi Berra reasoned: "I never blame myself when I'm not hitting. I just blame the bat, and if it keeps up, I change bats. After all, if I know it isn't my fault that I'm not hitting, how can I get mad at myself?" Larry Parrish had the opposite take: "It's not the arrow, it's the Indian!"

Later in my career when maple bats became popular, I would order a box in the same C271 specs. Those I would use for BP. Maple bats don't break as easily, so I figured instead of beating up my ash game bats I would just use the maple. Maple bats are harder, but I felt like the sweet spot on the ash bat, although smaller, is better and makes the ball jump off the bat. There is much more room for error with a maple bat, but you don't get rewarded as much for squaring it up. Teammates would borrow my bats all the time, and if a guy got a hit with one, then he fell in love with it and had me order more for him.

There is nothing quite like the adrenaline rush, the feel in your hands and the sound of getting good wood on a ball and driving it down the line, your spikes spraying clay as you dig in toward first. And then the anxious roar of the crowd as you try to stretch it out for a double. Pure fun. But, I also had fun every time I smacked a Wiffle ball with a broom handle in our basement when I was a kid. Hitters love hitting, period.

There are nearly as many ways to swing a bat as there are players. Different approaches, different stances; no two swings are the same. But successful hitters have two things in common: there is nothing else they would rather be doing and they stick to fundamentals. Let's review those and I will add some techniques that helped me.

**KNOW YOUR KRYPTONITE** No one in the world can hit every pitch. Some guys can't hit the inside pitch. Others have trouble with the high pitch. For others, the breaking ball is their kryptonite. Before stepping into the batter's box you should know your strengths and weaknesses. Once you are in pro ball, you can bet the pitcher will know what you can and can't hit. Know what you are good at and look for that pitch in the area that you like to hit the ball. If you like to see the ball from the middle to the outer part of the plate, sometimes you have to give the pitcher the inside part of the plate. You can't cover the whole plate. But, remember that the pitcher has to eventually throw strikes. Be patient.

**STANCE** I don't care how your stance looks. All that matters is that you are comfortable. We have seen so many different stances in the major leagues over the years, but the one constant among good hitters is that they get to a strong, balanced position before they swing the bat. One of the things in my stance that made a big difference

*Above left: Correct turn of head toward pitcher.*
*Above right: Head not turned far enough.*

was making sure that my head was fully turned towards the pitcher. I wanted to see him with both eyes. When you turn your head far enough to see him correctly, you should feel a little tug in your neck. Obviously, it is easier to hit the ball when you have clear vision of it with both eyes.

**HANDS** Once you are comfortable with the strike zone and know what part of the plate you like to cover, you are ready to go. For me, the most important part of hitting is the hands. Your hands start it off and become the trigger for your swing. Make sure your hands are nice and loose on the bat. Don't squeeze it as hard as you can because when your hands are tight, your arms will be, too, and you'll have a slow, long, tense swing. I liked to loosen both pointer fingers to where they were actually off the bat. I felt like this allowed me to get more of a snap or spring-like action with my hands. Imagine that you are using a hammer. If your pointer finger is tight on the ham-mer you will not get as much spring. The loose pointer finger al-lows for more whip to the point of contact. You need to have good rhythm in your swing, especially at the start when you are setting

*Above left: Correct, loose grip on bat.*
*Above right: Too tight.*

up. Also, if your hands are still or stagnant while you're setting up and awaiting the pitch, your swing won't be fluid.

**THE TRIGGER** Having loose hands will allow you to have a nice trigger as the pitcher gets ready to throw the ball. The trigger is so important and was the cause of many of my slumps. The trigger is simple. It is moving your hands straight back in a loaded position so you can get the most amount of force going through the ball at the point of contact. Think about a punch from a boxer. If a boxer was going to punch you he would bring his hand back first before throwing the punch. Of course, this would generate more power and you would feel it. If a boxer just threw the punch from a still position you would only feel a tap. The farther back your hands come in the swing, the more power you will generate. The trigger is also used as a timing device. I would always start moving my hands back early and slowly to avoid being late with my timing. A good rule of thumb is when the pitcher brings his hand back to throw the ball the hitter brings his hands back at the same time. When I was in a hitting slump, I would watch video of my at-bats and realize that my hands were getting started too late. Remember: if you start too late with your hands, you will be late getting the bat head to the ball. If you start too early, it's not a problem. You might not have as much power but you will still be on time to hit the ball. So when in doubt, always start your trigger early; it is better to be early than late. Sometimes if we don't see it, it can be tough to feel.

**MIRROR, MIRROR ON THE WALL** In the minor leagues, I would go home at the end of the day and watch myself in the mirror to make sure I was getting my hands back as far as I could without "barring out" my front arm—making it straight, like a bar. Barring out your front arm is the main thing you have to be careful of when getting your hands

back. If your front arm straightens out and locks you will have a long, tight, mechanical swing. Just make sure that you keep a little bit of a bend at the elbow of the front arm. Often, when I felt I was doing it right, I would get in front of the mirror and see that I wasn't getting my hands back as far as I thought. Use the mirror to see what it looks like and what it should feel like. You will notice a stretch in the front shoulder.

*Above: Correct. Below: Arm is too straight.*

That is a good sign that you are getting your hands back far enough and that you will be getting the most out of your hands and arms.

**STRIDE** The stride also varies from hitter to hitter. Find a stride that is comfortable and works for you. Make sure the stride is always toward the pitcher. The stride should put you in a good position as the ball is coming. If your stride is too open or too closed, your body won't be in a good position to hit the ball. I would sometimes incorrectly stride toward the pitcher with my toe leaking open toward him. To fix that, I came up with a way that helped me stay more consistent. Imagine that a rope is tied to the outside of your front heel and is being pulled toward the pitcher. That keeps your foot closed throughout your stride before the point of contact. Once you make contact with the ball your foot will open naturally just because of the violence and torque that the swing creates. By striding straight towards the pitcher it will allow you to handle both the inside and outside pitches. Walk away from your hands and reach with your foot. Don't jump or push forward. Preferably we would like to have a short stride with our foot landing softly on the ground. There is less room for error and we will be able to wait on the ball longer with a short stride. You will be able to see the ball better, which will prevent you from being fooled by off-speed pitches.

**STAY INSIDE** Young players sometimes have a hard time grasping this concept, but when they get it they immediately see how much difference it makes. Staying inside the ball will allow you to get backspin on the ball, which will make it jump off the bat and go farther. When you do the opposite and come around the ball, you will be taking a long swing and get a lot of groundballs. When making contact with the ball you want to hit the inside part of the ball: the part that is closest to you as opposed to the part that is farthest away. If you think about pointing the knob of the bat into the space between your body and where the

ball is, then you will be on the right track. If the knob of your bat starts to point at your body during your swing then you're doing it wrong. I like to imagine train tracks under my hands going from however far back my hands will go straight all the way out in front of the plate. I would always try to stay on the train tracks. The more length you get going back with your hands the more length you will get going forward. The more length you get going forward the easier it is to stay inside and swing through the baseball. Our bodies are designed to function in this way. It is the law of motion. Isaac Newton said, "To every action there is always an equal and opposite reaction." That is true in hit-

*Above: Staying inside (correct).*
*Below: Coming around (incorrect).*

ting. So get that action going back and you'll get the same action going forward. This will help you stay inside the ball. Staying on the train tracks will allow you to get good extension with your arms. Getting that extension will ensure that you are hitting the ball out in front of the plate and you won't be fighting it off in a defensive manner. When your hands don't trigger back, you will have the tendency to cut your swing off which leads to the shoulder and hips opening up too soon. Make sure at the point of contact you have one palm up and one palm down. If you swing around the ball it will be impossible to have your palms line up like that. You will roll your wrists and hit a lot of ground balls. To

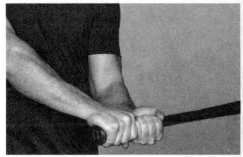

*Above left: Correct grip at point of contact. Above right: Rolled wrists.*

check yourself, hit off of a tee and get to the point of contact with one palm up and one palm down. Feel the way it is supposed to be so it will eventually come naturally.

**KEEP YOUR SHOULDER IN** It is important for your shoulder to be in as long as possible while using your hands and starting your swing at the ball. Your swing itself will force your shoulder to open. If your shoulder flies open too soon you will start pulling off the ball and will not be able to handle the pitch that is in the middle or outer part of the plate. This is very difficult for young hitters because they are not strong enough and they use too much of their body. So until you are stronger, try to over-exaggerate keeping the shoulder in and just throw your hands to the ball. That is a good way to train yourself to do it correctly. When your shoulder flies open too soon so will your hips. Your hips supply a lot of the power in your swing if used correctly, so by opening them too soon you are doing yourself an injustice. Don't get me wrong, your hips will start to open a little bit before contact. Again it is just because of how the human body is put together. But you really want to thrust your hips toward the pitcher upon contact. The torque in the hips will recruit your legs and create a powerful swing. I always knew if my hips were square to the pitcher at the end of my swing that I got the most amount of torque into the ball.

**WEIGHT SHIFT** When I was a kid, my coaches would always tell me to "squoosh a bug" with my back foot when I pivoted. They wanted my foot to be firmly planted on the ground and just rotate my hips. But

when you do that it is difficult to transfer weight from the

*Far left: Incorrect back foot plant.*

*Left: Correct weight shift as you drive through the ball.*

back to the front or even the middle of your body. When I

*Above left: Incorrect body position when transferring weight.*
*Above right: Correct weight shift.*

got to the minor leagues I learned that this was not the correct way anymore. The swing has evolved. When my dad was young the "squoosh a bug" is what was taught, but watch just about every major leaguer now and not many of them stay on their backside. Of course, there will always be the exception, but transferring the weight will allow you to make a positive move into the ball. When I finished my swing I was always on my back toe, not on my heel. If you are on your heel, your back shoulder will drop and you will hit a lot of pop ups. If you are on your back toe it shows me that there was a lot of torque in your hips, you stayed tall, your hands are above the ball and you have transferred your weight into the ball.

**THINK OFFENSE** Remember that as a hitter you are on the offense, not the defense. Don't be thinking defensively at the plate. Make a positive move into the ball. Think about other sports like bowling, football, soccer, basketball, boxing, nearly all of them; when you are on offense, you don't stay stagnant or make negative, defensive moves.

**GAME PLAN** There was never an at-bat in the major leagues that I did not have a game plan. Going up there without a plan is a recipe for disaster. Keep it simple. Ninety percent of the time I would look for a fastball out over the plate because that was the pitch that I handled the best. I would say to myself, "If I get a fastball out over the plate I am going to put a good swing on it and hit it hard." Reaffirming your plan to yourself in-between pitches is a good thing to do. It allows you to stay focused and confident in what you want to do. When making a plan, have your strengths and weaknesses in mind. Always be confident. Don't think once you get in the batter's box. Clear your head and know what you are looking for before you enter the box. There is nothing worse than talking to yourself in the box and convincing yourself to change your plan. Believe in your first instinct and go with it with one hundred percent confidence.

**PICKING UP THE BALL** Know (from your scouting reports and observations) what the pitcher might want to throw in certain situations. If he throws a lot of breaking balls, your approach might be different than if you were facing a guy who throws mostly fastballs. As you are waiting for the pitch, focus on an imaginary box next to the pitcher's ear where the ball will be released. That is the best way to pick up the ball. Don't follow his arm before the release and pay no attention to all of his other movements before the ball is pitched. Some guys flop their gloves around and do other things to try to distract you. Keep your eyes on that "box". Bring your eyes to the release point right before his hand gets there. Always be comfortable in the batter's box. If something affects your concentration call time out. Step out of the box, reaffirm your plan and step back in with a clear head. Sometimes just watching how the defense is playing you will help you determine how the pitcher might want to pitch to you. If the defense is shaded to the opposite field it might mean that the pitcher is going to pitch you away. Always keep an eye on that because it may just tip you off and give you an edge. That may help you adjust your plan.

**DRILLS** Over my career, I was able to weed out the drills that didn't help me and embrace the ones that seemed to get me locked in. Everyone is different so you'll need to find which ones you like and which ones you don't. Repetition of the drills is the most important part of getting better, especially for young players, because it teaches muscle memory.

- ONE-ARM  This one might be my favorite because of how well it strengthens each arm. I would get a small, lightweight bat and have someone flip me balls while kneeling to the side of me. With just my front arm, I would take ten to fifteen swings and then switch to the back arm. I always wanted to make sure each arm and hand was working correctly. I would focus on staying inside the ball making sure I was leading with the knob of the bat. Also, I would reach out toward the pitcher with the bat after contact to ensure I was getting the most amount of extension possible. I would do one-arm drills everyday before batting practice. When you do each arm separately you can find any weakness or flaw that may be the reason for the struggles you may be having at the plate.

- FRONT FLIPS  After I did my one-arm drills I would always go right into front flips where I could use both arms and hands working together. The coach would be about fifteen feet away behind an "L" screen and flip balls underhanded. He would flip five balls away, five in the middle, five inside and then I would finish off with five more away. Since the speed of the pitched balls was not very fast, I could really concentrate on feeling the mechanics of my swing and make sure that it was working correctly before I went on the field for live batting practice.

- WIFFLE GOLF BALL  Another drill I like and that I used a lot when I was a teenager at home is the Wiffle golf ball/broom handle drill. Cut a broom handle to a comfortable size (ask your parents first!) and get a bunch of Wiffle golf balls. Have someone flip the ball to you and try to hit it. It is not easy, especially at first but you will get the hang of it. The theory is if you can hit a tiny golf ball with a skinny broom stick handle, imagine how much easier it will be when you get to hit a much bigger ball with a much thicker bat. This drill really improves eye-hand co-ordination. It is great to do before a game and can also be done individually with each arm one at a time. And you don't even need to have a partner. Just tie a string through the Wiffle golf ball and attach it to the ceiling somewhere in the garage or base-ment (again, ask your parents!). The ball will always come back to you.

- TEE  I was never a big fan of hitting off a tee, but I did use one when I felt like I was not transferring the weight off my backside or getting good extension out front. I would put a tee way out in front of me and force myself to go get it with a good aggressive, positive move toward the ball. It would be impossible to hit the ball if I stayed on my back heel and "squooshed a bug." When I did this drill, I hit the ball up the middle or to the opposite field to make sure I was staying on the "train tracks" and not pulling off the ball. This drill always seemed to get my body in the right position: staying tall on the backside and not collapsing.

- RAPID FIRE  When I felt like my hands were getting lazy and not firing I would do a rapid fire drill. I would choke up on my bat a little and have someone flip ten to fifteen balls to me one at a time as fast as they could. The flipper would kneel down to the side of me and concentrate on putting the ball in the strike zone as quickly as possible. I would not care how well I hit the ball, it was all about getting my hands going. I wanted to feel my hands working and take my body out of it. It is impossible to reset your body and legs every time if you're doing rapid fire, so keep your feet planted and use only your hands.

- TRACKING DRILLS I would do tracking drills when I felt like I was not seeing the ball well. Tracking is simply watching the ball all the way into the catcher's glove once it is released from the pitcher's hand. I would stand in on a teammate's bullpen session or even just take some pitches from the coach during batting practice. Sometimes we take for granted the thing that does not take talent at all: seeing the ball. It is important to focus on the ball coming in and pick up the spin as quickly as possible once it is thrown. Picking up the spin can be a daunting task but once you start to figure it out it can help you tremendously. The fastball will spin upward or toward the pitcher. A curveball will spin downward since the pitcher will pull the ball down. A slider will have more of a diagonal spin. The change-up can be the toughest to pick up because the pitcher's arm speed is the same as with the fastball. If the pitcher is right-handed the change-up will have a sideways spin that goes away from a left-handed hitter, toward a right-handed hitter. If he is a left-handed pitcher it will spin sideways, away from the right-handed hitter and toward the left-handed hitter. Once again, focus on that imaginary box by the pitcher's ear where he will be releasing the ball. I would always try to see how quickly I could determine if it would be a pitch that I would swing at or not. Just by getting in there and making "seeing the ball" your only priority will help remind you that you can't take it for granted.

- RELAXATION and VISUALIZATION When you are in the batter's box, it is natural for your pulse to quicken and your adrenaline to rush. That's fine, it is part of the fight or flight mechanism that has ruled man since caveman days. But you want to harness that energy by controlling your breathing and slowing your heart rate. One way to do that is by putting positive thoughts in your head. Positive self-talk and doing deep breathing exercises where you breathe through your diaphragm, not shallow chest breathing will slow your heart rate and allow you to feel more in control. I would always visualize putting a good swing on the ball and seeing a positive result. In my mind, I always felt that I was in control of the at-bat. Ninety-nine percent of the time, I would look for a fastball out over the plate, something I could handle. If I was having trouble feeling confident, I would switch my thought process around, saying to myself that the pitcher, even if it was the best pitcher in the league, was not happy that he had to face me. I would remind myself that he still had to put the ball over the plate three times and when he did, I would hit it. The pitcher should feel the pressure, not me. it.

## BUNTING

Baseball changed in the mid-1980s. The focus shifted away from "small ball", where the strategy was to move runners around the bases. Big swingers who could hit home runs became fan favorites. Hitting twenty-five or more home runs in a season got them bigger contracts, even if they struck out the majority of the time. Reggie Jackson, the all-time leader in striking out, often led the league in both home runs and strikeouts. But, he was far down the rankings in batting average. He finished as a .262 lifetime hitter, but was a first-ballot Hall of Famer. Fans dug the long ball. The Home Run Derby at the All-Star Game did not begin until 1985. Bunting, unless you were a National League pitcher, became an overlooked and underused weapon. But it can be very effective when done correctly.

*Above left: Correct bunting stance.*    *Above right: Incorrect.*

You must use "soft" hands—don't grip the bat real hard so you can deaden the ball when it hits the bat. From your normal stance, just pivot on both feet toward the mound with your knees bent slightly, but don't square both feet off to the pitcher. You will put yourself in a vulnerable position, especially against a wild pitcher. Make sure you have a good base and balance. Point the bat head to the pitcher as you transfer your weight slightly to your front side. This will ensure that the bat is in fair territory. Your top hand should now slide up to the label of the bat. Make sure that you use only your thumb and index finger when gripping the bat with your top hand. The bottom hand should have a soft, loose grip on the handle. Hold the bat at the top of the strike zone. If the pitcher throws a low pitch just bend your knees to make the bat go lower. Don't lower your hands and stab at it. If the pitcher throws a pitch that is higher than where your bat is starting, don't attempt to bunt it. Those are the pitches that get popped up. The bat head should be above your hands when contact is made. Think about catching the ball with your bat—that way you won't stab at it. Your bottom hand will guide the direction of the ball, like a rudder on a ship.

*Above left: Correct bunting grip. Above right: Incorrect.*

## BUNTING DRILLS

- Place two bats on the grass parallel to each other ten to twenty feet down the line toward first, three to four feet apart. Try to bunt the pitched balls in between the bats. Repeat down the third base line.

- Have two or three teammates form an arc about twenty feet away as you stand squared in a bunt position. Have them take turns tossing you pitches that you bunt. Your job is to bunt each ball to a player who did not throw it.

**CAT'S KEYS**

Have a plan and stick to it.

*Know your strike zone.*

Know your strengths
and weaknesses.

*Stick to the fundamentals.*

Be aggressive, but selective.

*Stay balanced.*

Relax.

# 18

# FIELDING

*"The phrase 'off with the crack of the bat', while romantic, is really meaning-less, since the outfielder should be in motion long before he hears the sound of the ball meeting the bat." ~ Joe DiMaggio*

Few things, man-made at least, compare with the beauty of a perfectly executed double play. Even fewer are more thrilling than the rare triple play. Or, how about the leaping snow cone catch at the top of the outfield wall that robs a home run or stops a rally in its tracks? Pure artistry, especially when it is replayed in slow motion over and over on the television sports shows. But, we don't take fielding as seriously as we take hitting. Everyone wants to hit, hit, hit.

It wasn't that I did not take fielding seriously, I just wasn't as good at it as I was at hitting. Hitting was my bread and butter and what got me into the big leagues. Had I been blessed with blazing foot speed or quickness and was an exceptional defender at one position, I may have been able to be a starter for longer and, in turn, get more at-bats. Instead, I played a lot of positions because my teams were trying to find ways to get my bat in the lineup. I was a jack of all, master of none. Still, some of the greats of the game taught me how to play a bunch of differ-ent positions: 2B, 1B, 3B, LF and RF. I would like to touch on some of the things that fielders must do to be successful.

• KNOW THE PLAYING CONDITIONS  Before going into the game you should know about the field and what might happen during the game. Know what the outfield fence is made of.  Check to see if it is padded, brick, wood or chain link.  See how the ball might come off the wall. Look for things on or around the field that might get in the way like the tarp or bullpen mounds down the foul lines.  Know the playing surface and how the ball may bounce differently from other fields.  Some fields are soft, some are hard, some are slow and some are fast.  Is the grass long or has it just been cut short?  That will tell you whether you need to charge the ball or lay back on it.  Know the weather.  Check the wind. It is important to know which way the ball will blow once it is hit in the air.  Check to see where the sun will be.  You may need to wear sunglasses.  If you have sunglasses on and still lose the ball in the sun no one will say anything.  But, if you don't have them on and lose it in the sun you will probably get an earful from your coach or manager.  Better to be safe and know if you need them before you get out there.

• KNOW THE SITUATION BEFORE EACH PITCH  One sure way to get on a blooper reel is to catch a fly ball in the outfield for the out, start trotting toward the dugout and flip the ball into the stands as a souvenir when there were only TWO outs!  There is nothing worse than seeing a guy on the field who forgets how many outs there are or one who throws the ball to the wrong base.  Repeat in your head the number of outs and what you will do with the ball if it is hit to you.  Think of every different play that may happen and where you have to be or what you have to do.  Think about the count, the score and what the pitcher may throw to try to get the batter out.  That may determine where you position yourself on the field.  Even if a ball is not hit your way, you may still have to back up a base or be a cut-off man.  Always play it out in your mind ahead of time.

• REACT ON EVERY PITCH  Make sure you are moving whether the ball is hit or not.  Anticipate where the ball may be hit as the hitter prepares to make contact.  From the field, you can see if the hitter is going to be late or early on the pitched ball.  Adjust accordingly and make your first move in that direction.  If you can make an educated guess as to where the ball will be hit you will be able to get to many more balls.  If your first step is in the right direction before you even see where the ball is hit you will not have to rely solely on foot speed to get to it. A good time to practice this is during batting practice. React on every swing the hitter takes and try to anticipate which way the ball will be hit. Even if the hitter swings and misses you should still be moving one way or the other. You will be able to see if it would have been a pitch that he hit on the inside or outside part of the plate; if he is out in front or if he is getting jammed by the pitch. If you are playing the middle infield, you can watch the catcher's signs to know if the pitcher is throwing a fastball or an off-speed pitch. Also, you can check the location of where the catcher is setting up. This will help you position yourself knowing that the hitter might be late on the fastball and out in front on the off-speed pitch. If the catcher is set up inside you know that the pitch might be pulled as opposed to a pitch on the outer part of the plate that might be taken to the opposite field.

• COMMUNICATE Communication is such an important part of the game. Take charge in the field and do not expect someone else to be the vocal leader. Infielders and outfielders must let the fielders around them know when they are moving left or right so they will know how much ground they need to cover or if they should move over to cover the hole that the other fielder left vacant. Infielders and outfielders must communicate on pop-ups and fly balls. You must be vocal and yell loudly if you want to catch the ball. Middle infielders must talk and let each other know who will be covering the base on a steal attempt. Let each other know about the sun and the wind. Sometimes the sun will be in the left fielder's eyes but not the center fielder's. If you are that left fielder, make sure you tell the center fielder so he knows that if a ball is hit toward you, he may have to come over and try to catch it. Outfielders have to let the infielders know if they position themselves very shallow so the infielder is aware that the outfielder can get to any shallow fly ball. Communication eliminates a lot of guesswork and helps avoid collisions. The more we talk to our teammates, the more  cohesive our unit will be. Those who communicate well always seem to become the leaders on the team.

• CONCENTRATE Frankly, baseball can be boring at times. There is some old saying about it sometimes being as exciting as watching paint dry. Losing concentration while on the field is easy to do. But if there is one guarantee in baseball, it's that the minute you lose focus something bad will happen to you. Right then, the ball is hit to you and you make a mental mistake. There are a lot of causes for these mental lapses and one of the biggest is taking your last at-bat into the field on defense with you. You are kicking yourself for not swinging at that 3-2 fastball right down the middle, replaying it in your mind and you don't anticipate what may happen in the field. It is important to separate hitting from fielding. A baseball game usually lasts no longer than three hours. Keeping focused for three hours is not too much to ask. Try hard to concentrate and keep focused on what is in front of you while you are playing, otherwise you may turn a bad situation into a much worse one.

• MECHANICS Learning the basic mechanics of fielding is, of course, crucial. But, it is also important to make a checklist to remind yourself of some of the basics so you can stay sharp in the field. Write down what you learn and refer to it often. A good, comfortable ready position is how a fielder should start before the ball is pitched. A fielder has to have good rhythm. Standing still at your position will only make you stiff and slow. Make sure, whether you are an infielder or and outfielder, you are moving as the pitch is on the way to home plate. Some guys like to walk or creep into a good comfortable, ready stance before they react to the ball thrown by the pitcher. Others like to just pop up on their toes. As long as there is some movement with your body you will be quicker to react and quicker to the ball.

• LOW IS GOOD In the infield, once the ball is hit and you are going for the ball, it is important to keep your hands and arms close to your body. If a ball is hit to your right or left you will get there quicker by staying compact with your arms as opposed to flailing them all over the place. As you get ready to field the ball, break down with a good, wide base. The more your legs are spread out the easier it is to get your butt down and stay low. You won't be able to, if your legs are too close together. The lower you get, the easier it is to get your hands out in front of your body. When your hands are out in front of your body it allows them to be quicker and more fluid. But, if your hands are close to your body they tend to be tight and stiff, and that is when you are most likely to get eaten alive by a bad hop. Reacting to a bad hop is a lot easier when you are low and your hands are free. Also, it is much easier to see that screaming grounder when you are low and on the same plane. (See, it pays to pay attention in geometry class!) Being able to see the ball go right into the glove will make you a sure-handed fielder. Try to field everything in the middle of your body. That way if you do get a bad hop your body will be in the way to knock it down. Try not to be flat-footed and still when fielding the ball. Get on the balls of your feet and have your momentum going through the ball. This will allow you to play the ball and not let the ball play you.

• FAST-SLOW-FAST In the outfield, when you are fielding a ball and have to come up throwing to one of the bases make sure you bust your butt to the ball before breaking down and gathering yourself to receive the ball. Cutting down that distance is so important in keeping the runner from advancing to the next base. If the third base coach sees that you are not going hard to the ball he will send the runner to the next base. Just think, "Fast-Slow-Fast", and you will be on the right track. *Fast* to the ball, *Slow* when you breakdown to field the ball and then *Fast* with the transfer and release.

• RIGHT LEG FORWARD OR BACK? I was taught to field the ball with my left leg forward and right foot back. I was also taught to do it the opposite way with the right leg forward and the left leg back. There really is no right way to do it. Whatever feels comfortable for you is the way you should do it. I liked having my left foot forward, which was right next to my glove when I fielded the ball. I felt like I was able to get lower and really see the ball go into the glove better.

• RELEASE After deciding which foot feels most comfortable to put forward while fielding the ball, the next step is to work on your release. It is extremely important to get the ball out of the glove and into your bare hand quickly so you can get rid of it with a strong, quick release. When releasing the ball, a good way to make sure your throw stays straight is by pointing your shoulder to your target and replacing your feet. By that, I simply mean that if you are a right-handed thrower, your right foot goes to where your left foot was and your left foot goes directly to your target. This will ensure that you are headed in the right direction with your momentum going toward the base you want to throw the ball to. If your body momentum is going a different direction than where you are throwing the ball, you will have a tendency to fly open, causing your throw to be wild.

• DRILLS One of the best drills to do as soon as you get on the field for practice is the knee drill. Get on your knees and have a coach or teammate hit groundballs to you. You don't need to go all the way out in the dirt, just stay on the infield grass as the hitter hits the ball from about sixty to seventy-five feet away. Kneeling eliminates you having to move your feet and allows you to exclusively use your hands. It really makes you rely on your reactions with your glove hand. Make sure you reach out and snatch the ball, working through it instead of keeping your hand close to your body and getting tied up. Make sure you work both the backhand and the forehand.

The "ball rolling drill" is another of my favorites. This drill allows you to feel the right mechanics for fielding a groundball. Simply have a coach or teammate roll balls to you from ten to fifteen feet away. This way you don't have to worry about a bad hop or a fungo hitter that can't seem to hit a good groundball. Go slow at first so you can remind yourself of how it should feel and then speed it up as you go along. Start with balls right at you, then go to forehands, backhands and then finish with a few right at you again. Make sure you move your feet to get in the right position. Have your roller move farther back as you continue. This drill is great for young kids because the fear of a bad hop is eliminated. The success they have in this drill can help build their confidence.

When I played the outfield I liked doing a drop step drill. In this one, a coach would stand face-to-face with me about ten feet away. He would throw the ball over either one of my shoulders and I would have to drop step and chase down the ball. Most times, I wouldn't know which shoulder he would throw it over so I really had to react quickly, opening my shoulder with my drop step and go.

During batting practice I liked doing a reaction drill in the outfield. I'd stand in the outfield and would react to every batted ball from the hitter. I would try to get the best possible jump on the ball, anticipating where the ball would be hit right as it was getting in the hitting zone. I would try to determine where the ball would be hit as I watched the hitter's swing and where he was making contact. This really helped me and allowed me to make up for my lack of tremendous foot speed.

**CAT'S KEYS**

Be aware of field conditions.

*Know the situation
before each pitch.*

Concentrate, even during
slow moments.

*Communicate with your
teammates on the field.*

Learn fielding mechanics.
Low is good.

# 19

# CONDITIONING

*"While most are dreaming of success, winners wake up and work hard to achieve it."* ~ *Unknown*

Conditioning is an extremely important part of your success on the field. The baseball season is so long, you have to be in top shape to be able to endure the long, constant wear on your body. There is very little time for recovery. Rare days off and a punishing amount of travel (even though it is first-class) make the baseball season a grind. If you don't pay attention to your body, you won't be able to get through it.

I have tried all the conditioning techniques over the years and know what works well for a baseball player. I also know what may not work or may be unnecessary. There are so many different ways to train and several different exercises that essentially do the same thing. My hope is that having gone through this myself, I can help you get right to the good stuff and you won't waste your time on the less effective exercises. I understand that everyone is different and may not like some of the exercises that I like, but I am not putting them in only because I like them. These are all training techniques that most of my former teammates and strength trainers do themselves.

**Phase One** It all starts in the off-season. Putting together a good workout program is the first thing I did when the season ended. After taking two weeks off to rest my body, it was time to start building it back up so I could endure the upcoming eight-month season. During the first two months, I would concentrate strictly on strength training, building up the muscle that I had lost during the season. This involved working with a local strength trainer and some minor league guys from the area. I would focus mainly on baseball-specific muscles throughout the off-season. For me, the shoulders, forearms, hands, legs and core muscles were the most important. My workout would always start with an active warm-up to get the body loose and ready to go. Some think a static stretch is what you should start with before working out, but I have a different opinion. Your muscles need to be warm before doing a static stretch, so I wait until the end of my workout to do that. An active warm up includes some cardiovascular movements and really gets the muscles lubed up and ready to go. Here are some that I like the most and use everyday before my workout starts:

**Prisoner squats** - Squat down in a sitting position with the majority of your weight on your heels. Drive through your heels and return to the standing position. Make sure you put both hands behind your head. Do ten squats.

**Jumping Jacks** - Just like you learned as a kid: feet together, arms at your side. Jump, move your feet apart and raise your hands over your head. Then bring your hands back to your sides as you jump and move your feet back together. Repeat for a total of twenty times.

**Seal Jacks** - These are just like jumping jacks. The only difference is that you will start with your hands out in front of your body touching palm to palm. As you jump and spread your legs you will open your chest and bring your hands out to the side of your body at chest height. Twenty times.

**Fling Jacks** - Similar to seal jacks but now you will cross your feet and also your arms giving you more range of motion. Twenty times.

**Gate Swings** - Standing up, as you go to squat down, open your feet and get into a deep squat. When you come back up bring your feet together pointing straight in front. This movement should be done quickly and continuously until you have completed ten.

**Russian March** - Walk out and lift the right leg straight up. Touch the opposite hand to the toe. Repeat, lifting the left leg and touching the right hand. After ten, turn around and do ten coming back.

**Walking lunge** - Step out with right leg and get down into a lunge position. Rotate your upper body with arms out to the same side as the leg that is in front. Take ten steps out, turn around and come back for ten more steps.

**Knee Hugs** - Step out with your right foot, take your left knee and squeeze it into your chest with both hands. As you pull the knee into the chest, rise onto your toes and flex your calf. Take ten steps out and ten steps back.

**Leg Cradle** - Step out with your right foot, lift your left leg and grab your left foot. Lift foot as high as it will go into the stomach area, if possible. Repeat with the opposite leg. Take ten steps out and back.

**Ten Yard Skip** - Quickly skip for ten yards, but when you bring your foot down to touch the ground drive it down explosively.

Pick five or six of the above to do each day. Mix it up so it does not get boring. Doing these before you begin your exercise routine will really get the heart pumping and make you ready for a productive workout.

**STRENGTH TRAINING**  The following exercises build up the muscles you will need to endure the wear and tear of the long season.

## BACK

**One Arm Cable Rotations** - Start with your feet in a staggered position. Your knees should be bent and have one hand on the cable handle allowing your arm to stretch toward the machine as much as possible. Pull the cable back toward your side and squeeze as you rotate your midsection at the same time.

**Pull-Ups** - Grab the bar with both hands in a wide position. Pull yourself up until your chin reaches just above the bar and lower yourself back down after a short pause.

**Med Ball Throws** - Stand with feet hip-width apart, place right foot approximately twelve inches in front of left foot. Hold medicine ball with both hands and arms only slightly bent. Swing ball over to the left hip and forcefully underhand toss ball forward to a partner or wall. Switch sides. Catch the ball from your partner or off the wall and repeat.

**Dumbbell Row** - Put one knee on a bench and let the dumbbell hang down as close to the floor as possible. As you pull the free weights up, bend your elbow and keep it close to your side. Lift your elbow up to the sky. Pause for one second and lower back to start.

**Low Back Extension** - Begin by lying on either a bench or a stability ball. Allow your upper body to relax over the top part of the bench or ball. Place your hands where they are most comfortable. Slowly begin to lift your upper body by extending from your lower back and hips. Pause for one second at the top and then relax back to start.

# CHEST

**Dumbbell Press on Physioball** - Begin by sitting on a physioball. Gently roll down until you can relax your head on the ball. Place your ankles directly under your knees, and lift your hips up. Hold a dumbbell in each hand. Lift the dumbbells up by extending your arms. Don not lock your elbows. Pause here for one second and slowly lower the weight back down.

**Dumbbell Fly** - Hold a dumbbell in each hand. Palms should be facing each other. Lift the dumbbells up by extending your arms. Do not lock your elbows. Pause here for one second and slowly lower the weight back down.

**Push-Ups** - Begin in the upper push-up position. Your feet should be together and your hands are directly under your shoulders. Your back is flat and you are looking at the ground. Slowly begin lowering yourself to the ground. Allow your elbows to bend, but keep your back flat and strong. Pause just above the ground and then begin lifting yourself back up.

**Incline Dumbbell Press** - Begin by lying on an incline bench. Hold a dumbbell in each hand. Palms should be facing away from you. Lift the dumbbells by extending your arms up. Don't lock your elbows. Pause here for one second and slowly lower the weight back down.

**Medicine Ball Chest Pass** - Stand with legs comfortably spread apart. Hold medicine ball with both hands as if performing a basketball chest pass. Throw the medicine ball straight forward using a two-handed chest pass.

## ARMS

**Bicep Dumbbell Curl** - Begin with the dumbbells by your side and palms facing away from you. Your feet should be directly under your hips and your knees are slightly bent. Start to lift the weight up towards your shoulders. Once there, pause for one second and slowly lower the weight back down.

**Straight Bar Reverse Grip Curl -** Start out by holding the bar with your palms facing your body. Slowly begin to lift the weight towards your shoulders. Pause for a second and slowly lower down to the start position.

**Hammer Curl** - Begin with dumbbells by your side, palms facing your sides. Bend your knees slightly. Start to lift the weight up towards your shoulders. Once there, pause for one second and slowly lower the weight back down.

**Skull Crushers** - Begin by lying on a bench or on the floor. Hold the bar right above your forehead. Elbows are bent at a ninety degree angle. Begin to straighten out your arms by lifting the weight up. Pause for one second, and begin lowering the weight back down toward your forehead.

**Tricep Kick Backs** - Begin by placing a hand or knee on a bench and bending your back so it is near parallel to the floor. Hold a dumbbell in your hand with your palm facing your side and elbow bent to a ninety degree angle. Begin to straighten out your arms by lifting the weight up. Pause for one second, and begin lowering the free weight back down.

**Close Grip Push-Ups** - Start in a regular push-up position only with your hands close together. Begin to lower the body to just above the ground. Keep your elbows tucked into your sides. Pause here. Press back to the beginning.

**Tricep Press Downs** - Stand in front of the high pulley machine and grab the handlebar with both hands, upper arms pressed against your body, elbows at ninety degree angles. Push the bar down by straightening your arms and slowly bring your arms back to the starting point.

# SHOULDERS

**Front Raise** - Hold a dumbbell in each hand, palms facing your thighs. Keeping your arms straight, lift the dumbbells up until they are shoulder level. The only joint moving is your shoulder. Pause for a second and slowly lower back to start.

**Lateral Raise** - Hold a dumbbell in each hand, palms facing your sides. Lift both elbows and weights up to shoulder level. The only joint that is moving is your shoulder joint. Pause for one second at the top and slowly lower to the start of the shoulder exercise.

**Forty-Five Degree Raise** - Hold a dumbbell in each hand, palms facing your side. Keeping your arms straight, lift the dumbbells up on a forty-five degree angle until they are at shoulder level.

**Shrugs** - Standing with your feet under your hips and knees slightly bent, hold a free weight in each hand, palms facing your sides. Keep your arms relaxed and elbows extended. Pull your shoulders up to your ears. Pause for one second and lower back to start.

**External Rotation** - Sit on a bench with one foot on the floor and one foot on the bench. Put your elbow on your knee and rotate the dumbbell toward the ground as far as you comfortably can. After a slight pause return to the starting point.

# LEGS

**Walking Lunges** - Begin with your feet directly under your hips and hands by your sides. Take one step forward with your left leg. Take your back knee down so it almost touches the floor. Pause for a second and then step out with the other leg and repeat.

**Split Squats** - Begin with your feet directly under your hips and hands by your sides. Take one step forward with your left leg. Take your back knee down so it almost touches the floor. Pause for a second and lift back to start.

**Box Jumps** - Begin these with your feet separated and hands where you feel most comfortable. Make sure to have a sturdy box in front of you. Keeping the majority of your body weight on the heels, begin to sit down as though sitting on a chair. Go as low as feels comfortable, pause, and then jump up onto the box landing softly.

**Squat Jumps** - Start off with your feet separated and hands where you feel most comfortable. Keeping the majority of your body weight on the heels, begin to sit down as though sitting on a chair. Go as low as you feel comfortable, pause, and then jump up as high as you can.

**Physioball Hamstring Curls -** Begin by lying on your back. Hands on the floor. Bend your knees and place them directly over your hips. Your feet are up against the topside of the stability ball. Lift your hips to the sky as you press your feet into the ball. Keep your hips lifted as you begin to roll the ball away from you. Once you cannot roll it out further, pull the ball back towards you.

**Leg Press** - Sit down on the bench and place your feet on the footpads. Push the footpads by extending your legs and let them slowly come back after a short pause.

**Calf Raises** - Begin with your feet directly under your hips. Lift up onto your toes. Pause for a second and lower back down.

Choose three or four exercises for each body part. Mixing them up for each workout keeps your muscles confused and not accustomed to each movement. I like to pick two body parts per day to train. However, I would always do my legs by themselves on one day.

**Phase Two** In the middle of December, after I had added size and strength, I would usually start mixing in more agility workouts and speed training. All the phases of my off-season workouts were important, but these next two months were the most important and beneficial. For someone like myself, who was not born a physical specimen, I knew I had to be dedicated and remember what my ultimate goal was. I could not miss workouts or go through them half-heartedly. There were many days that I did not feel like doing it, days I was sick and days I was tired, but I pushed myself to go everyday. In New York during the cold winters, we were indoors for the workouts. It got monotonous but we pushed each other. Having good workout partners makes all the difference in the world. Doing baseball-specific agility drills helped me become a better athlete but I also felt like it protected me from injury. Every time you step on the field, injury is possible. Doing these drills helped limit the number and severity of the injuries. I liked doing a lot of rotational movements because being a baseball player meant I would be rotating my body a lot.

**AGILITY** These exercises are designed to maximize your body's ability to rapidly change directions without the loss of speed, balance or body control.

**Speed Ladder** - The speed ladder is a great agility-training tool. It is cheap and easy to use. The drills I would do were: Fast Feet, Lateral Fast

Feet, Base Shuffle, Scissors, Hops, Hop Scotch Drill, In-Out Drill, Lateral Feet Drill, Tango Drill and Five Count Drill.

**Cat and Mouse** - This is done with two people. Follow the person while they are sprinting and changing direction randomly. Stay as close to the person as possible at all times.

**Four Cone Square Drill** - Space the cones ten to fifteen feet apart. Begin by sprinting to the first cone, shuffling to the second cone, backpedaling to the third cone and carioca step to the last cone. You can start on your stomach for this drill and see how quickly you can get up. Make sure you time yourself.

**Side-to-Side Ball Rolls** - Have someone roll balls to your left and then to your right. Flip the ball back to the feeder as you are shuffling back to center. Stay low and watch the ball into your bare hands.

**SPEED** These exercises focus on improving your quickness over short distances.

**Falling Starts** - Lean forward as much as possible without actually falling on your face. Explode into the sprint when you feel like you are about to fall.

**Resisted Takeoffs** - Have a resistance band around your waist and have a partner holding the band. The partner should hold on tight for the first five steps than let go, making you feel like you are being shot out of a cannon.

**Up Hill Sprints** - Running up hill develops power and acceleration. Keep the distances short.

# CORE

In 2002, I was diagnosed with a back condition called spondylolisthesis. Briefly, it is a condition where a vertebra slips, either backward or frontward from the spine. Depending on how severe the slippage is, the symptoms range from pain in your back that can shoot down your legs, to stiffness and adding a waddle to the way you walk. Luckily, I was diagnosed early and from that point on I stuck to a strict core workout program. At the end of every weight-training workout I would do my core routine. Without that core routine I would not be able to play. If I missed a couple of days doing that routine my back would hurt so much it was tough to swing a bat. I could not neglect my back, not only during the season but during the off-season as well. I'll actually have to do it for the rest of my life if I want to keep my back in check. Mixing in yoga and Pilates helped out as well.

These core exercises focus on the central part of the body, the torso and the hips, which are the foundation for power and strength.

**Planks** - Face the floor, support yourself with only your forearms and your toes. Straighten out your body and hold it for thirty seconds.

**Russian Twist with Med Ball** - Start by sitting on the ground with med ball in your hands and feet lifted, lean back slightly and twist from side to side touching the area on the ground right next to each hip. Start with ten and increase as you get stronger.

**Bridges** - Lie on your back with your arms at your side. With your feet on the ground while your knees are up, raise your hips off the ground and squeeze your abs tightly. Pause at the top and feel your core working. Start with ten repetitions.

**Physioball Sit Up** - On the ball, simply do crunches with your arms folded across your chest. Start with twenty.

**Swimming** - With your stomach on floor lift your right arm and left leg at the same time and then switch to left arm and right leg. Pause one second at the top of the movement. Do for a count of twenty. (Also good on physioball.)

**Superman** - Begin with your stomach on the floor and lift both your arms and legs off the floor and pause for one 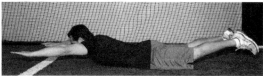 second at the top of the movement. Do not come more than five or six inches off the ground. Start with ten and then increase.

**Physioball Hyperextension** - With stomach on the physioball and hands on the floor, raise your feet off the ground until your back and legs become a flat table. Start with ten and increase.

**Dead Bug** - While lying flat on the floor, raise your arms and legs with your knees bent. Touch the left hand to the right knee and then switch. Go slow and make sure you keep your abs tight the whole time. Twenty reps.

# STRETCHING

When that was all done, I would go into a static stretching routine. Like I said, **static stretching is not good to do before a workout** when the muscles are cold but it is definitely good after a workout. Static stretching helps your muscles relax, and realigns the muscle fibers. Stretching can help you improve your flexibility which may improve your athletic performance and decrease your risk of injury.

 **IT Band** - On your back, bend knee of one leg and cross it over your opposite leg.

**Quad** - Standing up, grab one of your ankles. Slowly extend the hip back and hold. Your knee should be pointing downward.

**Hamstring** - Lying on your back, straighten your leg upward while keeping the toes flexed toward your body. Pull leg toward your head while keeping the leg straight.

**Groin** - On your back, put the soles of your shoes together in a butterfly position. Push down on inside of legs to get a deep stretch.

**Glute** - Stand up and pull one knee to the chest. Hug the knee with both hands and squeeze the thigh toward the chest.

**Trunk Twist** - On your back, bend both knees together and rotate to one side. Keep arms pinned down against the floor.

**Calf** - Standing on a step, let your heel hang down keeping only the toes on the step. Think about forcing your toes to your shins.

**Hip Flexor** - Knee on the ground and opposite leg bent out in front of the body. Push your hips forward while keeping your upper body erect.

**Forearm** - Pull fingers and hand up towards your forearm.

**Shoulder** - Straighten out your arm and pull it across your body.

**Tricep** - Bring your arm up and over your head and push down on your elbow.

All of these stretches should be held for thirty seconds.

## HITTING AND THROWING

I usually did not start hitting or throwing until right after the New Year. This was when my days got really long and busy. Most workouts would start at 9 a.m. and go until about 3 p.m. Often, we would throw in some racquetball, which is such a good workout; it helps your quickness, foot speed and hand-eye coordination. Usually for the first month of hitting in the off-season we would just do drills. One arm drills, flips and tee work. With two or three weeks left until spring training, we would start throwing batting practice to each other. All the hitting drills are detailed in the Hitting chapter.

Not only was strengthening my body very important to me, so was strengthening my eyes. In baseball, your eyes are your most important tool and I wanted to make sure mine were strong and that I was seeing as well as possible. I would see a vision training doctor once a week for the two months leading up to spring training. Dr. Arnold Sherman gave me many drills that not only helped me sharpen my vision but also give me confidence. If you feel your vision is its best, you will be confident and know you are seeing the ball well. Sometimes all it takes to lose confidence is for a little bit of doubt to enter your head and then you start questioning yourself and it snowballs. I would do these drills not only during the off-season but also during the season, especially when I felt like I was not seeing the ball.

# SportsView
Vision Training

---

## Vision Training
### "Continued Improvement"

Included here are some techniques top athletes use to warm up and improve their visual system. Note: These alone are not enough to optimize your visual system. Proper SportsView training sessions are required for optimization.

### Warm-Up

1) <u>Eye Tracking and Focusing</u>: Choose 6 spots on field greater than 20 feet away (choose a base, post, fence, etc.). Without moving your head move your eyes to each of the six spots, pause then focus, and move on to the next. Repeat six times.

2) <u>Eye Tracking and Focusing</u>: Look at your extended thumb and focus. Now pick out an object 300 feet away and focus. Return to the thumb and repeat six times.

3) <u>Eye Tracking</u>: Look at your extended thumb. Now move your arm in circular motions, watching your thumb at all times. Don't move your head. This warms up the eye muscles that control the eyes.

### Improvement

1) <u>Peripheral Vision</u>: Look straight ahead. Without moving your head point to an object far away in your peripheral vision. Now while pointing, move your head to see how accurate you pointed. Over time your peripheral vision will become more accurate and you will increase your visual world.

2) <u>Peripheral Vision</u>: While driving, look straight-ahead, but notice objects in your peripheral vision (posts, signs, etc.). Make sure you still concentrate on your driving!

3) <u>Eye Blinking/ Big Eyes</u>: Perform rapid eye blinking before an intense concentration moment such as an at-bat, or a tennis or racket ball hit. Blinking works like windshield wipers to clean the vision system. After blinking, use big eyes upon contact. Big eyes allow for optimum depth perception.

*Above: Several of the eye exercises I used year-round.*

*Right: Some of the eye exercise gear I took on the road with me.*

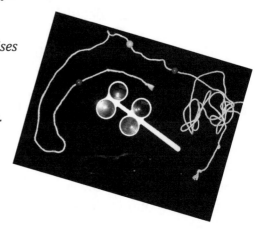

The off-season workouts were a process, introducing something new every couple of weeks; changing the workouts from time to time so the muscles did not get used to it; building the body up and not going too fast. There was a lot of repetition with the baseball-specific drills with the goal of creating muscle memory. I worked hard and never settled for the path of least resistance. If you don't take conditioning seriously, it may carry over onto practice and the game. Conditioning the right way and practicing the right way go hand in hand. By just going through the motions you create bad habits. And, the conditioning will pay off when you discover you can do a particular thing (whether it be making a play or hitting a certain pitch in practice) better or easier than before. You are strengthening your belief in yourself. When you do it right, over and over, you cannot help but be confident when put in that situation during the game.

*You can read much more about my conditioning routines and see additional photos at www.frankcatalanotto.com*

# INJURIES

*"When they operated on my arm, I asked them to put in Koufax's fastball.
They did. But, it turned out to be Mrs. Koufax." ~ Tommy John*

There wasn't one game in my fourteen-year major league career where I felt one hundred percent physically. For what is supposedly a "non-contact sport", there are a lot of injuries in baseball. Over the years, I had shoulder surgery, wrist surgery, sports hernia surgery, a broken hand (hit by pitch), groin pulls, hamstring pulls, plantar fasciitis, heel spurs, bicep tendonitis and a stress fracture in my back. I was also hit by seventy-eight pitches in the major leagues and forty-six in the minor leagues which left many welts and bruises. But, I did not injure every part of my body: my left big toe came away unscathed.

Although I had many minor injuries in the minor leagues, my first bite from the injury bug in the major leagues happened at what seemed, at the time, to be the worst possible moment in my career. After a successful September call-up to the major leagues in 1997, the Tigers asked me to go to the Arizona Fall League, which ran from the middle of October until the end of November. The Tigers wanted me to switch positions and solely play third base while I was there. Damion

Easley was entrenched as the Tigers' second baseman and in order to get my bat in the lineup they knew it had to be from a different position. I was excited to go and felt like I could make the adjustment to prove that I could play third in the big leagues. After being there for about two weeks, I was approached by my manager who told me that a scout for the Arizona Diamondbacks was in the stands and he really wanted me to show off my arm during my ground ball session at third base during practice. The expansion draft was approaching that winter and the Diamondbacks and Tampa Bay Devil Rays were checking guys out to see who they might want to select. I remember thinking that this could be my big chance to become an everyday starter on a young team and show the rest of the league what I could do. I was not known for having a great arm and since I played second base up until that point, I never had to make long throws across the diamond. Nevertheless, I was determined to "air it out" and impress this scout. I threw about twenty balls from third to first as hard as I could until my arm was hanging limply by my side. I stopped, walked to the dugout and realized that I could barely raise my arm. The pain was ridiculous and I knew that I had really overdone it. The next day at the ballpark, the team doctor checked me out and within hours I was on a plane to Alabama to see the pioneering sports surgeon, Dr. James Andrews. He examined my shoulder, took an M.R.I. and confirmed what I feared: I would need surgery. My labrum and rotator cuff were torn and I was on the operating table the next morning.

The timing was terrible. I had just made it to the major leagues, was performing well at my new position and had a chance to be taken in the expansion draft. But, just when I felt like I had a head of steam, I was headed for an off-season of grueling rehab. The surgery was a success, but the pain was excruciating and, for many days, I had doubts about my future. I was disappointed, thinking, "Will my shoulder be like new or be a constant problem?", "Will the team forget about me?", "Will I be ready for spring training?", "Have I blown my big opportunity?". The off-season was tough and there were many times that I did not think it would get any better. The rehab was boring and tedious. But, I knew if I wanted to get healthy I was going to have to do all the little things that the doctors and trainers were telling me to do and I did so diligently. When spring training came around my shoulder was not one hundred percent, but I felt like I was close. I was hoping that the team would be patient with me. Fortunately, they were. As the spring wore on, I gained more and more strength and flexibility and wound up performing well enough that I made the team out of spring training. The Tigers had me on the twenty-five man roster as a utility infielder. I played first base, second base and third base through spring training and, although I wasn't a Gold Glove infielder, Tigers' infield coach Perry Hill (the best infield coach I ever had) made me adequate at all three. Going through that injury was tough but it helped me realize that I could overcome any curve ball or bump in the road that this game had to offer.

Fast-forward six years to my first day of spring training with Toronto. One of the coaches walked up and introduced himself. His name was Brian Butterfield. He said "Frank, I've got a confession to make. I was the scout in the stands in Arizona in 1997 that asked your manager to have you show off your arm at third base." I said, "Thanks a lot." He laughed and said, "Sorry about that. I didn't intend on having you blow out your arm." Brian became one of my favorite coaches and we still get a kick out of that story when we see each other.

I played the game hard. I had only one gear. I never jogged to first base. But, I would have to say that most of my injuries did not happen because I was playing with reckless abandon. Other guys played hard and never got hurt. And there were guys who didn't play hard, but were always getting hurt. Some body types seem to be predisposed to injury. Some guys didn't prepare their bodies for the grind of the long, demanding season. I know my injuries weren't because I was physically unprepared or was out of shape. Playing hard and a bit of bad luck may have played roles but it's part of the game. If you play sports, especially as long as I did, you will inevitably have to deal with some injuries. Maybe the fact that I didn't take it easy caught up with me over the years. It is a long season and there are always nicks and bruises. Playing through some pain is expected. Managing the injuries is very important and knowing whether you should play and risk further injury can be tricky. Over the years, I learned how to listen to my body and was able to determine whether being out on the field would help the team or possibly hurt the team. Learning what your body is telling you is very important. Getting the proper treatment before and after games is vital.

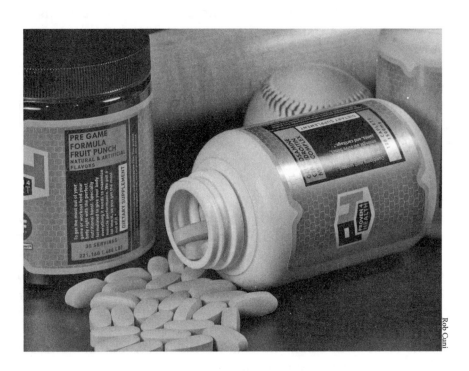

# SUPPLEMENTS

*"Adam and Eve ate the first vitamins, including the package."*
~ *E.R. Squibb*

When I graduated high school, I was a small kid, only five-ten and one hundred fifty-five pounds soaking wet, as the saying goes. When I got to the minor leagues, I realized that just about everyone was bigger and stronger than me, so I dedicated myself to putting on weight and muscle. I drank protein shakes and started taking creatine, which helps to provide energy to muscle cells. I made a habit of reading and understanding the labels on these products before I started taking them. I also made sure that I bought reputable brands that have tested "clean". There have been many players who tested positive for performance enhancing drugs and claimed that all they did was drink protein shakes or energy drinks. Here is the lesson that I learned from their suspensions: don't buy supplements that haven't been given a legitimate seal of approval, such as the one at right from NSF International, a lab that tests for banned substances.

    I have also learned how important it is to understand exactly what I am taking and to follow the instructions for those products, reading the labels carefully. For example, creatine requires its users to stay hydrated, meaning drink a lot of water. I made sure I did just that. I was always told that it is very difficult to get all our nutrients through food. My trainers made sure that I knew it could be done, but that I would have to eat an extraordinary amount of many different types of food just to get an effective amount of nutrients for my body. I thought it would help if I could get some muscle building nutrients through supplements. So, just like everything else related to baseball, I really got into nutrition and strength training. Starting when I was eighteen, I dedicated myself to getting stronger. Throughout my career, most of my teammates were also into it. However, there were always a few who did not want to work hard in the weight room. Maybe they were out of shape and did not care, or maybe they were afraid to gain weight and possibly lose a step. But, I felt that taking supplements helped me get stronger and faster which, in turn, helped me play better. I definitely felt an improvement on the field. I would also have a recovery drink, which contained glutamine, after my workout or game. Glutamine is said to promote muscle growth and recovery and I have always believed that feeding my muscles after a hard workout or long game is essential.

When I was playing in the minor leagues, coaches encouraged supplements but they did not always help us get the substances necessary for the healthy lifestyle they advised. Most of the time we were on our own to purchase supplements. However, in the major leagues, they were provided for us. After I got to the big leagues, the organizations woke up and had strength and conditioning coaches working with each minor league team. They also started providing minor leaguers with supplements.

Even in retirement, I work out most mornings and take supplements. I have a pre-workout formula that has an abundance of nutrients, caffeine to give me energy, glutamine, creatine and other ingredients to help me have a good workout. Afterward, I take a recovery drink that replenishes the nutrients and helps my body recover quickly. I don't have soreness after my workout and I have sustained energy the rest of the day. It truly works for me. Additionally, I will take a protein shake during the afternoon. With my body, I cannot get enough protein, so the shake is important. I also take omega-3 fish oil that I feel helps me with any inflammation I may have in my body and amino acids that may assist with the repair of muscles and ligaments.

My advice to the parents of kids who wish to explore nutrition and strength training? Speak with their medical professionals and discuss the possibility of adding protein shakes and nutritional supplements to their diet. Further, ensure that your child is drinking sufficient water to remain hydrated. If approved by their doctor, they may start strength training, but make sure they do not overexert themselves. They don't need to lift heavy weights, but I believe it's good to get into the habit of working out and exercising. Same goes for their diet. When I was a kid, we didn't know any better and would often have fast food and fried foods. Today we know more about proper nutrition. Kids have a better opportunity to eat healthier foods like grilled chicken, fruits and vegetables (which you also can get at many fast food restaurants. Just stay away from the fried stuff.) I encourage them to get on a nutritionally balanced diet and watch their caloric intake to make sure they're getting an appropriate amount of calories.

**A few words of caution:** There are a lot of products on the market that can do more harm than good. For example, many energy drinks on the market are loaded with sugar and caffeine. Be careful, you can overdo it. Also, keep in mind that eating the right foods and exercising appropriately for your age will give you energy that will last longer than most energy drinks.

Make sure you know exactly what you are putting in your body. Taking a product that may be contaminated could affect your health as well as your career. Again, you have to be certain that what it says on the label is what's going into your body.

> *Learn more about supplement safety at www.proven4.com*

# THE STEROIDS ERA

*"Competing against guys who were juiced was like taking a knife to a gunfight." ~ Unknown*

In an earlier chapter, I wrote about how, since baseball was invented, players have been trying to get an edge by doctoring the ball, corking the bat, stealing signs, etc. It turns out that performance enhancing drugs, and players willing to try them, were also around from the beginning. Wikipedia notes that in 1889, a pitcher named Pud Galvin was a user and vocal proponent of the Brown-Sequard Elixir, a testosterone supplement derived from the testicles of live animals such as dogs and guinea pigs.

Even Babe Ruth apparently gave in to the temptation of better baseball through chemistry. *The Baseball Hall of Shame's Warped Record Book* tells how he gave himself a shot of an extract from sheep testicles. The Babe's body apparently didn't respond well and he missed at least one game due to "a bellyache".

Tom House, who pitched in the big leagues during most of the 1970s, told the *Associated Press* in 2005 that he used "steroids they wouldn't give to horses" and that six or seven pitchers on every team were at least experimenting with steroids or human growth hormones in the 1960s and 1970s.

In the mid-1990s when I was in the minor leagues, we could see the effects of steroids. Guys were hitting home runs and putting up ridiculous numbers. Some were suddenly putting on a lot of weight, getting muscular, had bad acne on their back and started losing their hair. Whenever we saw those types of things, we wondered if a guy was on something. Other than a couple of players, I never knew for sure whether someone was on "the juice".

It was a very complicated issue at the time. I wrestled with the decision. The stakes were high. There were millions of dollars waiting for us in the big leagues and if something that other guys were doing could make our dreams come true, then why not? There were conversations in the clubhouses, all kind of hush-hush. Things like: "If you did steroids, do you think it would help you get to the big leagues?" "If you did it, would you get in trouble if you were caught?" The answers seemed to be "Yes" and "No". I totally understood why a player would do it. However, I also valued my health, my life and my body and I knew by juicing I would be putting myself in a bad spot. So, I passed.

I am never the type of guy who would say, "I cannot believe this guy is doing this", or "How can this guy even think about doing it?" There was a lot of pressure. I saw steroids helping other guys, so it was difficult enough for me to say "no", let alone judging someone else's decision. Once a teammate decided to "juice" and other players knew about it, that information did not leave the clubhouse. I never heard of a teammate blowing the whistle and telling on someone and I don't think it would happen. There is a type of brotherhood and even though someone might be doing something you would not do, you keep quiet about it. We would say, "Okay, maybe he will die when he is forty-five years old or there might be other consequences, but that is his business." There is definitely that brotherhood. You kept things in-house and you let them be.

But, even outside the clubhouse it was clear that something was juiced, either the balls, bats or the players. Fans were not packing the parks hoping to see a 1-0 pitchers' duel. They were there to see the long ball. Six home runs a game compared to one or two; games where frequently over twenty runs were scored. Steroid baseball was like a video game. Heroes were being made with every ball that sailed over the fence. Baseball was riding its biggest wave of popularity ever and at the time, no one seemed too concerned about how it was happening.

There are fans that now say a player who was a steroid user is a terrible person and should not be in the Hall of Fame. I disagree because when those gaudy numbers were packing stadiums, there was not a universal testing and enforcement policy. There were no extensive education and awareness programs for players. When Congress decided to look into it, the commissioner, owners and eventually the players' union got on board. There is plenty of blame to go around and to deny a player a place in the Hall of Fame because he used steroids during a time when there was widespread usage of them does not seem fair. I have a unique solution for this. We will likely never know every player who took steroids during that era and there is no way now to prove what happened back then. I propose that Hall of Fame officials figure out when the latest steroid era was, let's say it was 1993-2003, and have a wing in the Hall just for those years. That is not saying everyone in that era was on steroids, people can draw their own conclusions. There were guys who did it and got caught, guys who did it and did not get caught and guys who did not do it at all. All of them who had the required numbers should get in to that wing, and no other area of the Hall. Take a guy like Barry Bonds. He was a Hall of Famer before he was suspected of doing steroids. Or, a guy like Greg Maddux, who we all assume did not do steroids. They would both be in that same wing called: The Long Ball Era. Just a thought.

Would I vote for someone who took steroids? I would. There is no doubt that steroids can make you stronger and faster, but they will not help you make contact with the ball or improve hand-eye coordination. I know how difficult it is to hit a baseball traveling ninety miles an hour and I know how tough it is to play the game at that level. I would vote for everyone who had the numbers, even if I knew he did steroids.

What would I tell parents and kids about steroids? Do not use them. Not only are they now illegal and violators are being suspended for a minimum of fifty games—enough to kill some young careers—they may shorten your life. You have to think about your future. Eventually, you may want to have a family and you will want to be around for as long as you can. Doing steroids may improve your game in the short-term, but in the long-term, it is dangerous, deadly and stupid. Plus, there is no guarantee that just because you are doing steroids, you will turn into Superman. I have seen guys who juiced, got huge, but then their bodies broke down because they could not take all the stress.

*When it came to being sports parents, mine got it right. Mom and Dad were encouraging, enthusiastic and always there.*

# SPORTS PARENTS

*"Parents can really help, but they can also really hinder the development of their youngsters."*
*~ Coach Mike Krzyzewski*

*"Every word, facial expression, gesture, or action on the part of a parent gives the child some message about self-worth. It is sad that so many parents don't realize what messages they are sending." ~ Virginia Satir*

Whatever the kids' sport—baseball, softball, football, basketball, soccer, volleyball, hockey, lacrosse—all of us have seen "that parent", the crazed, wild-eyed one who screams at and berates the coach, the officials, other parents or, worst of all, his or her child. It has become so prevalent that psychologists have named it: "sports rage". They say it happens because those parents are trying to relive (and revise) their athletic history through their children and/or because parents have unrealistic expectations. They may think that because their five-year-old has advanced hand-eye coordination he's on his way to becoming a Major League All-Star or will be given a free college education.

I'm not a psychologist, but my guess is that every positive

thought I've had about myself—including when I was walking to the plate against some of the best pitchers who ever took the mound—had its roots in the way my parents talked to me and treated me when I was very, very young. Because they were supportive, encouraging and kind in everything from learning to tie my shoes to learning my multiplication tables, I developed an internal "voice" that was encouraging and supportive and gave me a can-do attitude.

*LARRY PARRISH: I saw that a lot in the minor leagues. Kids who came from supportive families were more coachable. They were likely to try things, like changing their swing. They'd come from a background where their parents had been in their corner and the kids got the concept of constructive criticism and that we, their coaches, were trying to help them, too. But, kids from tough backgrounds, a lot of times when you tried to correct them, they felt that you that you were just getting on them and they didn't trust that you were on their side. We had to approach them a little differently. But, if you spend any time around Frank, his manners and values tell you he comes from a supportive family. When you work with 180 young guys in camp, you can send the coaches out there for four days and they could pick out which kids came from a good family background. It's just so important.*

If my parents had been constantly putting me down, telling me I wasn't doing things right, belittling my efforts to try new things and discouraging me from being adventurous, I'm sure this book would have never been written because I wouldn't have had the career that I did.

## WHAT TYPE OF PARENT ARE YOU?

Let's begin this section with this fact: most kids, at some point in their lives, have that moment where they feel embarrassed by their parents. Below is a self-test, parts of which come from the Fair Play Canada website. I'm sure you can find others of similar value with a quick web search.

> ➢ THE SCREECHER
> The Screecher sees all the negative things on the field. Everything is going wrong and they yell constantly. They yell at all the players and the referee, umps and coaches. The Screecher

focuses on the negative and is sometimes verbally abusive to the players. The Screecher is most likely to wind up as the star of a YouTube video fighting another parent.

➤ THE TRY HARD
The Try Hard is the super positive one. For example, in soccer, Try Hards get so excited they yell every time their child even gets near the ball. They cheer so much their kids get embarrassed – especially when they use their kids' nicknames too often.

➤ THE ANALYST
This parent usually is taking notes and/or shooting video. He or she will use those notes and video to analyze the performance for days and weeks to come. Then, the Analyst will relive the game with their child, pointing out all the things they could do better. What might be particularly frustrating for the Analyst is that a child's attention span is sometimes so short that by the time he is ready to go over his charts and video, the child might have moved on to the next shiny thing.

➤ THE NOT REALLY THERE
These parents are sometimes grouped together or are by themselves. They are so busy catching up on the week's gossip or their heads are buried in their work e-mail on their smartphones, they pay no attention to the game. When it is over, they offer no encouragement and make no positive comments about improvement.

➤ THE WANNABES
The Wannabes are living their lives through their children. They remember their own skill levels (usually higher than they actually were) and assume that because their children have their DNA, they will be as good or better. They treat their child's game as if it was their own. At the extreme, the Wannabes may punish their children by scrapping the after-game social time or treat if the team loses the game. Even worse, after a loss or poor individual performance, the Wannabes may withdraw affection for their children.

➤ THE FOLD UP THE LAWNCHAIR AND STORM OFF

You felt bad for the child of this parent because you just knew that he or she was really going to hear about it (whatever *it* was that caused the parent to collapse the chair in anger and stalk off) when they got home.

> THE FIVE-STAR PARENTS
> Here are the ones we want: The Five-Star Parents focus on the effort and not the outcome. They respect the game, the officials and the players. They remember to thank the officials and offer encouragement to all of the players. They are actively involved, supportive, encouraging and are mindful of the important role they play on the sideline.

Look, I'm as competitive as they come but you have to remember where you are: it is a kids' game. It is for the kids. It is not about you. Sure, you can be disappointed by an umpire's bad call, but what good is yelling at the ump (who is probably making twenty-five dollars to do the game) going to do? It'll embarrass your child and your child's teammates. But worst of all, if you fit into one of the not-so-good categories above, your actions will turn what should be a joyful childhood moment into an activity that they dread. It is unlikely that your child will be a professional athlete, or even get an athletic scholarship to college. There are far more academic scholarships available than athletic ones. When children think that the sport they are playing has no value unless it translates into an economic gain like a scholarship or a signing bonus, they may be under too much pressure. Your child should be having fun and learning the values of teamwork and hard work. If that is not happening, you may be sacrificing valuable family time that could be better spent elsewhere.

*FRANK, SR.: I learned a valuable lesson when Frank was about nine years old. He was pitching and was struggling a little. I was the coach of the team yelling to him from the dugout, "Throw it, throw hard, Frankie". His mother was in the stands saying, "Take it easy, Frankie. Relax and calm down". All of a sudden a silence fell over the field as Frank stopped, looked at me with tears in his eyes and asked, "Dad, what do you want me to do? You want me to throw hard and mom wants me to relax!" At that point, I realized you can't put pressure on a nine-year-old.*

There should be a special place in Heaven for *good* Little League coaches. Not only do they have to motivate, inspire and manage their teams, they have to manage the parents. Here is my advice to parents... it is great to be involved and if you have suggestions, concerns or comments, you should definitely make yourself heard. But there is a time and a place, as well as a right way to talk to the coach. Don't be overbearing about it. You have to show an interest and let the coach know that you are there and you care, but there should be a relationship and dialogue. Be careful to not overstep boundaries. Telling a coach, "My kid is better, he has to play more," or, "You are doing this wrong, or that wrong," is not the right approach. And never, ever talk about another player, such as, "Why do you have Billy batting third? He can't hit."

## LESSONS

I am all for parents who want to buy their kids lessons, as long as the motives are in line with The Five-Star Parent.

Kids are funny when it comes to taking instruction from their parents. Even when their father has played fourteen seasons in the big leagues, children may not pay much attention to what he is attempting to teach. When I was trying to show one of my daughters how to hit, I got the, "What do you know?" attitude. My wife, Barbara, said to her, "You know, Daddy was a real good hitter in the big leagues for a long time. He knows what he's talking about". But it still seems to work better when the same instruction comes from someone who isn't their parent.

Another reason to consider private lessons is that your child's coaches may not be all that helpful. When I was a kid, some of my coaches were great at teaching us about being a good teammate, being on time and making the most out of practices, but when it came to teaching the nuts and bolts of baseball, they threw batting practice, hit fungos, filled out the lineup cards and that was about it.

Also, you don't only have to listen to one person when it comes to hitting, fielding or pitching mechanics. No one person knows it all. Take a little bit from every coach you have. Every hitter is different and when molding your swing you must use what works for you. Don't become a robot. I always took a little bit from each coach. Whatever felt comfortable and worked for me was what I implemented.

## VIDEO

With YouTube and MLB.com, it is easy to do side-by-side comparisons between your swing and the swings of the best players in the game. The same applies to pitchers. Have your dad, mom or a friend run the camera while you practice and during your games (as long as your parent is not The Analyst above!)

## PARENTS WITHOUT RESOURCES

Money does not have to be a barrier for parents who want to support their kids' enthusiasm. A bat, ball and hitting tee shouldn't cost a whole lot. You can set that up in the backyard or, if using a Wiffle ball, in the basement. The sawed-off broomstick handle and Wiffle golf ball don't cost much either. Even video cameras are so ubiquitous that a relative, friend or neighbor should have one you can borrow. Even a smartphone that shoots video will work, it does not have to be a professional job.

Whether parents can afford special lessons does not matter. What is most important is that they are there; that their child sees them being caring and being supportive. Odds are, they won't grow up to be a major league player, but whatever they do become, they will be better at it because of the encouragement, kindness and support they received from their parents when they were young.

*FRANK, SR.: As a parent, it's important to support your child one hundred percent in whatever their passion is. For the most part, we saw that Frank had a passion for athletics. Our daughter Christa (two years older) and son Michael (four years younger than Frank) both had a passion for academics. They were both active in athletics growing up, but Christa became a Special Ed teacher and Michael an attorney. I remember my parents were at every one of my games and that is something my wife Sharon and I wanted to do as parents. We make choices in life and one of the choices my wife and I made was to support our children and to be there for them. I could have taken some career paths that would have led me to make more money down the road, but I wanted to be there for Christa, Frank and Michael.*

*SHARON: Frankie's commitment to baseball was a family commitment. We all went to the games, my husband coached and I was the detail person (uniforms, field locations, etc.) and we all went together.*

*MICHAEL: I've told my parents a hundred times that I don't know how they did it but they got it right. They were at every game, every event and every teacher conference. There was nothing that came before their children. We knew we could always count on them and we knew we were loved. One of the things they were particularly good at was providing constructive criticism. It was never "You didn't do this right, you didn't do that right". It was a conversation about what had happened and by the end of it, we knew what we had done wrong and why we would never do it again. Always positive support.*

*CHRISTA: My parents were involved in all aspects of our lives growing up and they still are. They encouraged us to excel in music, sports and academics and they have been a huge inspiration to all three of us. Our parents were very accepting of who we were.*

School always came first. The first thing I did when I got home from school was homework. Mom and Dad were definitely on me about that. Schooling was very important, and baseball, or any other sport or activity, wouldn't get in the way of that. I knew that if I came home with bad grades, I couldn't play baseball.

**FUN**

One of the greatest gifts parents can give their children is helping them enjoy what they are doing. When I talk to kids, I tell them, "If you are not having fun playing baseball, then pick another sport. You don't want to be miserable playing a sport. If the only reason you are playing is because your dad says you have to, that is not good enough".

*FRANK, SR.: Don't put any pressure on your children to play a particular sport. Let them try different sports. If they enjoy the sport, that's fine. If they don't, that's fine, too. I see it so often when parents are yelling and screaming at games and practices, telling kids what to do. You just can't put that pressure on a kid in athletics, especially when he's just not able to perform at that level. It will leave a scar.*

If you are having fun, you are more likely to practice and the more you practice, the better you will get. The first thing I would do when I came home from school—after my homework—was to run outside and throw the ball around and hit the ball. I remember smiling a lot in those days. When I was hitting, throwing, catching and running, nothing else mattered. It was all I wanted to do.

So how does a parent make it fun? It isn't hard. In fact, the simple things can be the most fun. Take your child into the backyard or onto the street and make up games. For example, if you hit a ball past the driveway, it is four points, or past a tree, it is three points. Hit the street sign and you get ten. Silly things. Kids love that challenge. They love to try to beat their old scores. Even if it is away from the team, it is important for them to be out there, learning that it is fun. This will get them to want to go to practice.

Coaches need to incorporate simulated games into practices, as opposed to monotonous drills, the purpose of which kids sometimes don't see. Creating games during practice teaches kids how to compete in a fun way that will make them want to be there. In Little League, every child has to have the opportunity to play an equal amount of time regardless of his ability. Unfortunately, I see too many coaches who are more concerned about winning and who just put the best kids on the field and try to win, win, win. I think that's a bad message for really young kids. Winning doesn't matter as much at that age. It should be about having fun and creating a team atmosphere.

From Little League to the big leagues, it never stopped being fun for me. Although when Barbara and I began having kids and she wasn't able to travel with me as much, I would miss them terribly and hated being away from them. But once the game started and I was on the field, I always had fun. I loved that one-on-one competition with the pitcher.

Whether you had great parents or parents that were not so involved doesn't make a bit of difference when you are standing at the plate waiting for the pitch. The only thing that matters is whether you believe in yourself. If you're visualizing failure and fear, if the voice inside you is negative and is telling you to be afraid of the pitcher, or afraid to fail, you will inevitably fail.

## THE RIDE HOME

After many of my games, I would ride home with my dad and I couldn't wait to get in the car because, regardless of the score or how I did, I enjoyed talking with him about the game. He was always the same, so positive and encouraging, whether I had a good game or not. It was clear that he loved baseball, loved watching me play and loved that I loved it. What a gift! I cherished those rides home.

*LARRY PARRISH: When you have a kid like Frank to work with as a coach, you begin to think he's almost like your kid. You follow him throughout his career. It's like he is part of your family and I always thought that way about Frank. It was like if you had a daughter, you would've liked for her to bring him home.*

**CAT'S KEYS**

Make it fun.

*Be involved, but not overbearing.*

Be supportive, but not unrealistic.

*Be encouraging and positive.*

It isn't about you. It's their time.

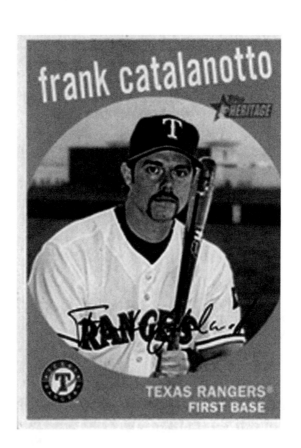

# frank catalanotto

TEXAS RANGERS®
FIRST BASE

# THE FANS

*"What is both surprising and delightful is that spectators are allowed, and even expected, to join in the vocal part of the game. There is no reason why the (fans) should not try to put the batsman off his stroke at the critical moment by neatly timed disparagements of his wife's fidelity and his mother's respectability."* ~ *George Bernard Shaw*

There is a story behind the Fu Manchu I am sporting in my baseball card photo on the preceding page. I will get to it later in this chapter.

I never stopped being a fan. There was always a little kid inside of me who got excited when I saw one of my heroes up close. The Yankees' Don Mattingly was my biggest hero. No matter what he did, I would emulate him. Like me, he was a left-handed hitter. Whenever he would change his batting stance, I would change mine. He played first base. As a kid, I wanted to play first base. He played fourteen years in the big leagues, I played fourteen years in the big leagues. (Of course, there was no way I could have planned that one, but I like the coincidence. We also both had back problems; again, unplanned.) I loved the way "Donnie Baseball" played the game. Whenever I went to the ballpark, he was always at the rail signing autographs and he seemed like a great guy. He could do it all, an overall great player. Mattingly retired two years before I made it to the big leagues and went on to become manager of the Dodgers in 2011. Eventually, after admiring him from afar, I did get to meet him and became friendly with him. That confirmed my suspicion that he is a great role model and hero to have. He is fun to talk with and when I saw him at a baseball alumni dinner in 2011 where he was receiving an award, he said, "Hey Frank, I need a left-handed bat off the bench. Would you mind coming back?" That was nice to hear from my hero.

Hockey Hall of Famer Mike Bossy was another of my sports heroes. He seemed to thrill me game after game. I grew up during the Islanders' dynasty when they won four consecutive Stanley Cups and my dad often took me to Nassau Coliseum to watch the Islanders. Of course I had a Mike Bossy jersey. Whenever he would be someplace signing autographs, I would try to go. In 2011, I did a photo shoot for my eye doctor. Mike Bossy was there, too and after all those years, I finally got a chance to speak with him. I mentioned that he was my favorite hockey player growing up, which I am sure he had heard thousands of times, but he was a really nice guy and it was great to meet another of my childhood heroes. I marveled at some of the things he was able to do, like the 1980-81 season when he scored 50 goals in the first 50 games! Only Maurice Richard had done it before and just a few since, including Wayne Gretzky.

One of my other favorite sports heroes was Ken Griffey Jr. I had his poster on my bedroom wall and I loved watching him as another left-handed hitter. I studied his swing; he had one of the sweetest swings ever. While playing in the major leagues our clubs faced each other and I got to meet him. That little boy fan inside me came out again. I had bought one of his jerseys and wanted to ask him to sign it. But it is a little awkward and embarrassing asking a competitor to sign something. Should I just take it out on the field during BP and ask him? Should I get someone from the clubhouse to ask him? About midway through my career when we were playing the Reds, I walked onto the field during batting practice and Junior just happened to be there, talking to another guy. I did not know if he even knew who I was, but sure enough, he saw me walking over.

"Hey Cat, how are you doing?" He gave me a big hug.

I was thinking, "This is awesome! One of my childhood heroes knows exactly who I am!" It broke the ice and I told him I wanted to send over a jersey to be signed.

He said, "Are you kidding me? Of course I'll do that."

It is framed and hanging in our basement next to my signed Don Mattingly jersey.

I never knew Michael Young would turn into the superstar that he did. When he was called up by the Rangers, I had been in the league for a few years. He was kind of a shy kid, so I took him under my wing and tried to help him out. He worked so hard. He is a great teammate and really cares about everyone on the team. That is a quality very important to me. You get to know guys and quickly learn which teammates are selfish and which ones are not. Even when he became a superstar he was selfless and never forgot where he came from. We shared many of the same values, which is probably why we became such great friends. I loved seeing Michael keep those values as he became a perennial All-Star. He never changed. Michael is just a great guy and we still keep in touch all these years later. Had I ever become a superstar I know, like Michael, I wouldn't have changed.

My ultimate hero is my dad. He is my hero for the way he raised us and the values he instilled. He always put his kids first. And, he never laid a hand on us; he didn't have to. I feared that I would disappoint him. He didn't have to smack us to get us to listen. Dad was so mild mannered and always had a calming effect on our family. I always wanted to be like him. He was such a hard worker and provided for the family. When you had a problem, he always seemed to have the answers to help you figure it out.

As for the fans who watched me play, there were many kinds. I loved the kids hanging over the rail asking you to sign cards. I collected cards when I was growing up and have a pretty nice collection now. When I was a kid, Dad would buy me baseball cards all the time. I would get so excited when he came home from work and had another pack of cards for me.

When my first pro card was printed, it was such a thrill. Here

I had been collecting all of my favorite players' cards and now, I had a real one of my own! Over the years, Topps and the other companies printed over one hundred ten different cards of me. Each time a new one came out, my dad would buy as many as he could. He has probably fifty of each of my cards.

When fans would ask me to sign one of my cards, I always got a kick out of it. I loved signing autographs whenever I could and I still get a lot of fan mail from people asking me to sign cards for them. I always make sure to sign them and send them back right away. It is a great hobby and I am glad I got into it as a kid. My favorite cards are my Don Mattingly and Dave Winfield rookie cards. My most valuable cards are a 1966 Topps Mickey Mantle and a 1969 Topps Reggie Jackson rookie card.

When I was playing, I would get a steady stream of fan mail. People would usually write that they enjoyed watching me play and that I was one of their favorite players. They would ask for a signature. Sometimes it would be for someone who was sick, a parent might write something like, "My son is sick and would love to get a letter from you". Others would ask questions about baseball. You would know for the most part who was sincere and who was just taking the cards and selling them. It got to be a little bit of a game and when I suspected the card might wind up on the Internet, I would sign it a little differently and then I'd try to find it. Over the years, some guys wrote me for autographs so often that I recognized their names. Sure enough, when I went on line, there were my cards for sale.

Young fans wanting autographs would usually ask me questions, too, which I would always answer. They often asked who was the toughest pitcher I had ever faced, how long I played in the minors, who was my best friend on the team, or how I thought the team would do that year. I enjoyed meeting young fans and loved getting their fan mail.

Some of my teammates did not like answering fan mail and either didn't send a response right way, or at all. Some guys would save them up all season, pack them up and take them home where they may or may not have gotten around to them over the winter. I would take home however many I had each day, maybe ten or fifteen, and I would respond within the next couple of days.

There were some fans at the ballpark I tried to ignore: the trash talkers. You hear every word they yell when you are standing in the outfield and most of the time I would ignore them. I would pretend I couldn't hear them in hopes that they would stop. In Toronto, I played left field and Vernon Wells played center. He was the opposite of me. He loved hecklers and all game long, he would go back and forth with them. They would yell things like, "Vernon, you suck!" And, he would return the greeting. The really good hecklers would do their homework and yell things that might be true. When they get personal, it stings a little more.

A lot of the insults were about your wife, mother or sister and I would think to myself, "What losers these guys are. Instead of enjoying the game, they are sitting there from the first through the ninth inning just ragging on me non-stop." Usually, I had a good head about me, but once in a while I would snap back. That only egged them on and made it worse. But Vernon never took anything personally and always had a smile on his face. There were a couple of times when I caught Vernon turned around talking to these guys when the pitch was on the way. I would yell, "Hey Vernon, you missed the pitch!" He'd just say, "Oh, really?"

The hecklers love it when you're in a slump. They would yell, "Cat, you haven't gotten a hit in 20 times at bat. You shouldn't be here. You belong in Triple A. Go back to the minor leagues". Usually the hecklers were on the road, but I was heckled at home in Toronto. I platooned in left field with Reed Johnson. When there was a righty on the mound I was in left field. There was a guy who loved Reed and whenever I was playing left, he would give me hell the whole time. "Hey Cat, what are you doing here? You suck. We want Reed!" It didn't make me feel great, but when we went into the dugout, I would tell Reed what a big fan he had in left.

One more fan story and this was one of the funniest things I have ever seen, so I hope it translates well into print. I was with the Tigers in 1998. We were at the old Tiger Stadium. Our pitcher, Frank Castillo had just given up a bunch of runs. He finally got out of the inning and was so furious, he stormed through the dugout, threw his glove down and then went into a tunnel that separated the dugout from the club-house. The tunnel was all concrete and cracked, with water coming down the sides. It was usually muddy, dark and damp. In one corner of the tunnel, there was a huge fan, one of those giant commercial fans, maybe four feet across, on a pedestal that was used to dry out the tun-nel. Castillo headed into the tunnel, kicking the walls as he went. When he got to the fan (which was off) he started kicking the pedestal part as hard as he could, over and over again. Now, there were four of us sitting on the end of the bench who could see him doing all of this. As we are watching him try to destroy this fan, all of a sudden the fan tips over, he slips, his legs fly out from under him and the huge fan comes down on top of him. Frank is wrestling with this fan and he is rolling around in the mud trying to get it off of him. We didn't know what to do. We thought about going to help him, but we were cracking up and he was so pissed off. We were afraid he would punch us in the face if we went to help him and he saw how much we were enjoying his show. Finally, he pushes the fan off of him and disappears into the clubhouse. But shortly after that the inning was over and he had to come back out on the field. So, he comes running out of the dugout and his whole back is full of mud and you could barely see his name and number. The four of us were dying laughing on the bench.

Now, about the Fu Manchu. At the end of the 2007 season one of my Ranger teammates dared all of us to grow mustaches for the fol-lowing spring training's photo day. Photo day was during the first week of spring training. All types of media outlets would come and put us through a series of photo shoots. There were photo stations set up on the various minor league fields, on the major league field and even in-side the clubhouse. The video game guys, the AP photo guys, the jum-botron guys, most of the baseball card companies and other photographers were there. This was the day that you wanted to make sure you looked your best or, at least, however you wanted your big face up on the humongous screen at every ballpark to look. I basically looked the same every year in my photos and baseball cards and thought that it would be cool to have some that looked different. There were about eight players who said they would do it. But when spring training rolled around, only three of us actually had significant facial hair, not including the guy who came up with the idea! He said that his wife did not want to have to look at his face with a bad mustache every time he got up to bat, so he decided not to do it. I, being a man of my word, went through with it. The morning of photo day, I carved out a Fu Manchu, then shaved it right after we were done taking photos. About a month later when we got to Texas, in my first at-bat I looked up and saw this funny photo of me on the screen. I could hear the guys laughing in the dugout. Shortly after that, I received a baseball card in the mail with the Fu Manchu. To this day, that is the one I get the most questions about. Although my wife didn't care to look at my face on the jumbotron, the guys and I got a kick out of it. I will always have a story about, "Why the mustache?"

*In the cage during my final season.*

# THE TAP

*"...today I consider myself the luckiest man on the face of this earth. I have been in ballparks for seventeen years and have never received anything but kindness from you fans. Look at these grand men. Which of you wouldn't consider it the highlight of his career to associate with them for even one day? Sure, I'm lucky."*

*~ Lou Gehrig*
*July 4, 1939*
*Yankee Stadium*

Hollywood couldn't have written my final major league at-bat any better. It was game seven of the World Series at Citi Field. We had a big lead over the Yankees in the bottom of the eighth and would go on to win, but my personal highlight was about to happen. It was my turn to bat. Word had leaked out just before the Series that I was going to retire and everyone in the stadium knew it would be my final trip to the plate as a Major League Baseball player. As the public address announcer's booming voice lingered on the syllables of my last name, giving each a little extra emphasis, the crowd's roar was deafening! As I strolled toward the plate, I swear the ground was shaking a little. I stopped a few feet from the batter's box, looked around and soaked it all in. Everyone was standing and applauding, including Yankees fans and players. Through my tears I could see my family. Barbara and the girls, Mom and Dad, Christa and Michael and their families. I used my forearm to wipe my eyes, doffed my cap and did a slow, grateful wave to all corners of the field.

That is how I wish my career had ended. Not because I craved the adoration, but because I would have loved the opportunity to display the respect and love I had for the game that had been my life as long as I could remember. And, winning a World Series would have been great, too.

After the September day in 1997 when I was called up, the only thing I knew for sure about my major league career was that it would end. How and when it would end and everything else about it was a mystery that unfolded with each at-bat.

How many years would it last? *Fourteen in the big leagues, nineteen total.*

How many hits would I get? *1,113 in the big leagues.*

Would I be a career .300 hitter? *Close. .291.*

Would I win a batting title? *Close again. In late September of 2001 I was within striking distance of Ichiro Suzuki, but would have had to finish the season 14-14 to have a chance. I went 0-14 and came in fifth with a .330 average.*

Would I be an All-Star? *No.*

Would I be on a World Series winning team? *No.*

And, when it ended, would I miss it? Would I miss the battle at the plate, the thrill of getting a hit, or driving in a run, or robbing a hit with a dive or leap, or the beauty of turning a double play? Would I miss the applause? Would I miss the butterflies just before I ran onto the field for each first inning? Would my family like having me around full-time? What would I do with the rest of my year, let alone the rest of my life?

In what would become my final year in the big leagues, I found my role had changed completely. Rather than a starting player, which I had been for most of thirteen years, I became a role player. Over eleven seasons, from 1998 through 2008, I had 4,292 plate appearances, an average of 370 per season. There were a few seasons where I had over 500 plate appearances, and a few years where injuries pulled the numbers down into the 200s. But, in 2009 with Milwaukee, I had only 162 plate appearances in 77 games. And through the first five weeks of the 2010 season with the Mets, I had 26 trips to the plate in 25 games, mostly as a pinch hitter. I played only 3 games in the field; twice in the outfield and once at first base. I knew the end was near, but I didn't want it to come until I was ready, until I decided that I was done. I did not want to be one of the guys who got "the tap".

In that 2010 season, I found myself becoming more of a fan, not only of other players, but of the fans themselves. I enjoyed the fan interaction. When I walked on the field before games, they would yell my name and ask me to sign memorabilia. There was a moment when I told myself to really enjoy this time because it could end at any moment. Once you are no longer a major league player, people aren't going to care that much about you or your autograph. The major league lifestyle would also be gone unless you stay on as a coach or manager and I didn't have much interest in doing that. So, I shifted a little in terms of understanding how lucky I was, really appreciating every moment. Even my routine—the training room, the hot tub, the video room, the stretching and batting practice—I knew it could not go on forever and I savored it all. I miss that routine to this day.

*SCOTT PUCINO, AGENT: I could see that Cat's career was nearing an end. In his final year at Texas, 2008, his playing time had dropped off quite a bit. We helped him get a job in Milwaukee the next year, where he had even fewer opportunities and in 2010, it was harder to find him a job. It was frustrating because he still had skills, but teams were looking to go with their younger guys. We were glad he got the job with the Mets, near his home.*

Suspecting I was a "dead man walking" was motivation for me at the plate. Each could be my last at-bat and I wanted to go out on a good note. I was healthy, I felt great, was a proven big league hitter and was sure I could contribute if given the chance.

But, then...

May 10th, at Citi Field, it was the bottom of the ninth . We were trailing the Nationals 3 to 1. I led off as a pinch hitter for Jenrry Mejia. Miguel Batista was on the mound and I got behind in the count 1 and 2 when I grounded out to second base. One out. Angel Pagan homered on the next at-bat, but that's how the game ended, 3-2. In the usual post-loss clubhouse silence, I was sitting at my locker, about to get undressed and showered when Dave Jauss, our bench coach tapped me on the shoulder.

"Frank, Jerry (Manuel, the manager) would like to talk to you."

Right when I felt him touch me, I knew what it meant. I had been there when other guys had gotten the tap and everyone in the room knew the guy was probably being sent down or released. I had observed their reactions, whether they were upset or confused. As I got up to walk to Jerry's office, I felt like there were a lot of eyes on me. I didn't say anything to anyone and was just trying to think of what I wanted to say to Jerry in the thirty seconds it was going to take me to get to his door. I was pretty sure I knew what was going to be said to me, but I wanted to figure out what I was going to say. Waiting for me were general manager Omar Minaya, Jerry Manuel and John Ricco, the assistant general manager. They asked me to sit down. Omar said, "We had to make a move today and you're the odd man out. Thank you for everything you've given us and we're sorry we didn't get you more playing time. We're going to have to let you go. If you would like to go to AAA, we could send you there and you might get called up eventually".

I was fighting back tears. When I had gone in there, I thought it would be easy to say what I wanted and get closure. But I was cracking and I had tears in my eyes.

"No", I said, "I knew this was coming and I think I'm done. I want to stay home and be with my family. I appreciate the opportunity and I'm sorry it didn't work out."

I stood up, thanked them and shook hands. The meeting felt like it went on a long time, but it was probably three or four minutes. And that was it. My major league career was over.

From Jerry's office, I had to do the "walk of shame" back to my locker. Some guys watched, some looked down or turned away. There were nineteen years of thoughts racing through my head, including, "What do I do now?" Well, I thought, right now, I have to pack up. But, when I got back to my locker, the clubhouse guy already had my bag out and was pulling my jerseys off of the hangers. It was kind of, "There ya go kid, pack your stuff and you're out of here". They had to start the process because there was a new guy coming to take over my locker. They took down my nameplate, "Catalanotto 27", and replaced it with his. My mind was swimming and I wanted to make sure I took care of everything. I knew I had to tip the clubhouse guys and the trainers and had to pack all my stuff. I wanted to take some bats with me. As I walked around, still with tape on my ankles from the game, several guys were looking at me. I was not sure who knew and who didn't and some of them came over. "We'll miss you. Take care. We'll keep in touch." It is a very awkward moment and guys don't quite know how to react. Should they go over and say something? Should they just look away, knowing somewhere deep inside that their day will come?

I was keeping my emotions in check, but when a teammate came up to me and said something, I started to lose it a little. Then the media came over and started asking questions, "What happened in the office? Are you going to retire?" It was really hard for me to speak and get it out. I tried to keep it brief. I was emotional not because I was released, but because I knew this was the end of my baseball career. I was done. My playing career, my life for the last nineteen years, was over. I stayed at the locker for about an hour and a half and when I left it was even weird walking out to my car. The security guards were still there, they said "See ya tomorrow, Cat". Obviously, they had no idea. I knew it was the last time I would walk out of a clubhouse as a major leaguer and I wouldn't be going back as a player. It was pretty difficult. I realized how fortunate I was to have had a major league career, but to have it end, and not on my terms, was tough.

I had not had a chance to talk to anyone outside the stadium yet. There were text messages on my phone from people who heard it through the media. There was a message from my dad saying, "I heard the news and I want to talk to you." When I got in the car, I called him. Of course, he was so supportive and told me what a great career I had. But, it was hard and I had a tough time talking. I wasn't necessarily sad because it was my decision to stop instead of going to AAA or possibly signing with another team. It was just the finality. That is what pulled at the heart strings.

*FRANK, SR.: I think he was ready. His oldest daughter was eleven; he had four girls and his wife at home. He played fourteen years in big leagues, five in minors. Nineteen years is a long time to be away from your family, especially given the closeness in our family and closeness he has with his kids.*

*SHARON: He was ready and told me that it was time, he prayed about it and he made his decision. And he thanked management for allowing him to play the game he loved. It doesn't get better than that.*

My family told me what a great career I had and how proud they were of me. Barbara said how happy they were to now have me home. Everyone was supportive. No one pressured me to continue playing. They knew this was the end. I had some calls from teams. Scotty and Alan said the Marlins were interested. But, I would not leave the girls for that offer. I told them, "If the Yankees or the Red Sox want me, give me a call". Otherwise I didn't want to talk about coming back.

*LARRY PARRISH: Did I see anything in the eighteen-year-old Frank that would make me think he'd have a fourteen year career in the big leagues? Well, I didn't really think about it at the time, but later on, after doing some scouting and talking to scouts, I saw how important that hand-eye coordination is. That ability to put the ball in play for different pitches. You can't teach it. Scouts would talk about guys who were swing and miss guys and how they tend to stay that way. When you look at a guy like Frank, even in first instructional league, if he swung at the ball, he hit it.*

*It didn't matter if he swung at a ball or a strike, he hit it. He put his bat on it. I used to say that the thing about Cat that makes him a great bench guy or everyday player is you can play him against a starter, he can hit breaking balls, change-ups; he can hit everything in the pitchers' repertoire. And, he has the ability to sit on the bench for seven innings and hit the fast ball late in the game. That's tough to do. If you can't hit, you can't play in the big leagues. Cat could hit.*

After enjoying my first summer at home, I did have some second thoughts in October when Larry Parrish got the Atlanta Braves hitting coach job. I thought how great it would be if I could sign there and work with Larry again. He could be so helpful with my swing. Why not come back to play for the season? I thought, maybe I can do this! I did not want to be one of these guys who lost their skills and still stuck around, but my skills had not totally diminished. I contemplated that for a little while, but realized I loved being home and didn't want to leave my girls again.

*BARBARA: I would never have wanted him to leave with regrets. I think he was done. A year after he left, he helped coach the Italian National Team and he mentioned how glad he was that he wasn't playing anymore. His last few years, he had to go to the ballpark very early, get wrapped up and taped up and needed many hours of preparation before even getting on the field. So, although he may not have been convinced of it at the time, he realized the following year that he had made the right decision.*

It was not a tough transition. I had always been very involved with the family during off seasons. Some players go off to winter ball, but I was home full time the four months. Some players have a tough time with their families when they retire. Maybe because Barbara and I were high school sweethearts and had been together so long, it was not a big deal to be home all the time. At first, it was like an extended off-season. But, it changed everything around the family for the better because there was less of a sense of urgency. We were not trying to cram in so many things with the kids between October and February because I wasn't going to have to leave again for spring training.

*BARBARA: When I look back over the last couple of years since he retired,*

*I don't know how I would have gotten half the things done without him! He helped with the carpooling and driving the kids here and there. He's such a great husband and partner. But—and this is funny—as you've read, Frank loves to make lists. In the first week or so after he retired, he would take out his lists and tell the girls and me what we were going to do the next day. I had to tell him, "Oh, no we're not. It may be what you're going to do, but it's certainly not in our plans for tomorrow". He had to get used to how we roll and what our priorities were. It took awhile for him to realize we already had a schedule and a way of doing things and he/we had to compromise to accommodate everyone's needs. It was a bit of an adjustment, but he's such a wonderful father, fully involved with his kids. Just like his parents were.*

Yeah, I think retirement impacted the family more than it changed my life; all of a sudden, Daddy was home 24/7. I had never viewed myself as an absentee father, but I think the times we were apart made us grow stronger. We couldn't wait to see each other. That old saying about absence making the heart grow fonder? There's something to that and even now, when I have to go away on vitamin company business, or Barbara goes away with friends, we think it's a good thing.

Later in the summer when I spoke to a reporter, he said he had heard that I wasn't sure I was retiring. I may not have been convinced of it, but I assured him that I was done. His report regarding my retirement spawned a number of others as well as numerous website mentions. In May of 2011, I was inducted into the Suffolk County Sports Hall of Fame. That served as my send-off banquet. I was able to stand at the podium and thank everyone I had always wanted to.

At this point in the book, you know how important my family was to my big league career. It was not just my career, it was *our* career and I cannot imagine it being any other way. I couldn't have done it without them. Most of the values that helped make me a good baseball player were instilled in me at home: discipline, respect, faith, loyalty, compassion, diligence and humility.

I am so fortunate and blessed to have played baseball for as long as I did. It still amazes me that I got paid to play the game that I had always dreamed of playing when I was a little boy in Smithtown. Through the years, there were so many different experiences; most good, some bad, but I learned from them all. Thanks to baseball, I traveled the country and the world. I met countless, unforgettable people who made my life richer. Baseball is my passion, my love, my life. I owe so much to the game. It changed my life and helped mold me into the man, husband and father I am today.

To paraphrase a quote by Yankees' legend Jim Bouton, I spent nineteen years of my adult life gripping a baseball bat, but in the end it turned out that the whole time, it was the other way around.

Thank you for reading my book. My hope is that you found it useful, positive and enjoyable.

And, thank you, baseball, for all the wonderful memories.

# CAT'S BEST

*"You know it's summertime at Candlestick when the fog rolls in, the wind kicks up, and you see the center fielder slicing open a caribou to survive the ninth inning."*
*~ Bob Sarlette*

Playing baseball in thirty of North America's largest cities gave me the opportunity to form opinions on "the best" in a variety of categories.

## BEST AMERICAN LEAGUE BALLPARK

1. The Ballpark in Arlington (Rangers)
   I just love the character of the stadium and the "jet stream" to right center field is great for hitters.
2. Safeco Field (Mariners)
3. Jacobs Field (Indians)
4. Angel Stadium ((Angels)
5. Camden Yards (Orioles)

## BEST NATIONAL LEAGUE BALLPARK

1. Miller Park (Brewers)
   It is very unique in its design. I like that the roof can open
   and close. At night, it is probably the best hitting
   background in the league.
2. Busch Stadium (Cardinals)
3. Great American Ballpark (Reds)
4. Pac Bell Park (Giants)
5. Coors Field (Rockies)

## BEST FANS

1. Boston Red Sox
   They know the game.  Very smart fans. They will even cheer
   for the opponent if he makes a nice play.
2. St. Louis Cardinals
3. Chicago Cubs
4. Milwaukee Brewers
5. New York Yankees

## BEST ROAD CITY

1. Chicago
   There is so much to do in the Windy City.  So
   many great restaurants and a lot of good shopping.
2. Boston
3. Toronto
4. Seattle
5. San Francisco

## BEST ATMOSPHERE AT BALLPARK

1. Fenway
   It is always packed and the fans are into the game from the first pitch to the last pitch. "Sweet Caroline" sung by 38,000 in the seventh inning is pretty awesome, too.
2. Yankee Stadium
3. Wrigley Field
4. Safeco Field in Seattle
5. Citizen's Bank Park in Philadelphia

## BEST ROAD CLUBHOUSE

1. Tampa Bay
   Everything is first class. Clubhouse manager Guy Gallagher does a great job. The food is awesome, the place is very clean and the staff is always ready to tend to all your needs. There is even someone to cut your hair.
2. Cleveland
3. Seattle
4. Anaheim
5. Colorado

## BEST POSTGAME SPREAD

1. New York Yankees
   No surprise here. New York City has the best food. The Italian food the clubbies brought in was especially good.
2. Tampa Bay
3. Texas
4. St. Louis
5. Seattle

## CAT AT BAT

When you are a major league hitter for fourteen seasons, you put on a lot of miles just walking from the dugout to the plate. In my 4,292 plate appearances, figuring an average of forty feet from dugout to batter's box, I walked thirty-two and a half miles.

I faced 763 major league pitchers. Some of them are, or will be, in the Hall of Fame. Most of them are not and will not be. Some of them owned me and I owned some of them. On the following pages are my stats against each of them.

Statistics courtesy of www.baseball-reference.com

# FRANK CATALANOTTO CAREER HITTING VS. PITCHERS

| PITCHER | PA | AB | H | 2B | 3B | HR | RBI | BB | SO | BA | OBP | SLG | OPS |
|---------|-----|-----|---|----|----|-----|-----|----|----|-----|------|------|------|
| David Aardsma | 1 | 0 | 0 | 0 | 0 | 0 | 0 | 1 | 0 | | 1.000 | | 1.000 |
| Paul Abbott | 17 | 13 | 7 | 1 | 0 | 1 | 3 | 3 | 0 | 0.538 | 0.647 | 0.846 | 1.493 |
| Winston Abreu | 1 | 1 | 0 | 0 | 0 | 0 | 0 | 0 | 1 | 0.000 | 0.000 | 0.000 | 0.000 |
| Jeremy Accardo | 3 | 3 | 2 | 0 | 0 | 1 | 1 | 0 | 0 | 0.667 | 0.667 | 1.667 | 2.333 |
| Juan Acevedo | 6 | 6 | 0 | 0 | 0 | 0 | 0 | 0 | 1 | 0.000 | 0.000 | 0.000 | 0.000 |
| Manny Acosta | 1 | 0 | 0 | 0 | 0 | 0 | 0 | 1 | 0 | | 1.000 | | |
| Mike Adams | 1 | 1 | 0 | 0 | 0 | 0 | 0 | 0 | 0 | 0.000 | 0.000 | 0.000 | 0.000 |
| Jon Adkins | 2 | 2 | 1 | 0 | 0 | 0 | 1 | 0 | 0 | 0.500 | 0.500 | 0.500 | 1.000 |
| Jeremy Affeldt | 5 | 3 | 1 | 1 | 0 | 0 | 1 | 2 | 0 | 0.333 | 0.600 | 0.667 | 1.267 |
| Rick Aguilera | 1 | 1 | 0 | 0 | 0 | 0 | 0 | 0 | 1 | 0.000 | 0.000 | 0.000 | 0.000 |
| Kurt Ainsworth | 3 | 2 | 0 | 0 | 0 | 0 | 2 | 0 | 1 | 0.000 | 0.000 | 0.000 | 0.000 |
| Matt Albers | 1 | 1 | 0 | 0 | 0 | 0 | 0 | 0 | 1 | 0.000 | 0.000 | 0.000 | 0.000 |
| Scott Aldred | 1 | 0 | 0 | 0 | 0 | 0 | 0 | 0 | 0 | | 1.000 | | |
| Antonio Alfonseca | 1 | 1 | 0 | 0 | 0 | 0 | 0 | 0 | 1 | 0.000 | 0.000 | 0.000 | 0.000 |
| Brian Anderson | 7 | 7 | 4 | 0 | 0 | 0 | 1 | 0 | 0 | 0.571 | 0.571 | 0.571 | 1.143 |
| Jason Anderson | 2 | 2 | 0 | 0 | 0 | 0 | 0 | 0 | 0 | 0.000 | 0.000 | 0.000 | 0.000 |
| Matt Anderson | 2 | 2 | 1 | 0 | 1 | 0 | 0 | 0 | 0 | 0.500 | 0.500 | 1.500 | 2.000 |
| Kevin Appier | 10 | 7 | 1 | 0 | 0 | 0 | 1 | 2 | 2 | 0.143 | 0.400 | 0.143 | 0.543 |
| Tony Armas | 7 | 6 | 2 | 0 | 0 | 0 | 1 | 0 | 0 | 0.333 | 0.429 | 0.333 | 0.762 |
| Jose Arredondo | 1 | 1 | 0 | 0 | 0 | 0 | 0 | 0 | 0 | 0.000 | 0.000 | 0.000 | 0.000 |
| Rolando Arrojo | 21 | 17 | 4 | 2 | 0 | 0 | 2 | 1 | 2 | 0.235 | 0.333 | 0.353 | 0.686 |

| Cat vs. | PA | AB | H | 2B | 3B | HR | RBI | BB | SO | BA | OBP | SLG | OPS |
|---|---|---|---|---|---|---|---|---|---|---|---|---|---|
| Bronson Arroyo | 29 | 27 | 6 | 2 | 2 | 1 | 1 | 2 | 1 | 0.222 | 0.276 | 0.556 | 0.831 |
| Miguel Asencio | 3 | 3 | 2 | 2 | 0 | 0 | 0 | 0 | 0 | 0.667 | 0.667 | 1.333 | 2.000 |
| Paul Assenmacher | 3 | 3 | 0 | 0 | 0 | 0 | 0 | 0 | 0 | 0.000 | 0.000 | 0.000 | 0.000 |
| Pedro Astacio | 8 | 8 | 2 | 2 | 0 | 0 | 1 | 0 | 2 | 0.250 | 0.250 | 0.500 | 0.750 |
| Scott Atchison | 1 | 1 | 0 | 0 | 0 | 0 | 0 | 0 | 0 | 0.000 | 0.000 | 0.000 | 0.000 |
| Bryan Augenstein | 1 | 1 | 0 | 0 | 0 | 0 | 0 | 0 | 0 | 0.000 | 0.000 | 0.000 | 0.000 |
| Jeff Austin | 1 | 1 | 1 | 0 | 0 | 0 | 0 | 0 | 0 | 1.000 | 1.000 | 1.000 | 2.000 |
| Bobby Ayala | 1 | 1 | 0 | 0 | 0 | 0 | 0 | 0 | 0 | 0.000 | 0.000 | 0.000 | 0.000 |
| Luis Ayala | 2 | 2 | 0 | 0 | 0 | 0 | 0 | 0 | 0 | 0.000 | 0.000 | 0.000 | 0.000 |
| Manny Aybar | 1 | 1 | 0 | 0 | 0 | 0 | 0 | 0 | 0 | 0.000 | 0.000 | 0.000 | 0.000 |
| Brandon Backe | 3 | 3 | 1 | 0 | 0 | 0 | 0 | 0 | 0 | 0.333 | 0.333 | 0.333 | 0.667 |
| Burke Badenhop | 3 | 2 | 0 | 0 | 0 | 0 | 0 | 1 | 0 | 0.000 | 0.333 | 0.000 | 0.333 |
| Cha-Seung Baek | 10 | 9 | 2 | 1 | 1 | 0 | 2 | 1 | 0 | 0.222 | 0.300 | 0.556 | 0.856 |
| Danys Baez | 15 | 13 | 5 | 1 | 0 | 0 | 1 | 2 | 2 | 0.385 | 0.467 | 0.462 | 0.928 |
| Cory Bailey | 3 | 3 | 0 | 0 | 0 | 0 | 0 | 0 | 0 | 0.000 | 0.000 | 0.000 | 0.000 |
| Scott Baker | 2 | 2 | 0 | 0 | 0 | 0 | 0 | 0 | 0 | 0.000 | 0.000 | 0.000 | 0.000 |
| James Baldwin | 29 | 27 | 7 | 1 | 1 | 0 | 1 | 1 | 2 | 0.259 | 0.310 | 0.370 | 0.681 |
| John Bale | 1 | 1 | 0 | 0 | 0 | 0 | 0 | 0 | 1 | 0.000 | 0.000 | 0.000 | 0.000 |
| Collin Balester | 3 | 3 | 1 | 1 | 0 | 0 | 0 | 0 | 1 | 0.333 | 0.333 | 0.667 | 1.000 |
| Grant Balfour | 2 | 1 | 1 | 0 | 0 | 0 | 2 | 1 | 0 | 1.000 | 1.000 | 1.000 | 2.000 |
| Brian Bannister | 7 | 7 | 1 | 0 | 0 | 0 | 0 | 0 | 0 | 0.143 | 0.143 | 0.143 | 0.286 |
| Lorenzo Barcelo | 2 | 2 | 2 | 1 | 1 | 0 | 3 | 0 | 0 | 1.000 | 1.000 | 2.500 | 3.500 |
| Miguel Batista | 16 | 14 | 3 | 1 | 0 | 0 | 0 | 2 | 0 | 0.214 | 0.313 | 0.286 | 0.598 |
| Denny Bautista | 2 | 2 | 1 | 0 | 0 | 0 | 0 | 0 | 0 | 0.500 | 0.500 | 0.500 | 1.000 |

| Cat vs. | PA | AB | H | 2B | 3B | HR | RBI | BB | SO | BA | OBP | SLG | OPS |
|---|---|---|---|---|---|---|---|---|---|---|---|---|---|
| Yorman Bazardo | 1 | 1 | 0 | 0 | 0 | 0 | 0 | 0 | 0 | 0.000 | 0.000 | 0.000 | 0.000 |
| Rod Beck | 5 | 5 | 1 | 1 | 0 | 0 | 1 | 0 | 0 | 0.200 | 0.200 | 0.400 | 0.600 |
| Josh Beckett | 16 | 12 | 3 | 1 | 0 | 0 | 0 | 4 | 1 | 0.250 | 0.438 | 0.333 | 0.771 |
| Erik Bedard | 6 | 6 | 1 | 1 | 0 | 0 | 0 | 0 | 1 | 0.167 | 0.167 | 0.333 | 0.500 |
| Joe Beimel | 2 | 2 | 0 | 0 | 0 | 0 | 0 | 0 | 0 | 0.000 | 0.000 | 0.000 | 0.000 |
| Tim Belcher | 6 | 5 | 3 | 0 | 0 | 1 | 2 | 1 | 0 | 0.600 | 0.667 | 1.200 | 1.867 |
| Ronald Belisario | 1 | 1 | 1 | 1 | 0 | 0 | 0 | 0 | 0 | 1.000 | 1.000 | 2.000 | 3.000 |
| Matt Belisle | 4 | 4 | 1 | 1 | 0 | 0 | 1 | 0 | 1 | 0.250 | 0.250 | 0.500 | 0.750 |
| Heath Bell | 1 | 1 | 0 | 0 | 0 | 0 | 0 | 0 | 0 | 0.000 | 0.000 | 0.000 | 0.000 |
| Rob Bell | 4 | 3 | 2 | 1 | 0 | 0 | 1 | 1 | 0 | 0.667 | 0.750 | 1.000 | 1.750 |
| Francis Beltran | 1 | 1 | 0 | 0 | 0 | 0 | 0 | 0 | 0 | 0.000 | 0.000 | 0.000 | 0.000 |
| Armando Benitez | 5 | 3 | 0 | 0 | 0 | 0 | 0 | 2 | 2 | 0.000 | 0.400 | 0.000 | 0.400 |
| Joaquin Benoit | 8 | 8 | 3 | 2 | 1 | 0 | 1 | 0 | 0 | 0.375 | 0.375 | 0.875 | 1.250 |
| Kris Benson | 17 | 16 | 4 | 0 | 0 | 0 | 0 | 1 | 2 | 0.250 | 0.294 | 0.250 | 0.544 |
| Jason Bere | 5 | 5 | 2 | 1 | 0 | 0 | 0 | 0 | 0 | 0.400 | 0.400 | 0.600 | 1.000 |
| Justin Berg | 1 | 1 | 0 | 0 | 0 | 0 | 0 | 0 | 0 | 0.000 | 0.000 | 0.000 | 0.000 |
| Jason Bergmann | 3 | 2 | 0 | 0 | 0 | 0 | 0 | 1 | 0 | 0.000 | 0.333 | 0.000 | 0.333 |
| Adam Bernero | 6 | 5 | 1 | 0 | 0 | 0 | 0 | 1 | 1 | 0.200 | 0.333 | 0.200 | 0.533 |
| Rafael Betancourt | 8 | 7 | 2 | 1 | 0 | 1 | 5 | 1 | 1 | 0.286 | 0.375 | 0.857 | 1.232 |
| Jason Beverlin | 1 | 1 | 1 | 0 | 0 | 0 | 0 | 0 | 0 | 1.000 | 1.000 | 1.000 | 2.000 |
| Rocky Biddle | 2 | 2 | 1 | 1 | 0 | 0 | 1 | 0 | 0 | 0.500 | 0.500 | 1.000 | 1.500 |
| Randor Bierd | 1 | 1 | 0 | 0 | 0 | 0 | 0 | 0 | 0 | 0.000 | 0.000 | 0.000 | 0.000 |
| Chad Billingsley | 3 | 3 | 1 | 0 | 0 | 0 | 1 | 0 | 0 | 0.333 | 0.333 | 0.333 | 0.667 |
| Kurt Birkins | 1 | 1 | 0 | 0 | 0 | 0 | 0 | 0 | 0 | 0.000 | 0.000 | 0.000 | 0.000 |

| Cat vs. | PA | AB | H | 2B | 3B | HR | RBI | BB | SO | BA | OBP | SLG | OPS |
|---|---|---|---|---|---|---|---|---|---|---|---|---|---|
| Nick Blackburn | 4 | 3 | 1 | 0 | 0 | 0 | 0 | 1 | 1 | 0.333 | 0.500 | 0.333 | 0.833 |
| Willie Blair | 3 | 2 | 0 | 0 | 0 | 0 | 0 | 1 | 0 | 0.000 | 0.333 | 0.000 | 0.333 |
| Joe Blanton | 25 | 23 | 8 | 1 | 0 | 0 | 2 | 1 | 0 | 0.348 | 0.360 | 0.391 | 0.751 |
| Jeremy Bonderman | 22 | 20 | 4 | 1 | 0 | 1 | 3 | 1 | 4 | 0.200 | 0.273 | 0.400 | 0.673 |
| Ricky Bones | 1 | 0 | 0 | 0 | 0 | 0 | 0 | 1 | 0 |  | 1.000 |  |  |
| Boof Bonser | 9 | 9 | 3 | 2 | 0 | 0 | 0 | 0 | 1 | 0.333 | 0.333 | 0.556 | 0.889 |
| Chris Bootcheck | 2 | 1 | 0 | 0 | 0 | 0 | 1 | 0 | 1 | 0.000 | 0.000 | 0.000 | 0.000 |
| Pedro Borbon | 1 | 1 | 0 | 0 | 0 | 0 | 0 | 0 | 0 | 0.000 | 0.000 | 0.000 | 0.000 |
| Dave Borkowski | 5 | 4 | 1 | 1 | 0 | 0 | 0 | 0 | 0 | 0.250 | 0.400 | 0.500 | 0.900 |
| Joe Borowski | 5 | 3 | 1 | 0 | 0 | 0 | 0 | 2 | 1 | 0.333 | 0.600 | 0.333 | 0.933 |
| Ricky Bottalico | 3 | 3 | 1 | 0 | 0 | 1 | 2 | 0 | 1 | 0.333 | 0.333 | 1.333 | 1.667 |
| Kent Bottenfield | 3 | 3 | 0 | 0 | 0 | 0 | 0 | 0 | 1 | 0.000 | 0.000 | 0.000 | 0.000 |
| Chad Bradford | 8 | 8 | 3 | 1 | 0 | 0 | 1 | 0 | 0 | 0.375 | 0.375 | 0.500 | 0.875 |
| Ryan Braun | 2 | 2 | 0 | 0 | 0 | 0 | 0 | 0 | 0 | 0.000 | 0.000 | 0.000 | 0.000 |
| Bill Bray | 1 | 1 | 1 | 0 | 0 | 0 | 1 | 0 | 0 | 1.000 | 1.000 | 1.000 | 2.000 |
| Dewon Brazelton | 12 | 12 | 3 | 1 | 0 | 0 | 3 | 0 | 0 | 0.250 | 0.250 | 0.333 | 0.583 |
| Jamie Brewington | 3 | 2 | 2 | 0 | 0 | 0 | 1 | 0 | 0 | 1.000 | 0.667 | 1.000 | 1.667 |
| Doug Brocail | 2 | 1 | 0 | 0 | 0 | 0 | 0 | 0 | 0 | 0.000 | 0.500 | 0.000 | 0.500 |
| Jim Brower | 2 | 1 | 0 | 0 | 0 | 0 | 0 | 1 | 0 | 0.000 | 0.500 | 0.000 | 0.500 |
| Andrew Brown | 2 | 1 | 1 | 0 | 0 | 0 | 0 | 1 | 0 | 1.000 | 1.000 | 1.000 | 2.000 |
| Kevin Brown | 4 | 4 | 0 | 0 | 0 | 0 | 0 | 0 | 1 | 0.000 | 0.000 | 0.000 | 0.000 |
| Jonathan Broxton | 1 | 0 | 0 | 0 | 0 | 0 | 1 | 0 | 0 |  | 0.000 |  |  |
| Brian Bruney | 1 | 1 | 1 | 0 | 0 | 0 | 0 | 0 | 0 | 1.000 | 1.000 | 1.000 | 2.000 |
| Billy Buckner | 3 | 2 | 0 | 0 | 0 | 0 | 0 | 1 | 0 | 0.000 | 0.333 | 0.000 | 0.333 |

| Cat vs. | PA | AB | H | 2B | 3B | HR | RBI | BB | SO | BA | OBP | SLG | OPS |
|---|---|---|---|---|---|---|---|---|---|---|---|---|---|
| Mark Buehrle | 4 | 3 | 0 | 0 | 0 | 0 | 0 | 0 | 1 | 0.000 | 0.000 | 0.000 | 0.000 |
| Ryan Bukvich | 2 | 2 | 1 | 0 | 0 | 0 | 0 | 0 | 0 | 0.500 | 0.500 | 0.500 | 1.000 |
| Jason Bulger | 1 | 1 | 0 | 0 | 0 | 0 | 0 | 0 | 0 | 0.000 | 0.000 | 0.000 | 0.000 |
| Melvin Bunch | 1 | 1 | 1 | 1 | 0 | 0 | 0 | 0 | 0 | 1.000 | 1.000 | 2.000 | 3.000 |
| Dave Burba | 28 | 26 | 6 | 1 | 0 | 1 | 2 | 1 | 1 | 0.231 | 0.286 | 0.385 | 0.670 |
| Ambiorix Burgos | 1 | 1 | 1 | 1 | 0 | 0 | 3 | 0 | 0 | 1.000 | 1.000 | 2.000 | 3.000 |
| John Burkett | 14 | 12 | 6 | 2 | 0 | 0 | 1 | 1 | 1 | 0.500 | 0.571 | 0.667 | 1.238 |
| A.J. Burnett | 7 | 7 | 4 | 3 | 0 | 0 | 3 | 0 | 1 | 0.571 | 0.571 | 1.000 | 1.571 |
| Brian Burres | 2 | 1 | 1 | 0 | 0 | 0 | 1 | 1 | 0 | 1.000 | 1.000 | 1.000 | 2.000 |
| Jared Burton | 2 | 2 | 0 | 0 | 0 | 0 | 0 | 0 | 1 | 0.000 | 0.000 | 0.000 | 0.000 |
| Dave Bush | 2 | 2 | 0 | 0 | 0 | 0 | 1 | 0 | 0 | 0.000 | 0.000 | 0.000 | 0.000 |
| Paul Byrd | 15 | 13 | 3 | 2 | 0 | 0 | 1 | 1 | 0 | 0.231 | 0.333 | 0.385 | 0.718 |
| Tim Byrdak | 5 | 3 | 0 | 0 | 0 | 0 | 0 | 1 | 0 | 0.000 | 0.250 | 0.000 | 0.250 |
| Daniel Cabrera | 30 | 26 | 6 | 2 | 0 | 0 | 0 | 4 | 8 | 0.231 | 0.333 | 0.308 | 0.641 |
| Fernando Cabrera | 2 | 2 | 0 | 0 | 0 | 0 | 0 | 0 | 0 | 0.000 | 0.000 | 0.000 | 0.000 |
| Greg Cadaret | 1 | 1 | 0 | 0 | 0 | 0 | 0 | 0 | 1 | 0.000 | 0.000 | 0.000 | 0.000 |
| Matt Cain | 3 | 3 | 0 | 0 | 0 | 0 | 0 | 0 | 0 | 0.000 | 0.000 | 0.000 | 0.000 |
| Kiko Calero | 9 | 7 | 2 | 0 | 0 | 0 | 0 | 2 | 0 | 0.286 | 0.444 | 0.286 | 0.730 |
| Mickey Callaway | 3 | 3 | 0 | 0 | 0 | 0 | 0 | 0 | 0 | 0.000 | 0.000 | 0.000 | 0.000 |
| Shawn Camp | 6 | 6 | 4 | 1 | 1 | 0 | 3 | 0 | 1 | 0.667 | 0.667 | 1.167 | 1.833 |
| Tom Candiotti | 4 | 4 | 0 | 0 | 0 | 0 | 0 | 0 | 0 | 0.000 | 0.000 | 0.000 | 0.000 |
| Jose Capellan | 1 | 1 | 0 | 0 | 0 | 0 | 0 | 0 | 0 | 0.000 | 0.000 | 0.000 | 0.000 |
| Chris Capuano | 3 | 2 | 1 | 0 | 0 | 1 | 1 | 0 | 0 | 0.500 | 0.667 | 2.000 | 2.667 |
| Jesse Carlson | 1 | 1 | 0 | 0 | 0 | 0 | 0 | 0 | 0 | 0.000 | 0.000 | 0.000 | 0.000 |

| Cat vs. | PA | AB | H | 2B | 3B | HR | RBI | BB | SO | BA | OBP | SLG | OPS |
|---|---|---|---|---|---|---|---|---|---|---|---|---|---|
| Fausto Carmona | 7 | 7 | 0 | 0 | 0 | 0 | 0 | 0 | 2 | 0.000 | 0.000 | 0.000 | 0.000 |
| Rafael Carmona | 1 | 1 | 0 | 0 | 0 | 0 | 0 | 0 | 1 | 0.000 | 0.000 | 0.000 | 0.000 |
| Chris Carpenter | 23 | 20 | 8 | 0 | 0 | 0 | 3 | 1 | 3 | 0.400 | 0.455 | 0.400 | 0.855 |
| Giovanni Carrara | 3 | 2 | 1 | 0 | 1 | 0 | 0 | 1 | 1 | 0.500 | 0.667 | 1.500 | 2.167 |
| D.J. Carrasco | 3 | 3 | 1 | 0 | 0 | 0 | 1 | 0 | 0 | 0.333 | 0.333 | 0.333 | 0.667 |
| Hector Carrasco | 6 | 5 | 1 | 0 | 0 | 1 | 3 | 1 | 2 | 0.200 | 0.333 | 0.800 | 1.133 |
| Lance Carter | 6 | 6 | 0 | 0 | 0 | 0 | 0 | 0 | 1 | 0.000 | 0.000 | 0.000 | 0.000 |
| Santiago Casilla | 3 | 2 | 2 | 0 | 0 | 0 | 2 | 1 | 0 | 1.000 | 1.000 | 1.000 | 2.000 |
| Scott Cassidy | 1 | 1 | 0 | 0 | 0 | 0 | 0 | 0 | 0 | 0.000 | 0.000 | 0.000 | 0.000 |
| Alberto Castillo | 1 | 1 | 0 | 0 | 0 | 0 | 0 | 0 | 1 | 0.000 | 0.000 | 0.000 | 0.000 |
| Carlos Castillo | 1 | 1 | 0 | 0 | 0 | 0 | 0 | 0 | 1 | 0.000 | 0.000 | 0.000 | 0.000 |
| Frank Castillo | 11 | 10 | 3 | 0 | 0 | 0 | 0 | 0 | 1 | 0.300 | 0.364 | 0.300 | 0.664 |
| Fabio Castro | 1 | 1 | 0 | 0 | 0 | 0 | 0 | 0 | 0 | 0.000 | 0.000 | 0.000 | 0.000 |
| Shawn Chacon | 21 | 18 | 3 | 0 | 0 | 0 | 0 | 2 | 0 | 0.167 | 0.286 | 0.167 | 0.452 |
| Jesse Chavez | 1 | 1 | 0 | 0 | 0 | 0 | 0 | 0 | 0 | 0.000 | 0.000 | 0.000 | 0.000 |
| Rocky Cherry | 1 | 1 | 0 | 0 | 0 | 0 | 0 | 0 | 0 | 0.000 | 0.000 | 0.000 | 0.000 |
| Travis Chick | 2 | 2 | 0 | 0 | 0 | 0 | 0 | 0 | 1 | 0.000 | 0.000 | 0.000 | 0.000 |
| Randy Choate | 2 | 1 | 0 | 0 | 0 | 0 | 0 | 1 | 0 | 0.000 | 0.500 | 0.000 | 0.500 |
| Jason Christiansen | 2 | 2 | 2 | 1 | 0 | 0 | 0 | 0 | 0 | 1.000 | 1.000 | 1.500 | 2.500 |
| Roger Clemens | 32 | 31 | 8 | 0 | 0 | 0 | 0 | 1 | 14 | 0.258 | 0.281 | 0.258 | 0.539 |
| Matt Clement | 24 | 20 | 6 | 3 | 0 | 1 | 5 | 4 | 2 | 0.300 | 0.417 | 0.600 | 1.017 |
| Tyler Clippard | 1 | 1 | 0 | 0 | 0 | 0 | 0 | 0 | 1 | 0.000 | 0.000 | 0.000 | 0.000 |
| Ken Cloude | 4 | 4 | 3 | 2 | 0 | 0 | 0 | 0 | 0 | 0.750 | 0.750 | 1.250 | 2.000 |
| Jesus Colome | 7 | 7 | 1 | 0 | 0 | 0 | 0 | 0 | 0 | 0.143 | 0.143 | 0.143 | 0.286 |

255

| Cat vs. | PA | AB | H | 2B | 3B | HR | RBI | BB | SO | BA | OBP | SLG | OPS |
|---|---|---|---|---|---|---|---|---|---|---|---|---|---|
| Bartolo Colon | 30 | 26 | 4 | 1 | 0 | 0 | 1 | 3 | 4 | 0.154 | 0.241 | 0.192 | 0.434 |
| Roman Colon | 3 | 2 | 1 | 0 | 0 | 0 | 1 | 0 | 0 | 0.500 | 0.333 | 0.500 | 0.833 |
| David Cone | 19 | 16 | 7 | 2 | 0 | 0 | 1 | 1 | 2 | 0.438 | 0.526 | 0.563 | 1.089 |
| Jose Contreras | 16 | 15 | 5 | 3 | 0 | 0 | 2 | 1 | 2 | 0.333 | 0.375 | 0.533 | 0.908 |
| Aaron Cook | 3 | 3 | 1 | 0 | 0 | 0 | 0 | 0 | 1 | 0.333 | 0.333 | 0.333 | 0.667 |
| Brian Cooper | 1 | 1 | 0 | 0 | 0 | 0 | 0 | 0 | 0 | 0.000 | 0.000 | 0.000 | 0.000 |
| Chad Cordero | 1 | 1 | 0 | 0 | 0 | 0 | 0 | 0 | 1 | 0.000 | 0.000 | 0.000 | 0.000 |
| Francisco Cordero | 9 | 8 | 1 | 0 | 0 | 0 | 0 | 0 | 1 | 0.125 | 0.222 | 0.125 | 0.347 |
| Francisco Cordova | 1 | 1 | 0 | 0 | 0 | 0 | 0 | 0 | 0 | 0.000 | 0.000 | 0.000 | 0.000 |
| Bryan Corey | 4 | 3 | 0 | 0 | 0 | 0 | 0 | 1 | 2 | 0.000 | 0.250 | 0.000 | 0.250 |
| Rheal Cormier | 3 | 2 | 0 | 0 | 0 | 0 | 0 | 1 | 0 | 0.000 | 0.333 | 0.000 | 0.333 |
| Nate Cornejo | 11 | 10 | 3 | 1 | 0 | 0 | 3 | 1 | 0 | 0.300 | 0.364 | 0.400 | 0.764 |
| Kevin Correia | 5 | 4 | 0 | 0 | 0 | 0 | 0 | 1 | 0 | 0.000 | 0.200 | 0.000 | 0.200 |
| Jim Corsi | 2 | 2 | 1 | 0 | 0 | 0 | 0 | 0 | 0 | 0.500 | 0.500 | 0.500 | 1.000 |
| Neal Cotts | 1 | 1 | 0 | 0 | 0 | 0 | 0 | 0 | 1 | 0.000 | 0.000 | 0.000 | 0.000 |
| Jon Coutlangus | 1 | 0 | 0 | 0 | 0 | 0 | 0 | 0 | 0 |  |  |  |  |
| Tim Crabtree | 2 | 1 | 0 | 0 | 0 | 0 | 0 | 1 | 1 | 0.000 | 0.500 | 0.000 | 0.500 |
| Jesse Crain | 3 | 3 | 1 | 0 | 0 | 0 | 0 | 0 | 1 | 0.333 | 0.333 | 0.333 | 0.667 |
| Doug Creek | 2 | 1 | 0 | 0 | 0 | 0 | 0 | 1 | 0 | 0.000 | 0.500 | 0.000 | 0.500 |
| Jack Cressend | 1 | 1 | 0 | 0 | 0 | 0 | 0 | 0 | 1 | 0.000 | 0.000 | 0.000 | 0.000 |
| Rich Croushore | 1 | 1 | 0 | 0 | 0 | 0 | 0 | 0 | 0 | 0.000 | 0.000 | 0.000 | 0.000 |
| Juan Cruz | 2 | 1 | 1 | 0 | 0 | 0 | 1 | 0 | 0 | 1.000 | 0.500 | 1.000 | 1.500 |
| Nelson Cruz | 4 | 4 | 1 | 0 | 0 | 0 | 1 | 0 | 1 | 0.250 | 0.250 | 0.250 | 0.500 |
| Jeff D'Amico | 3 | 2 | 0 | 0 | 0 | 0 | 0 | 0 | 0 | 0.000 | 0.333 | 0.000 | 0.333 |

| Cat vs. | PA | AB | H | 2B | 3B | HR | RBI | BB | SO | BA | OBP | SLG | OPS |
|---|---|---|---|---|---|---|---|---|---|---|---|---|---|
| Omar Daal | 3 | 3 | 0 | 0 | 0 | 0 | 0 | 0 | 0 | 0.000 | 0.000 | 0.000 | 0.000 |
| Vic Darensbourg | 1 | 1 | 0 | 0 | 0 | 0 | 0 | 2 | 0 | 0.000 | 0.000 | 0.000 | 0.000 |
| Kyle Davies | 9 | 6 | 2 | 1 | 0 | 0 | 0 | 0 | 0 | 0.333 | 0.556 | 0.500 | 1.056 |
| Doug Davis | 2 | 1 | 1 | 0 | 0 | 0 | 0 | 0 | 0 | 1.000 | 1.000 | 1.000 | 2.000 |
| Jason Davis | 2 | 2 | 0 | 0 | 0 | 0 | 0 | 0 | 1 | 0.000 | 0.000 | 0.000 | 0.000 |
| Zach Day | 1 | 1 | 1 | 0 | 0 | 0 | 0 | 0 | 0 | 1.000 | 1.000 | 1.000 | 2.000 |
| Jorge De La Rosa | 1 | 1 | 1 | 0 | 0 | 0 | 0 | 0 | 0 | 1.000 | 1.000 | 1.000 | 2.000 |
| Mike DeJean | 3 | 2 | 2 | 0 | 0 | 0 | 1 | 0 | 0 | 1.000 | 1.000 | 1.000 | 2.000 |
| Manny Delcarmen | 6 | 6 | 3 | 1 | 1 | 0 | 1 | 0 | 0 | 0.500 | 0.500 | 1.000 | 1.500 |
| Ryan Dempster | 8 | 7 | 3 | 1 | 0 | 0 | 0 | 1 | 2 | 0.429 | 0.500 | 0.571 | 1.071 |
| Julio DePaula | 3 | 1 | 0 | 0 | 0 | 0 | 0 | 1 | 0 | 0.000 | 0.667 | 0.000 | 0.667 |
| Elmer Dessens | 3 | 2 | 0 | 0 | 0 | 0 | 0 | 0 | 0 | 0.000 | 0.333 | 0.000 | 0.333 |
| Joey Devine | 1 | 1 | 0 | 0 | 0 | 0 | 0 | 0 | 0 | 0.000 | 0.000 | 0.000 | 0.000 |
| Matt DeWitt | 2 | 2 | 1 | 0 | 0 | 0 | 0 | 0 | 0 | 0.500 | 0.500 | 0.500 | 1.000 |
| R.A. Dickey | 9 | 8 | 2 | 0 | 0 | 0 | 0 | 1 | 3 | 0.250 | 0.333 | 0.250 | 0.583 |
| Jason Dickson | 5 | 3 | 1 | 0 | 0 | 1 | 2 | 2 | 0 | 0.333 | 0.600 | 1.333 | 1.933 |
| Lenny DiNardo | 4 | 4 | 2 | 1 | 0 | 0 | 2 | 0 | 0 | 0.500 | 0.500 | 0.750 | 1.250 |
| Juan Dominguez | 1 | 1 | 1 | 0 | 0 | 1 | 3 | 0 | 0 | 1.000 | 1.000 | 4.000 | 5.000 |
| Brendan Donnelly | 5 | 3 | 0 | 0 | 0 | 0 | 0 | 0 | 1 | 0.000 | 0.250 | 0.000 | 0.250 |
| Octavio Dotel | 3 | 3 | 1 | 1 | 0 | 0 | 0 | 0 | 1 | 0.333 | 0.333 | 0.667 | 1.000 |
| Sean Douglass | 9 | 7 | 3 | 1 | 0 | 0 | 0 | 2 | 0 | 0.429 | 0.556 | 0.571 | 1.127 |
| Darren Dreifort | 5 | 3 | 0 | 0 | 0 | 0 | 0 | 2 | 2 | 0.000 | 0.400 | 0.000 | 0.400 |
| Ryan Drese | 13 | 13 | 4 | 1 | 0 | 1 | 1 | 0 | 1 | 0.308 | 0.308 | 0.615 | 0.923 |
| Tim Drew | 2 | 2 | 1 | 0 | 0 | 0 | 0 | 0 | 0 | 0.500 | 0.500 | 0.500 | 1.000 |

| Cat vs. | PA | AB | H | 2B | 3B | HR | RBI | BB | SO | BA | OBP | SLG | OPS |
|---|---|---|---|---|---|---|---|---|---|---|---|---|---|
| Travis Driskill | 3 | 3 | 1 | 0 | 0 | 0 | 1 | 0 | 1 | 0.333 | 0.333 | 0.333 | 0.667 |
| Eric DuBose | 7 | 7 | 1 | 1 | 0 | 0 | 0 | 0 | 2 | 0.143 | 0.143 | 0.286 | 0.429 |
| Justin Duchscherer | 6 | 6 | 2 | 2 | 0 | 0 | 0 | 0 | 1 | 0.333 | 0.333 | 0.667 | 1.000 |
| Scott Dunn | 1 | 1 | 0 | 0 | 0 | 0 | 0 | 0 | 0 | 0.000 | 0.000 | 0.000 | 0.000 |
| Chad Durbin | 9 | 8 | 1 | 0 | 0 | 0 | 0 | 1 | 0 | 0.125 | 0.222 | 0.125 | 0.347 |
| Mike Duvall | 1 | 1 | 0 | 0 | 0 | 0 | 0 | 0 | 1 | 0.000 | 0.000 | 0.000 | 0.000 |
| Dennis Eckersley | 2 | 2 | 0 | 0 | 0 | 0 | 0 | 0 | 0 | 0.000 | 0.000 | 0.000 | 0.000 |
| Joey Eischen | 2 | 2 | 0 | 0 | 0 | 0 | 0 | 0 | 1 | 0.000 | 0.000 | 0.000 | 0.000 |
| Scott Elarton | 11 | 9 | 3 | 1 | 0 | 0 | 0 | 2 | 0 | 0.333 | 0.455 | 0.444 | 0.899 |
| Scott Elbert | 1 | 1 | 0 | 0 | 0 | 0 | 0 | 0 | 0 | 0.000 | 0.000 | 0.000 | 0.000 |
| Dave Elder | 1 | 1 | 0 | 0 | 0 | 0 | 0 | 0 | 0 | 0.000 | 0.000 | 0.000 | 0.000 |
| Cal Eldred | 2 | 2 | 0 | 0 | 0 | 0 | 0 | 0 | 0 | 0.000 | 0.000 | 0.000 | 0.000 |
| Robert Ellis | 3 | 2 | 1 | 0 | 0 | 0 | 0 | 1 | 0 | 0.500 | 0.667 | 0.500 | 1.167 |
| Alan Embree | 9 | 9 | 1 | 0 | 0 | 0 | 1 | 0 | 4 | 0.111 | 0.111 | 0.111 | 0.222 |
| Todd Erdos | 1 | 1 | 0 | 0 | 0 | 0 | 0 | 0 | 0 | 0.000 | 0.000 | 0.000 | 0.000 |
| Scott Erickson | 5 | 4 | 0 | 0 | 0 | 0 | 0 | 1 | 0 | 0.000 | 0.200 | 0.000 | 0.200 |
| Kelvim Escobar | 25 | 24 | 3 | 2 | 0 | 0 | 1 | 1 | 4 | 0.125 | 0.160 | 0.208 | 0.368 |
| Shawn Estes | 3 | 2 | 0 | 0 | 0 | 0 | 0 | 1 | 0 | 0.000 | 0.333 | 0.000 | 0.333 |
| Seth Etherton | 2 | 1 | 1 | 0 | 0 | 1 | 1 | 1 | 0 | 1.000 | 1.000 | 4.000 | 5.000 |
| Scott Eyre | 1 | 1 | 1 | 0 | 0 | 0 | 0 | 0 | 0 | 1.000 | 1.000 | 1.000 | 2.000 |
| Willie Eyre | 2 | 1 | 0 | 0 | 0 | 0 | 0 | 1 | 0 | 0.000 | 0.500 | 0.000 | 0.500 |
| Kyle Farnsworth | 5 | 4 | 1 | 1 | 0 | 0 | 2 | 1 | 2 | 0.250 | 0.400 | 0.500 | 0.900 |
| Jeff Fassero | 2 | 2 | 1 | 1 | 0 | 0 | 2 | 0 | 0 | 0.500 | 0.500 | 1.000 | 1.500 |
| Ryan Feierabend | 1 | 1 | 1 | 0 | 0 | 0 | 0 | 0 | 0 | 1.000 | 1.000 | 1.000 | 2.000 |

| Cat vs. | PA | AB | H | 2B | 3B | HR | RBI | BB | SO | BA | OBP | SLG | OPS |
|---|---|---|---|---|---|---|---|---|---|---|---|---|---|
| Mike Fetters | 3 | 3 | 0 | 0 | 0 | 0 | 0 | 0 | 1 | 0.000 | 0.000 | 0.000 | 0.000 |
| Nate Field | 1 | 1 | 0 | 0 | 0 | 0 | 0 | 0 | 0 | 0.000 | 0.000 | 0.000 | 0.000 |
| Chuck Finley | 4 | 4 | 1 | 0 | 0 | 0 | 0 | 0 | 1 | 0.250 | 0.250 | 0.250 | 0.500 |
| Tony Fiore | 4 | 3 | 0 | 0 | 0 | 0 | 0 | 1 | 1 | 0.000 | 0.250 | 0.000 | 0.250 |
| Carlos Fisher | 2 | 2 | 0 | 0 | 0 | 0 | 0 | 0 | 1 | 0.000 | 0.000 | 0.000 | 0.000 |
| Brian Fitzgerald | 1 | 1 | 0 | 0 | 0 | 0 | 0 | 0 | 0 | 0.000 | 0.000 | 0.000 | 0.000 |
| Ron Flores | 1 | 1 | 1 | 0 | 0 | 0 | 0 | 0 | 0 | 1.000 | 1.000 | 1.000 | 2.000 |
| Bryce Florie | 3 | 3 | 1 | 0 | 0 | 0 | 0 | 0 | 1 | 0.333 | 0.333 | 0.333 | 0.667 |
| Gavin Floyd | 3 | 2 | 1 | 0 | 0 | 0 | 0 | 1 | 0 | 0.500 | 0.667 | 0.500 | 1.167 |
| Josh Fogg | 3 | 2 | 1 | 0 | 0 | 0 | 0 | 1 | 0 | 0.500 | 0.667 | 0.500 | 1.167 |
| Tony Fossas | 1 | 0 | 0 | 0 | 0 | 0 | 0 | 1 | 0 |  | 1.000 |  |  |
| Casey Fossum | 5 | 4 | 0 | 0 | 0 | 0 | 1 | 1 | 2 | 0.000 | 0.200 | 0.000 | 0.200 |
| Keith Foulke | 25 | 22 | 4 | 0 | 0 | 1 | 3 | 2 | 5 | 0.182 | 0.280 | 0.318 | 0.598 |
| Chad Fox | 2 | 1 | 0 | 0 | 0 | 0 | 0 | 1 | 1 | 0.000 | 0.500 | 0.000 | 0.500 |
| Ryan Franklin | 18 | 15 | 8 | 1 | 0 | 1 | 6 | 3 | 4 | 0.533 | 0.611 | 0.800 | 1.411 |
| Wayne Franklin | 1 | 1 | 0 | 0 | 0 | 0 | 0 | 0 | 1 | 0.000 | 0.000 | 0.000 | 0.000 |
| John Frascatore | 3 | 2 | 0 | 0 | 0 | 0 | 1 | 0 | 1 | 0.000 | 0.000 | 0.000 | 0.000 |
| Jason Frasor | 1 | 0 | 0 | 0 | 0 | 0 | 1 | 0 | 0 |  | 1.000 |  |  |
| Emiliano Fruto | 2 | 2 | 0 | 0 | 0 | 0 | 0 | 0 | 0 | 0.000 | 0.000 | 0.000 | 0.000 |
| Brian Fuentes | 2 | 1 | 0 | 0 | 0 | 0 | 0 | 0 | 0 | 0.000 | 0.500 | 0.000 | 0.500 |
| Jeff Fulchino | 3 | 2 | 1 | 1 | 0 | 0 | 0 | 1 | 0 | 0.500 | 0.667 | 1.000 | 1.667 |
| Aaron Fultz | 6 | 4 | 1 | 0 | 0 | 0 | 1 | 1 | 2 | 0.250 | 0.333 | 0.250 | 0.583 |
| Chris Fussell | 1 | 1 | 0 | 0 | 0 | 0 | 0 | 0 | 0 | 0.000 | 0.000 | 0.000 | 0.000 |
| Mike Fyhrie | 2 | 2 | 0 | 0 | 0 | 0 | 0 | 0 | 0 | 0.000 | 0.000 | 0.000 | 0.000 |

| Cat vs. | PA | AB | H | 2B | 3B | HR | RBI | BB | SO | BA | OBP | SLG | OPS |
|---|---|---|---|---|---|---|---|---|---|---|---|---|---|
| Kason Gabbard | 1 | 1 | 0 | 0 | 0 | 0 | 0 | 0 | 1 | 0.000 | 0.000 | 0.000 | 0.000 |
| Eric Gagne | 1 | 1 | 0 | 0 | 0 | 0 | 0 | 0 | 0 | 0.000 | 0.000 | 0.000 | 0.000 |
| Rich Garces | 4 | 4 | 2 | 2 | 0 | 0 | 0 | 0 | 0 | 0.500 | 0.500 | 1.000 | 1.500 |
| Freddy Garcia | 26 | 24 | 7 | 1 | 0 | 2 | 5 | 2 | 1 | 0.292 | 0.346 | 0.583 | 0.929 |
| Rosman Garcia | 1 | 1 | 1 | 0 | 0 | 0 | 0 | 0 | 0 | 1.000 | 1.000 | 1.000 | 2.000 |
| Jon Garland | 44 | 39 | 12 | 4 | 0 | 0 | 2 | 2 | 2 | 0.308 | 0.386 | 0.410 | 0.797 |
| Matt Garza | 11 | 11 | 4 | 0 | 0 | 1 | 1 | 0 | 0 | 0.364 | 0.364 | 0.636 | 1.000 |
| Chad Gaudin | 22 | 18 | 5 | 2 | 0 | 0 | 3 | 3 | 2 | 0.278 | 0.409 | 0.389 | 0.798 |
| Geoff Geary | 1 | 0 | 0 | 0 | 0 | 0 | 0 | 1 | 0 | | 1.000 | | |
| Chris George | 9 | 9 | 4 | 1 | 1 | 0 | 1 | 0 | 2 | 0.444 | 0.444 | 0.778 | 1.222 |
| Franklyn German | 3 | 2 | 0 | 0 | 0 | 0 | 0 | 1 | 0 | 0.000 | 0.333 | 0.000 | 0.333 |
| Samuel Gervacio | 1 | 0 | 0 | 0 | 0 | 0 | 0 | 1 | 0 | | 1.000 | | |
| Jason Gilfillan | 1 | 1 | 0 | 0 | 0 | 0 | 0 | 0 | 0 | 0.000 | 0.000 | 0.000 | 0.000 |
| Matt Ginter | 2 | 2 | 1 | 1 | 0 | 0 | 0 | 0 | 0 | 0.500 | 0.500 | 1.000 | 1.500 |
| Gary Glover | 8 | 7 | 2 | 1 | 0 | 0 | 0 | 0 | 1 | 0.286 | 0.375 | 0.429 | 0.804 |
| Ryan Glynn | 3 | 3 | 3 | 0 | 0 | 1 | 1 | 0 | 0 | 1.000 | 1.000 | 2.000 | 3.000 |
| Geremi Gonzalez | 6 | 6 | 1 | 0 | 0 | 0 | 0 | 0 | 0 | 0.167 | 0.167 | 0.167 | 0.333 |
| Andrew Good | 3 | 2 | 0 | 0 | 0 | 0 | 0 | 0 | 0 | 0.000 | 0.333 | 0.000 | 0.333 |
| Dwight Gooden | 6 | 6 | 1 | 0 | 0 | 0 | 0 | 0 | 2 | 0.167 | 0.167 | 0.167 | 0.333 |
| Tom Gordon | 5 | 5 | 2 | 0 | 0 | 0 | 0 | 0 | 1 | 0.400 | 0.400 | 0.400 | 0.800 |
| Danny Graves | 2 | 2 | 1 | 0 | 0 | 0 | 0 | 0 | 0 | 0.500 | 0.500 | 0.500 | 1.000 |
| Sean Green | 2 | 2 | 1 | 1 | 0 | 0 | 0 | 0 | 0 | 0.500 | 0.500 | 1.000 | 1.500 |
| Kevin Gregg | 2 | 2 | 0 | 0 | 0 | 0 | 0 | 0 | 1 | 0.000 | 0.000 | 0.000 | 0.000 |
| Zack Greinke | 9 | 9 | 3 | 1 | 0 | 0 | 2 | 0 | 1 | 0.333 | 0.333 | 0.444 | 0.778 |

| Cat vs. | PA | AB | H | 2B | 3B | HR | RBI | BB | SO | BA | OBP | SLG | OPS |
|---|---|---|---|---|---|---|---|---|---|---|---|---|---|
| Jason Grilli | 1 | 1 | 0 | 0 | 0 | 0 | 0 | 0 | 0 | 0.000 | 0.000 | 0.000 | 0.000 |
| Jason Grimsley | 8 | 7 | 2 | 0 | 0 | 0 | 3 | 1 | 0 | 0.286 | 0.375 | 0.571 | 0.946 |
| Buddy Groom | 6 | 6 | 1 | 0 | 0 | 0 | 1 | 0 | 1 | 0.167 | 0.167 | 0.167 | 0.333 |
| Kevin Gryboski | 1 | 1 | 0 | 0 | 0 | 0 | 0 | 0 | 0 | 0.000 | 0.000 | 0.000 | 0.000 |
| Eddie Guardado | 4 | 3 | 0 | 0 | 0 | 0 | 0 | 0 | 2 | 0.000 | 0.000 | 0.000 | 0.000 |
| Matt Guerrier | 4 | 4 | 1 | 0 | 0 | 0 | 0 | 0 | 0 | 0.250 | 0.250 | 0.250 | 0.500 |
| Eric Gunderson | 1 | 0 | 0 | 0 | 0 | 0 | 0 | 0 | 0 | | 1.000 | | |
| Jeremy Guthrie | 9 | 9 | 3 | 1 | 0 | 0 | 0 | 0 | 1 | 0.333 | 0.333 | 0.444 | 0.778 |
| Mark Guthrie | 6 | 5 | 1 | 0 | 0 | 0 | 0 | 0 | 1 | 0.200 | 0.333 | 0.200 | 0.533 |
| John Halama | 6 | 6 | 1 | 0 | 0 | 0 | 0 | 0 | 1 | 0.167 | 0.167 | 0.167 | 0.333 |
| Roy Halladay | 40 | 33 | 7 | 1 | 2 | 0 | 6 | 4 | 4 | 0.212 | 0.308 | 0.364 | 0.671 |
| Joey Hamilton | 8 | 8 | 3 | 1 | 0 | 1 | 1 | 0 | 2 | 0.375 | 0.375 | 0.875 | 1.250 |
| Jason Hammel | 4 | 4 | 1 | 0 | 1 | 0 | 1 | 0 | 0 | 0.250 | 0.250 | 0.750 | 1.000 |
| Chris Hammond | 4 | 3 | 0 | 0 | 0 | 0 | 0 | 1 | 0 | 0.000 | 0.250 | 0.000 | 0.250 |
| Chris Haney | 2 | 1 | 0 | 0 | 0 | 0 | 1 | 0 | 0 | 0.000 | 0.500 | 0.000 | 0.500 |
| Joel Hanrahan | 2 | 2 | 1 | 0 | 0 | 0 | 1 | 0 | 0 | 0.500 | 0.500 | 0.500 | 1.000 |
| Devern Hansack | 3 | 3 | 2 | 1 | 0 | 0 | 0 | 0 | 0 | 0.667 | 0.667 | 1.000 | 1.667 |
| Craig Hansen | 1 | 1 | 1 | 0 | 0 | 0 | 0 | 0 | 0 | 1.000 | 1.000 | 1.000 | 2.000 |
| Tommy Hanson | 3 | 2 | 2 | 0 | 0 | 0 | 0 | 1 | 0 | 1.000 | 1.000 | 1.000 | 2.000 |
| Aaron Harang | 9 | 8 | 1 | 1 | 0 | 0 | 1 | 0 | 0 | 0.125 | 0.111 | 0.250 | 0.361 |
| Rich Harden | 7 | 4 | 1 | 1 | 0 | 0 | 0 | 2 | 1 | 0.250 | 0.571 | 0.500 | 1.071 |
| Dan Haren | 24 | 24 | 9 | 1 | 1 | 1 | 4 | 0 | 2 | 0.375 | 0.375 | 0.625 | 1.000 |
| Tim Harikkala | 1 | 1 | 1 | 0 | 0 | 0 | 0 | 0 | 0 | 1.000 | 1.000 | 1.000 | 2.000 |
| Travis Harper | 8 | 8 | 4 | 1 | 0 | 0 | 2 | 0 | 1 | 0.500 | 0.500 | 0.625 | 1.125 |

| Cat vs. | PA | AB | H | 2B | 3B | HR | RBI | BB | SO | BA | OBP | SLG | OPS |
|---|---|---|---|---|---|---|---|---|---|---|---|---|---|
| Jeff Harris | 2 | 2 | 1 | 0 | 0 | 0 | 0 | 0 | 1 | 0.500 | 0.500 | 0.500 | 1.000 |
| Pep Harris | 2 | 2 | 0 | 0 | 0 | 0 | 0 | 0 | 0 | 0.000 | 0.000 | 0.000 | 0.000 |
| Kevin Hart | 6 | 6 | 2 | 0 | 0 | 0 | 0 | 0 | 0 | 0.333 | 0.333 | 0.333 | 0.667 |
| Shigetoshi Hasegawa | 14 | 13 | 3 | 2 | 0 | 0 | 1 | 1 | 0 | 0.231 | 0.286 | 0.385 | 0.670 |
| LaTroy Hawkins | 13 | 9 | 1 | 0 | 0 | 0 | 0 | 4 | 2 | 0.111 | 0.385 | 0.111 | 0.496 |
| Blake Hawksworth | 1 | 1 | 0 | 0 | 0 | 0 | 0 | 0 | 0 | 0.000 | 0.000 | 0.000 | 0.000 |
| Jimmy Haynes | 14 | 13 | 5 | 2 | 0 | 0 | 2 | 1 | 4 | 0.385 | 0.429 | 0.538 | 0.967 |
| Aaron Heilman | 1 | 1 | 0 | 0 | 0 | 0 | 0 | 0 | 0 | 0.000 | 0.000 | 0.000 | 0.000 |
| Rick Helling | 19 | 16 | 6 | 1 | 0 | 0 | 2 | 1 | 4 | 0.375 | 0.421 | 0.438 | 0.859 |
| Mark Hendrickson | 1 | 0 | 0 | 0 | 0 | 0 | 0 | 0 | 0 | | 1.000 | | |
| Doug Henry | 2 | 2 | 0 | 0 | 0 | 0 | 0 | 0 | 0 | 0.000 | 0.000 | 0.000 | 0.000 |
| Pat Hentgen | 11 | 8 | 1 | 1 | 0 | 0 | 0 | 2 | 1 | 0.125 | 0.364 | 0.250 | 0.614 |
| Felix Heredia | 2 | 2 | 0 | 0 | 0 | 0 | 0 | 0 | 1 | 0.000 | 0.000 | 0.000 | 0.000 |
| Gil Heredia | 13 | 13 | 2 | 1 | 0 | 0 | 2 | 0 | 3 | 0.154 | 0.154 | 0.231 | 0.385 |
| Matt Herges | 5 | 5 | 0 | 0 | 0 | 0 | 0 | 0 | 1 | 0.000 | 0.000 | 0.000 | 0.000 |
| Dustin Hermanson | 4 | 4 | 2 | 2 | 0 | 0 | 1 | 0 | 1 | 0.500 | 0.500 | 1.000 | 1.500 |
| Felix Hernandez | 22 | 22 | 5 | 0 | 0 | 0 | 1 | 0 | 2 | 0.227 | 0.227 | 0.227 | 0.455 |
| Livan Hernandez | 16 | 13 | 3 | 0 | 0 | 0 | 0 | 1 | 0 | 0.231 | 0.375 | 0.231 | 0.606 |
| Orlando Hernandez | 33 | 32 | 7 | 2 | 0 | 1 | 6 | 0 | 5 | 0.219 | 0.212 | 0.375 | 0.587 |
| Roberto Hernandez | 7 | 6 | 2 | 0 | 0 | 0 | 0 | 1 | 2 | 0.333 | 0.429 | 0.333 | 0.762 |
| Runelvys Hernandez | 20 | 19 | 10 | 3 | 1 | 0 | 4 | 1 | 1 | 0.526 | 0.550 | 0.789 | 1.339 |
| Danny Herrera | 2 | 2 | 0 | 0 | 0 | 0 | 0 | 0 | 0 | 0.000 | 0.000 | 0.000 | 0.000 |
| Ken Hill | 6 | 4 | 1 | 0 | 0 | 1 | 1 | 1 | 1 | 0.250 | 0.500 | 1.000 | 1.500 |
| Shawn Hill | 3 | 3 | 2 | 1 | 0 | 0 | 1 | 0 | 1 | 0.667 | 0.667 | 1.000 | 1.667 |

| Cat vs. | PA | AB | H | 2B | 3B | HR | RBI | BB | SO | BA | OBP | SLG | OPS |
|---|---|---|---|---|---|---|---|---|---|---|---|---|---|
| Sterling Hitchcock | 9 | 9 | 3 | 0 | 0 | 0 | 0 | 0 | 2 | 0.333 | 0.333 | 0.333 | 0.667 |
| Jim Hoey | 1 | 1 | 1 | 0 | 0 | 0 | 0 | 0 | 0 | 1.000 | 1.000 | 1.000 | 2.000 |
| Darren Holmes | 2 | 2 | 0 | 0 | 0 | 0 | 0 | 0 | 1 | 0.000 | 0.000 | 0.000 | 0.000 |
| Chris Holt | 3 | 3 | 1 | 1 | 0 | 0 | 1 | 0 | 0 | 0.333 | 0.333 | 0.667 | 1.000 |
| Mike Holtz | 5 | 5 | 1 | 0 | 0 | 0 | 1 | 0 | 1 | 0.200 | 0.200 | 0.200 | 0.400 |
| J.P. Howell | 7 | 7 | 2 | 1 | 0 | 0 | 0 | 0 | 0 | 0.286 | 0.286 | 0.429 | 0.714 |
| Bob Howry | 16 | 15 | 3 | 0 | 0 | 0 | 1 | 0 | 3 | 0.200 | 0.200 | 0.200 | 0.400 |
| Jon Huber | 1 | 1 | 0 | 0 | 0 | 0 | 0 | 0 | 0 | 0.000 | 0.000 | 0.000 | 0.000 |
| Luke Hudson | 6 | 5 | 1 | 1 | 0 | 0 | 1 | 0 | 0 | 0.200 | 0.167 | 0.400 | 0.567 |
| Tim Hudson | 31 | 26 | 6 | 4 | 0 | 0 | 2 | 5 | 2 | 0.231 | 0.355 | 0.385 | 0.739 |
| Hideki Irabu | 11 | 11 | 3 | 0 | 0 | 0 | 2 | 0 | 2 | 0.273 | 0.273 | 0.273 | 0.545 |
| Jason Isringhausen | 3 | 3 | 0 | 0 | 0 | 0 | 0 | 0 | 1 | 0.000 | 0.000 | 0.000 | 0.000 |
| Edwin Jackson | 6 | 6 | 0 | 0 | 0 | 0 | 0 | 0 | 2 | 0.000 | 0.000 | 0.000 | 0.000 |
| Michael Jackson | 7 | 7 | 1 | 1 | 0 | 0 | 0 | 0 | 1 | 0.143 | 0.143 | 0.286 | 0.429 |
| Steven Jackson | 1 | 1 | 1 | 0 | 1 | 0 | 0 | 0 | 0 | 1.000 | 1.000 | 3.000 | 4.000 |
| Mike James | 1 | 1 | 0 | 0 | 0 | 0 | 0 | 0 | 1 | 0.000 | 0.000 | 0.000 | 0.000 |
| Casey Janssen | 1 | 1 | 0 | 0 | 0 | 0 | 0 | 0 | 0 | 0.000 | 0.000 | 0.000 | 0.000 |
| Kevin Jarvis | 6 | 6 | 4 | 3 | 0 | 0 | 1 | 0 | 0 | 0.667 | 0.667 | 1.167 | 1.833 |
| Bobby Jenks | 3 | 3 | 1 | 0 | 0 | 0 | 0 | 0 | 0 | 0.333 | 0.333 | 0.333 | 0.667 |
| Ryan Jensen | 3 | 3 | 1 | 0 | 0 | 0 | 0 | 0 | 0 | 0.333 | 0.333 | 0.333 | 0.667 |
| Cesar Jimenez | 1 | 0 | 0 | 0 | 0 | 0 | 0 | 1 | 0 |  | 1.000 |  |  |
| Jose Jimenez | 4 | 4 | 2 | 0 | 0 | 1 | 2 | 0 | 1 | 0.500 | 0.500 | 1.250 | 1.750 |
| Doug Johns | 1 | 0 | 0 | 0 | 0 | 0 | 1 | 0 | 0 |  | 0.000 |  |  |
| Jason Johnson | 21 | 18 | 6 | 3 | 0 | 0 | 2 | 2 | 3 | 0.333 | 0.381 | 0.500 | 0.881 |

| Cat vs. | PA | AB | H | 2B | 3B | HR | RBI | BB | SO | BA | OBP | SLG | OPS |
|---|---|---|---|---|---|---|---|---|---|---|---|---|---|
| Jim Johnson | 2 | 1 | 0 | 0 | 0 | 0 | 1 | 0 | 0 | 0.000 | 0.000 | 0.000 | 0.000 |
| Josh Johnson | 4 | 3 | 1 | 0 | 0 | 0 | 0 | 1 | 0 | 0.333 | 0.500 | 0.333 | 0.833 |
| John Johnstone | 1 | 1 | 1 | 0 | 0 | 0 | 0 | 0 | 0 | 1.000 | 1.000 | 1.000 | 2.000 |
| Bobby Jones | 3 | 3 | 2 | 0 | 0 | 0 | 0 | 0 | 1 | 0.667 | 0.667 | 0.667 | 1.333 |
| Doug Jones | 3 | 2 | 0 | 0 | 0 | 0 | 0 | 1 | 0 | 0.000 | 0.333 | 0.000 | 0.333 |
| Todd Jones | 7 | 6 | 1 | 0 | 0 | 0 | 2 | 1 | 1 | 0.167 | 0.286 | 0.167 | 0.452 |
| Jorge Julio | 8 | 7 | 1 | 0 | 0 | 0 | 1 | 1 | 0 | 0.143 | 0.250 | 0.143 | 0.393 |
| Jair Jurrjens | 3 | 3 | 1 | 0 | 0 | 0 | 0 | 0 | 0 | 0.333 | 0.333 | 0.333 | 0.667 |
| Scott Kamieniecki | 3 | 3 | 2 | 1 | 0 | 0 | 0 | 0 | 0 | 0.667 | 0.667 | 1.000 | 1.667 |
| Scott Karl | 2 | 1 | 0 | 0 | 0 | 0 | 0 | 1 | 0 | 0.000 | 0.500 | 0.000 | 0.500 |
| Steve Karsay | 1 | 1 | 0 | 0 | 0 | 0 | 0 | 0 | 0 | 0.000 | 0.000 | 0.000 | 0.000 |
| Jeff Karstens | 8 | 7 | 1 | 0 | 0 | 0 | 0 | 1 | 0 | 0.143 | 0.250 | 0.143 | 0.393 |
| Logan Kensing | 2 | 2 | 0 | 0 | 0 | 0 | 0 | 0 | 0 | 0.000 | 0.000 | 0.000 | 0.000 |
| Byung-Hyun Kim | 8 | 8 | 3 | 2 | 0 | 0 | 1 | 0 | 3 | 0.375 | 0.375 | 0.625 | 1.000 |
| Sun-Woo Kim | 5 | 5 | 0 | 0 | 0 | 0 | 0 | 0 | 0 | 0.000 | 0.000 | 0.000 | 0.000 |
| Matt Kinney | 3 | 2 | 0 | 0 | 0 | 0 | 0 | 1 | 0 | 0.000 | 0.333 | 0.000 | 0.333 |
| Steve Kline | 1 | 1 | 0 | 0 | 0 | 0 | 0 | 0 | 0 | 0.000 | 0.000 | 0.000 | 0.000 |
| Brandon Knight | 1 | 1 | 0 | 0 | 0 | 0 | 0 | 0 | 0 | 0.000 | 0.000 | 0.000 | 0.000 |
| Gary Knotts | 1 | 1 | 0 | 0 | 0 | 0 | 0 | 0 | 0 | 0.000 | 0.000 | 0.000 | 0.000 |
| Billy Koch | 16 | 15 | 4 | 1 | 0 | 0 | 1 | 1 | 4 | 0.267 | 0.313 | 0.333 | 0.646 |
| Shane Komine | 3 | 3 | 0 | 0 | 0 | 0 | 0 | 0 | 0 | 0.000 | 0.000 | 0.000 | 0.000 |
| John Koronka | 7 | 7 | 2 | 0 | 0 | 0 | 1 | 0 | 0 | 0.286 | 0.286 | 0.286 | 0.571 |
| Hiroki Kuroda | 3 | 1 | 0 | 0 | 0 | 0 | 1 | 1 | 0 | 0.000 | 0.667 | 0.000 | 0.667 |
| John Lackey | 19 | 15 | 2 | 1 | 0 | 0 | 2 | 3 | 3 | 0.133 | 0.316 | 0.200 | 0.516 |

| Cat vs. | PA | AB | H | 2B | 3B | HR | RBI | BB | SO | BA | OBP | SLG | OPS |
|---|---|---|---|---|---|---|---|---|---|---|---|---|---|
| Mark Langston | 1 | 1 | 0 | 0 | 0 | 0 | 0 | 0 | 1 | 0.000 | 0.000 | 0.000 | 0.000 |
| Andy Larkin | 1 | 1 | 1 | 0 | 0 | 1 | 4 | 0 | 0 | 1.000 | 1.000 | 4.000 | 5.000 |
| Brandon League | 1 | 0 | 0 | 0 | 0 | 0 | 0 | 0 | 0 | | 1.000 | | |
| Wil Ledezma | 3 | 2 | 0 | 0 | 0 | 0 | 0 | 1 | 0 | 0.000 | 0.333 | 0.000 | 0.333 |
| Cliff Lee | 1 | 1 | 1 | 0 | 0 | 0 | 0 | 0 | 0 | 1.000 | 1.000 | 1.000 | 2.000 |
| David Lee | 3 | 3 | 0 | 0 | 0 | 0 | 0 | 0 | 1 | 0.000 | 0.000 | 0.000 | 0.000 |
| Justin Lehr | 2 | 1 | 0 | 0 | 0 | 0 | 0 | 1 | 0 | 0.000 | 0.500 | 0.000 | 0.500 |
| Jon Leicester | 4 | 3 | 0 | 0 | 0 | 0 | 0 | 0 | 0 | 0.000 | 0.250 | 0.000 | 0.250 |
| Al Leiter | 1 | 1 | 0 | 0 | 0 | 0 | 0 | 0 | 0 | 0.000 | 0.000 | 0.000 | 0.000 |
| Al Levine | 11 | 11 | 3 | 1 | 1 | 0 | 0 | 0 | 1 | 0.273 | 0.273 | 0.545 | 0.818 |
| Colby Lewis | 4 | 4 | 2 | 0 | 0 | 1 | 2 | 0 | 1 | 0.500 | 0.500 | 1.250 | 1.750 |
| Jensen Lewis | 4 | 3 | 0 | 0 | 0 | 0 | 0 | 0 | 1 | 0.000 | 0.000 | 0.000 | 0.000 |
| Brad Lidge | 2 | 2 | 0 | 0 | 0 | 0 | 0 | 0 | 1 | 0.000 | 0.000 | 0.000 | 0.000 |
| Cory Lidle | 27 | 23 | 8 | 2 | 0 | 1 | 1 | 3 | 1 | 0.348 | 0.444 | 0.565 | 1.010 |
| Jon Lieber | 7 | 7 | 2 | 0 | 0 | 0 | 1 | 0 | 0 | 0.286 | 0.286 | 0.286 | 0.571 |
| Ted Lilly | 1 | 1 | 0 | 0 | 0 | 0 | 0 | 0 | 0 | 0.000 | 0.000 | 0.000 | 0.000 |
| Jose Lima | 6 | 5 | 2 | 0 | 0 | 0 | 0 | 0 | 1 | 0.400 | 0.500 | 0.400 | 0.900 |
| Matt Lindstrom | 1 | 1 | 0 | 0 | 0 | 0 | 0 | 0 | 1 | 0.000 | 0.000 | 0.000 | 0.000 |
| Felipe Lira | 2 | 2 | 0 | 0 | 0 | 0 | 0 | 0 | 1 | 0.000 | 0.000 | 0.000 | 0.000 |
| Jesse Litsch | 6 | 6 | 2 | 1 | 0 | 0 | 0 | 0 | 2 | 0.333 | 0.333 | 0.500 | 0.833 |
| Wes Littleton | 1 | 1 | 0 | 0 | 0 | 0 | 0 | 0 | 0 | 0.000 | 0.000 | 0.000 | 0.000 |
| Radhames Liz | 2 | 2 | 1 | 0 | 0 | 0 | 0 | 0 | 1 | 0.500 | 0.500 | 0.500 | 1.000 |
| Graeme Lloyd | 2 | 2 | 0 | 0 | 0 | 0 | 0 | 0 | 0 | 0.000 | 0.000 | 0.000 | 0.000 |
| Esteban Loaiza | 35 | 33 | 11 | 2 | 0 | 2 | 4 | 2 | 2 | 0.333 | 0.371 | 0.576 | 0.947 |

| Cat vs. | PA | AB | H | 2B | 3B | HR | RBI | BB | SO | BA | OBP | SLG | OPS |
|---|---|---|---|---|---|---|---|---|---|---|---|---|---|
| Kyle Lohse | 11 | 9 | 0 | 0 | 0 | 0 | 1 | 1 | 0 | 0.000 | 0.091 | 0.000 | 0.091 |
| Albie Lopez | 9 | 5 | 1 | 0 | 0 | 0 | 0 | 3 | 1 | 0.200 | 0.500 | 0.200 | 0.700 |
| Aquilino Lopez | 1 | 1 | 1 | 0 | 0 | 0 | 0 | 0 | 0 | 1.000 | 1.000 | 1.000 | 2.000 |
| Javier Lopez | 1 | 0 | 0 | 0 | 0 | 0 | 0 | 1 | 0 |  | 1.000 |  |  |
| Rodrigo Lopez | 21 | 20 | 7 | 3 | 0 | 1 | 3 | 1 | 4 | 0.350 | 0.381 | 0.650 | 1.031 |
| Andrew Lorraine | 1 | 1 | 0 | 0 | 0 | 0 | 0 | 0 | 1 | 0.000 | 0.000 | 0.000 | 0.000 |
| Shane Loux | 3 | 3 | 1 | 0 | 1 | 0 | 2 | 0 | 0 | 0.333 | 0.333 | 1.000 | 1.333 |
| Derek Lowe | 27 | 26 | 8 | 0 | 0 | 1 | 2 | 1 | 2 | 0.308 | 0.333 | 0.423 | 0.756 |
| Mark Lowe | 3 | 3 | 2 | 0 | 0 | 0 | 1 | 0 | 0 | 0.667 | 0.667 | 0.667 | 1.333 |
| Sean Lowe | 6 | 6 | 3 | 1 | 0 | 0 | 3 | 0 | 1 | 0.500 | 0.500 | 0.667 | 1.167 |
| Ruddy Lugo | 5 | 5 | 2 | 1 | 0 | 0 | 3 | 0 | 0 | 0.400 | 0.400 | 0.600 | 1.000 |
| Mark Lukasiewicz | 3 | 3 | 2 | 0 | 0 | 0 | 2 | 0 | 0 | 0.667 | 0.667 | 0.667 | 1.333 |
| David Lundquist | 1 | 1 | 0 | 0 | 0 | 0 | 0 | 0 | 0 | 0.000 | 0.000 | 0.000 | 0.000 |
| Brandon Lyon | 5 | 5 | 0 | 0 | 0 | 0 | 0 | 0 | 0 | 0.000 | 0.000 | 0.000 | 0.000 |
| Mike MacDougal | 8 | 5 | 1 | 1 | 0 | 0 | 0 | 3 | 0 | 0.200 | 0.500 | 0.400 | 0.900 |
| Calvin Maduro | 5 | 5 | 2 | 0 | 0 | 0 | 0 | 0 | 0 | 0.400 | 0.400 | 0.400 | 0.800 |
| Mike Magnante | 10 | 10 | 1 | 1 | 0 | 0 | 0 | 0 | 0 | 0.100 | 0.100 | 0.200 | 0.300 |
| Ron Mahay | 2 | 2 | 0 | 0 | 0 | 0 | 0 | 0 | 0 | 0.000 | 0.000 | 0.000 | 0.000 |
| John Maine | 8 | 6 | 1 | 0 | 0 | 0 | 0 | 2 | 0 | 0.167 | 0.375 | 0.167 | 0.542 |
| Gary Majewski | 1 | 1 | 0 | 0 | 0 | 0 | 0 | 0 | 0 | 0.000 | 0.000 | 0.000 | 0.000 |
| Mark Malaska | 3 | 3 | 0 | 0 | 0 | 0 | 0 | 0 | 1 | 0.000 | 0.000 | 0.000 | 0.000 |
| Julio Manon | 1 | 0 | 0 | 0 | 0 | 0 | 0 | 1 | 0 |  | 1.000 |  |  |
| Matt Mantei | 1 | 1 | 1 | 0 | 0 | 0 | 1 | 0 | 0 | 1.000 | 1.000 | 1.000 | 2.000 |
| Shaun Marcum | 7 | 7 | 3 | 1 | 0 | 0 | 1 | 0 | 0 | 0.429 | 0.429 | 0.571 | 1.000 |

| Cat vs. | PA | AB | H | 2B | 3B | HR | RBI | BB | SO | BA | OBP | SLG | OPS |
|---|---|---|---|---|---|---|---|---|---|---|---|---|---|
| Carlos Marmol | 2 | 2 | 0 | 0 | 0 | 0 | 0 | 0 | 2 | 0.000 | 0.000 | 0.000 | 0.000 |
| Mike Maroth | 3 | 3 | 1 | 0 | 0 | 0 | 0 | 0 | 0 | 0.333 | 0.333 | 0.333 | 0.667 |
| Jason Marquis | 6 | 6 | 1 | 0 | 0 | 1 | 1 | 0 | 1 | 0.167 | 0.167 | 0.667 | 0.833 |
| Damaso Marte | 6 | 5 | 0 | 0 | 0 | 0 | 0 | 1 | 1 | 0.000 | 0.167 | 0.000 | 0.167 |
| J.D. Martin | 3 | 3 | 1 | 0 | 0 | 0 | 0 | 0 | 0 | 0.333 | 0.333 | 0.333 | 0.667 |
| Tom Martin | 1 | 1 | 1 | 0 | 0 | 0 | 0 | 0 | 0 | 1.000 | 1.000 | 1.000 | 2.000 |
| Carlos Martinez | 1 | 1 | 1 | 0 | 0 | 0 | 0 | 0 | 0 | 1.000 | 1.000 | 1.000 | 2.000 |
| Pedro Martinez | 29 | 29 | 4 | 1 | 0 | 0 | 0 | 0 | 8 | 0.138 | 0.138 | 0.172 | 0.310 |
| Tom Mastny | 2 | 2 | 0 | 0 | 0 | 0 | 0 | 0 | 1 | 0.000 | 0.000 | 0.000 | 0.000 |
| Julio Mateo | 5 | 5 | 3 | 0 | 1 | 0 | 1 | 0 | 0 | 0.600 | 0.600 | 1.000 | 1.600 |
| T.J. Mathews | 3 | 2 | 1 | 0 | 0 | 0 | 1 | 0 | 0 | 0.500 | 0.667 | 0.500 | 1.167 |
| Terry Mathews | 2 | 2 | 0 | 0 | 0 | 0 | 0 | 0 | 1 | 0.000 | 0.000 | 0.000 | 0.000 |
| Daisuke Matsuzaka | 8 | 8 | 2 | 1 | 0 | 1 | 2 | 0 | 1 | 0.250 | 0.250 | 0.750 | 1.000 |
| Darrell May | 4 | 3 | 0 | 0 | 0 | 0 | 1 | 0 | 0 | 0.000 | 0.000 | 0.000 | 0.000 |
| Joe Mays | 27 | 26 | 10 | 3 | 0 | 1 | 3 | 0 | 3 | 0.385 | 0.370 | 0.615 | 0.986 |
| Macay McBride | 1 | 1 | 0 | 0 | 0 | 0 | 0 | 0 | 0 | 0.000 | 0.000 | 0.000 | 0.000 |
| Brandon McCarthy | 2 | 2 | 1 | 1 | 0 | 0 | 2 | 0 | 0 | 0.500 | 0.500 | 1.000 | 1.500 |
| Kyle McClellan | 2 | 1 | 0 | 0 | 0 | 0 | 0 | 1 | 0 | 0.000 | 0.500 | 0.000 | 0.500 |
| Seth McClung | 19 | 17 | 6 | 0 | 0 | 0 | 2 | 2 | 3 | 0.353 | 0.421 | 0.353 | 0.774 |
| Allen McDill | 3 | 3 | 2 | 1 | 0 | 0 | 3 | 0 | 0 | 0.667 | 0.667 | 1.000 | 1.667 |
| James McDonald | 1 | 1 | 0 | 0 | 0 | 0 | 0 | 0 | 0 | 0.000 | 0.000 | 0.000 | 0.000 |
| Jack McDowell | 3 | 3 | 0 | 0 | 0 | 0 | 0 | 0 | 1 | 0.000 | 0.000 | 0.000 | 0.000 |
| Chuck McElroy | 3 | 3 | 0 | 0 | 0 | 0 | 0 | 0 | 0 | 0.000 | 0.000 | 0.000 | 0.000 |
| Dustin McGowan | 4 | 4 | 2 | 0 | 0 | 1 | 1 | 0 | 0 | 0.500 | 0.500 | 1.250 | 1.750 |

| Cat vs. | PA | AB | H | 2B | 3B | HR | RBI | BB | SO | BA | OBP | SLG | OPS |
|---|---|---|---|---|---|---|---|---|---|---|---|---|---|
| Tony McKnight | 3 | 3 | 1 | 1 | 0 | 0 | 1 | 0 | 0 | 0.333 | 0.333 | 0.667 | 1.000 |
| Rusty Meacham | 1 | 1 | 0 | 0 | 0 | 0 | 0 | 0 | 0 | 0.000 | 0.000 | 0.000 | 0.000 |
| Brian Meadows | 8 | 8 | 4 | 0 | 0 | 1 | 3 | 0 | 1 | 0.500 | 0.500 | 0.875 | 1.375 |
| Chris Mears | 2 | 2 | 2 | 0 | 0 | 2 | 2 | 0 | 0 | 1.000 | 1.000 | 4.000 | 5.000 |
| Gil Meche | 20 | 18 | 5 | 1 | 1 | 0 | 1 | 1 | 3 | 0.278 | 0.316 | 0.444 | 0.760 |
| Jim Mecir | 11 | 9 | 3 | 0 | 0 | 0 | 1 | 1 | 1 | 0.333 | 0.364 | 0.333 | 0.697 |
| Kris Medlen | 1 | 1 | 0 | 0 | 0 | 0 | 0 | 0 | 0 | 0.000 | 0.000 | 0.000 | 0.000 |
| Evan Meek | 1 | 1 | 1 | 0 | 0 | 0 | 0 | 0 | 0 | 1.000 | 1.000 | 1.000 | 2.000 |
| Ramiro Mendoza | 7 | 7 | 1 | 0 | 1 | 0 | 0 | 0 | 2 | 0.143 | 0.143 | 0.429 | 0.571 |
| Jose Mercedes | 5 | 5 | 2 | 2 | 0 | 0 | 1 | 0 | 1 | 0.400 | 0.400 | 0.800 | 1.200 |
| Kent Mercker | 2 | 1 | 0 | 0 | 0 | 0 | 0 | 1 | 0 | 0.000 | 0.500 | 0.000 | 0.500 |
| Jose Mesa | 3 | 3 | 2 | 0 | 0 | 1 | 1 | 0 | 1 | 0.667 | 0.667 | 1.667 | 2.333 |
| Randy Messenger | 1 | 1 | 1 | 0 | 0 | 0 | 0 | 0 | 0 | 1.000 | 1.000 | 1.000 | 2.000 |
| Dan Meyer | 1 | 1 | 0 | 0 | 0 | 0 | 0 | 0 | 0 | 0.000 | 0.000 | 0.000 | 0.000 |
| Bart Miadich | 3 | 2 | 0 | 0 | 0 | 0 | 0 | 1 | 0 | 0.000 | 0.333 | 0.000 | 0.333 |
| Dan Miceli | 6 | 5 | 0 | 0 | 0 | 0 | 0 | 1 | 0 | 0.000 | 0.167 | 0.000 | 0.167 |
| Chris Michalak | 1 | 0 | 0 | 0 | 0 | 0 | 0 | 1 | 0 |  | 1.000 |  |  |
| Travis Miller | 3 | 2 | 1 | 0 | 0 | 0 | 1 | 1 | 0 | 0.500 | 0.667 | 0.500 | 1.167 |
| Trever Miller | 4 | 3 | 0 | 0 | 0 | 0 | 1 | 0 | 0 | 0.000 | 0.000 | 0.000 | 0.000 |
| Wade Miller | 6 | 5 | 2 | 0 | 0 | 1 | 2 | 1 | 2 | 0.400 | 0.500 | 1.000 | 1.500 |
| Alan Mills | 3 | 3 | 1 | 0 | 0 | 0 | 0 | 0 | 0 | 0.333 | 0.333 | 0.333 | 0.667 |
| Kevin Millwood | 9 | 9 | 3 | 0 | 0 | 0 | 1 | 0 | 2 | 0.333 | 0.333 | 0.333 | 0.667 |
| Zach Miner | 4 | 4 | 0 | 0 | 0 | 0 | 0 | 0 | 0 | 0.000 | 0.000 | 0.000 | 0.000 |
| Sergio Mitre | 3 | 3 | 0 | 0 | 0 | 0 | 0 | 0 | 0 | 0.000 | 0.000 | 0.000 | 0.000 |

| Cat vs. | PA | AB | H | 2B | 3B | HR | RBI | BB | SO | BA | OBP | SLG | OPS |
|---|---|---|---|---|---|---|---|---|---|---|---|---|---|
| Dave Mlicki | 6 | 6 | 1 | 0 | 0 | 1 | 1 | 0 | 0 | 0.167 | 0.167 | 0.667 | 0.833 |
| Garrett Mock | 3 | 3 | 0 | 0 | 0 | 0 | 0 | 0 | 1 | 0.000 | 0.000 | 0.000 | 0.000 |
| Brian Moehler | 12 | 10 | 5 | 1 | 0 | 1 | 1 | 2 | 1 | 0.500 | 0.583 | 0.900 | 1.483 |
| Mike Mohler | 1 | 1 | 0 | 0 | 0 | 0 | 0 | 0 | 0 | 0.000 | 0.000 | 0.000 | 0.000 |
| Gabe Molina | 1 | 0 | 0 | 0 | 0 | 0 | 0 | 1 | 0 |  | 1.000 |  |  |
| Carlos Monasterios | 1 | 1 | 0 | 0 | 0 | 0 | 0 | 0 | 0 | 0.000 | 0.000 | 0.000 | 0.000 |
| Steve Montgomery | 1 | 0 | 0 | 0 | 0 | 0 | 0 | 1 | 0 |  | 1.000 |  |  |
| Matt Morris | 4 | 4 | 2 | 0 | 0 | 0 | 1 | 0 | 0 | 0.500 | 0.500 | 0.500 | 1.000 |
| Brandon Morrow | 6 | 5 | 1 | 0 | 0 | 0 | 0 | 0 | 1 | 0.200 | 0.200 | 0.200 | 0.400 |
| Charlie Morton | 3 | 3 | 1 | 0 | 0 | 0 | 0 | 0 | 0 | 0.333 | 0.333 | 0.333 | 0.667 |
| Dustin Moseley | 5 | 4 | 0 | 0 | 0 | 0 | 0 | 0 | 0 | 0.000 | 0.000 | 0.000 | 0.000 |
| Danny Mota | 1 | 1 | 1 | 1 | 0 | 0 | 0 | 0 | 0 | 1.000 | 1.000 | 2.000 | 3.000 |
| Jamie Moyer | 13 | 13 | 3 | 0 | 0 | 0 | 0 | 0 | 2 | 0.231 | 0.231 | 0.231 | 0.462 |
| Edward Mujica | 1 | 1 | 0 | 0 | 0 | 0 | 0 | 0 | 0 | 0.000 | 0.000 | 0.000 | 0.000 |
| Mark Mulder | 7 | 7 | 2 | 1 | 0 | 0 | 0 | 0 | 1 | 0.286 | 0.286 | 0.429 | 0.714 |
| Terry Mulholland | 1 | 1 | 0 | 0 | 0 | 0 | 0 | 0 | 1 | 0.000 | 0.000 | 0.000 | 0.000 |
| Scott Mullen | 2 | 2 | 0 | 0 | 0 | 0 | 0 | 0 | 0 | 0.000 | 0.000 | 0.000 | 0.000 |
| Kevin Mulvey | 3 | 3 | 1 | 0 | 0 | 0 | 0 | 0 | 1 | 0.333 | 0.333 | 0.333 | 0.667 |
| Dan Murray | 1 | 1 | 0 | 0 | 0 | 0 | 0 | 0 | 0 | 0.000 | 0.000 | 0.000 | 0.000 |
| Mike Mussina | 67 | 61 | 28 | 8 | 0 | 2 | 10 | 3 | 7 | 0.459 | 0.507 | 0.689 | 1.196 |
| Mike Myers | 1 | 1 | 0 | 0 | 0 | 0 | 0 | 0 | 0 | 0.000 | 0.000 | 0.000 | 0.000 |
| Rodney Myers | 1 | 1 | 0 | 0 | 0 | 0 | 0 | 0 | 0 | 0.000 | 0.000 | 0.000 | 0.000 |
| Charles Nagy | 17 | 16 | 6 | 1 | 1 | 0 | 1 | 0 | 1 | 0.375 | 0.412 | 0.563 | 0.974 |
| Joe Nathan | 3 | 2 | 0 | 0 | 0 | 0 | 0 | 1 | 0 | 0.000 | 0.333 | 0.000 | 0.333 |

| Cat vs. | PA | AB | H | 2B | 3B | HR | RBI | BB | SO | BA | OBP | SLG | OPS |
|---|---|---|---|---|---|---|---|---|---|---|---|---|---|
| Jaime Navarro | 7 | 7 | 0 | 0 | 0 | 0 | 0 | 0 | 2 | 0.000 | 0.000 | 0.000 | 0.000 |
| Blaine Neal | 1 | 1 | 1 | 0 | 0 | 0 | 0 | 0 | 0 | 1.000 | 1.000 | 1.000 | 2.000 |
| Jeff Nelson | 8 | 7 | 1 | 0 | 0 | 0 | 0 | 1 | 0 | 0.143 | 0.250 | 0.143 | 0.393 |
| Joe Nelson | 1 | 1 | 0 | 0 | 0 | 0 | 0 | 0 | 1 | 0.000 | 0.000 | 0.000 | 0.000 |
| Robb Nen | 1 | 1 | 0 | 0 | 0 | 0 | 0 | 0 | 0 | 0.000 | 0.000 | 0.000 | 0.000 |
| Pat Neshek | 2 | 2 | 1 | 0 | 0 | 0 | 0 | 0 | 1 | 0.500 | 0.500 | 0.500 | 1.000 |
| Michael Neu | 1 | 0 | 0 | 0 | 0 | 0 | 0 | 1 | 0 |  | 1.000 |  |  |
| Fernando Nieve | 3 | 3 | 2 | 1 | 0 | 0 | 0 | 0 | 0 | 0.667 | 0.667 | 1.000 | 1.667 |
| C.J. Nitkowski | 1 | 1 | 0 | 0 | 0 | 0 | 0 | 0 | 0 | 0.000 | 0.000 | 0.000 | 0.000 |
| Hideo Nomo | 19 | 17 | 6 | 0 | 0 | 0 | 0 | 2 | 2 | 0.353 | 0.421 | 0.353 | 0.774 |
| Bud Norris | 4 | 4 | 0 | 0 | 0 | 0 | 0 | 0 | 4 | 0.000 | 0.000 | 0.000 | 0.000 |
| Darren O'Day | 1 | 1 | 0 | 0 | 0 | 0 | 0 | 0 | 0 | 0.000 | 0.000 | 0.000 | 0.000 |
| Eric O'Flaherty | 1 | 1 | 0 | 0 | 0 | 0 | 0 | 0 | 0 | 0.000 | 0.000 | 0.000 | 0.000 |
| Wes Obermueller | 1 | 1 | 0 | 0 | 0 | 0 | 0 | 0 | 0 | 0.000 | 0.000 | 0.000 | 0.000 |
| Tomo Ohka | 15 | 13 | 3 | 1 | 0 | 0 | 0 | 2 | 0 | 0.231 | 0.333 | 0.308 | 0.641 |
| Ross Ohlendorf | 5 | 4 | 2 | 0 | 0 | 0 | 0 | 1 | 0 | 0.500 | 0.600 | 0.500 | 1.100 |
| Will Ohman | 1 | 1 | 1 | 0 | 0 | 0 | 0 | 0 | 0 | 1.000 | 1.000 | 1.000 | 2.000 |
| Hideki Okajima | 1 | 1 | 0 | 0 | 0 | 0 | 0 | 0 | 0 | 0.000 | 0.000 | 0.000 | 0.000 |
| Omar Olivares | 7 | 6 | 1 | 0 | 1 | 0 | 0 | 1 | 2 | 0.167 | 0.286 | 0.500 | 0.786 |
| Darren Oliver | 3 | 3 | 0 | 0 | 0 | 0 | 0 | 0 | 0 | 0.000 | 0.000 | 0.000 | 0.000 |
| Gregg Olson | 1 | 1 | 0 | 0 | 0 | 0 | 0 | 0 | 0 | 0.000 | 0.000 | 0.000 | 0.000 |
| Mike Oquist | 10 | 10 | 4 | 1 | 1 | 0 | 3 | 0 | 3 | 0.400 | 0.400 | 0.700 | 1.100 |
| Jesse Orosco | 1 | 1 | 0 | 0 | 0 | 0 | 0 | 0 | 1 | 0.000 | 0.000 | 0.000 | 0.000 |
| Ramon Ortiz | 37 | 33 | 11 | 3 | 0 | 0 | 5 | 4 | 0 | 0.333 | 0.405 | 0.424 | 0.830 |

| Cat vs. | PA | AB | H | 2B | 3B | HR | RBI | BB | SO | BA | OBP | SLG | OPS |
|---|---|---|---|---|---|---|---|---|---|---|---|---|---|
| Russ Ortiz | 3 | 3 | 2 | 1 | 0 | 0 | 0 | 0 | 0 | 0.667 | 0.667 | 1.000 | 1.667 |
| Chad Orvella | 3 | 2 | 1 | 1 | 0 | 0 | 0 | 1 | 0 | 0.500 | 0.667 | 1.000 | 1.667 |
| Antonio Osuna | 2 | 2 | 0 | 0 | 0 | 0 | 0 | 0 | 2 | 0.000 | 0.000 | 0.000 | 0.000 |
| Roy Oswalt | 23 | 22 | 7 | 0 | 0 | 0 | 1 | 1 | 3 | 0.318 | 0.348 | 0.318 | 0.666 |
| Juan Oviedo | 5 | 4 | 2 | 0 | 0 | 1 | 1 | 1 | 0 | 0.500 | 0.600 | 1.250 | 1.850 |
| Juan Padilla | 3 | 2 | 0 | 0 | 0 | 0 | 0 | 1 | 0 | 0.000 | 0.333 | 0.000 | 0.333 |
| Vicente Padilla | 6 | 6 | 2 | 0 | 0 | 1 | 2 | 0 | 0 | 0.333 | 0.333 | 0.833 | 1.167 |
| Lance Painter | 1 | 0 | 0 | 0 | 0 | 0 | 0 | 1 | 0 |  | 1.000 |  |  |
| Jose Paniagua | 3 | 1 | 1 | 0 | 0 | 0 | 0 | 1 | 0 | 1.000 | 1.000 | 1.000 | 2.000 |
| Jonathan Papelbon | 10 | 10 | 5 | 1 | 0 | 0 | 0 | 0 | 1 | 0.500 | 0.500 | 0.600 | 1.100 |
| Jim Parque | 2 | 2 | 1 | 0 | 0 | 0 | 0 | 0 | 0 | 0.500 | 0.500 | 0.500 | 1.000 |
| John Parrish | 2 | 2 | 0 | 0 | 0 | 0 | 0 | 0 | 0 | 0.000 | 0.000 | 0.000 | 0.000 |
| Danny Patterson | 6 | 6 | 5 | 1 | 0 | 0 | 1 | 0 | 1 | 0.833 | 0.833 | 1.000 | 1.833 |
| John Patterson | 2 | 1 | 0 | 0 | 0 | 0 | 0 | 1 | 0 | 0.000 | 0.500 | 0.000 | 0.500 |
| David Pauley | 4 | 4 | 2 | 1 | 0 | 0 | 0 | 0 | 0 | 0.500 | 0.500 | 0.750 | 1.250 |
| Carl Pavano | 7 | 6 | 3 | 1 | 0 | 0 | 0 | 0 | 1 | 0.500 | 0.571 | 0.667 | 1.238 |
| Mike Pelfrey | 1 | 1 | 1 | 0 | 0 | 0 | 0 | 0 | 0 | 1.000 | 1.000 | 1.000 | 2.000 |
| Hayden Penn | 3 | 2 | 1 | 0 | 0 | 0 | 1 | 1 | 0 | 0.500 | 0.667 | 0.500 | 1.167 |
| Joel Peralta | 2 | 2 | 0 | 0 | 0 | 0 | 0 | 0 | 0 | 0.000 | 0.000 | 0.000 | 0.000 |
| Troy Percival | 10 | 9 | 2 | 0 | 0 | 0 | 0 | 1 | 1 | 0.222 | 0.300 | 0.222 | 0.522 |
| Dan Perkins | 3 | 3 | 2 | 0 | 0 | 0 | 1 | 0 | 0 | 0.667 | 0.667 | 0.667 | 1.333 |
| Glen Perkins | 1 | 1 | 0 | 0 | 0 | 0 | 0 | 0 | 1 | 0.000 | 0.000 | 0.000 | 0.000 |
| Robert Person | 2 | 0 | 0 | 0 | 0 | 0 | 0 | 2 | 0 |  | 1.000 |  |  |
| Andy Pettitte | 6 | 6 | 3 | 0 | 0 | 0 | 0 | 0 | 1 | 0.500 | 0.500 | 0.500 | 1.000 |

| Cat vs. | PA | AB | H | 2B | 3B | HR | RBI | BB | SO | BA | OBP | SLG | OPS |
|---|---|---|---|---|---|---|---|---|---|---|---|---|---|
| Travis Phelps | 2 | 2 | 1 | 0 | 0 | 0 | 1 | 0 | 1 | 0.500 | 0.500 | 0.500 | 1.000 |
| Jason Phillips | 2 | 1 | 0 | 0 | 0 | 0 | 0 | 1 | 1 | 0.000 | 0.500 | 0.000 | 0.500 |
| Luis Pineda | 2 | 2 | 2 | 0 | 0 | 0 | 0 | 0 | 0 | 1.000 | 1.000 | 1.000 | 2.000 |
| Joel Pineiro | 22 | 20 | 5 | 2 | 0 | 0 | 0 | 2 | 2 | 0.250 | 0.318 | 0.350 | 0.668 |
| Renyel Pinto | 1 | 1 | 0 | 0 | 0 | 0 | 0 | 0 | 1 | 0.000 | 0.000 | 0.000 | 0.000 |
| Jim Pittsley | 1 | 0 | 0 | 0 | 0 | 0 | 0 | 1 | 0 |  | 1.000 |  |  |
| Dan Plesac | 2 | 2 | 1 | 0 | 0 | 0 | 0 | 0 | 1 | 0.500 | 0.500 | 0.500 | 1.000 |
| Eric Plunk | 1 | 1 | 0 | 0 | 0 | 0 | 0 | 0 | 1 | 0.000 | 0.000 | 0.000 | 0.000 |
| Sidney Ponson | 49 | 45 | 16 | 2 | 0 | 0 | 4 | 3 | 4 | 0.356 | 0.388 | 0.400 | 0.788 |
| Mark Portugal | 4 | 4 | 3 | 0 | 0 | 1 | 1 | 0 | 0 | 0.750 | 0.750 | 1.500 | 2.250 |
| Mike Porzio | 1 | 0 | 0 | 0 | 0 | 0 | 0 | 1 | 0 |  | 1.000 |  |  |
| Lou Pote | 4 | 4 | 0 | 0 | 0 | 0 | 0 | 0 | 1 | 0.000 | 0.000 | 0.000 | 0.000 |
| Jay Powell | 2 | 2 | 0 | 0 | 0 | 0 | 0 | 0 | 0 | 0.000 | 0.000 | 0.000 | 0.000 |
| Mark Prior | 3 | 3 | 1 | 0 | 0 | 0 | 0 | 0 | 1 | 0.333 | 0.333 | 0.333 | 0.667 |
| Scott Proctor | 5 | 5 | 1 | 1 | 0 | 0 | 0 | 0 | 0 | 0.200 | 0.200 | 0.400 | 0.600 |
| Luke Prokopec | 11 | 9 | 3 | 1 | 0 | 0 | 0 | 1 | 0 | 0.333 | 0.455 | 0.444 | 0.899 |
| Brandon Puffer | 1 | 1 | 0 | 0 | 0 | 0 | 0 | 0 | 0 | 0.000 | 0.000 | 0.000 | 0.000 |
| Bill Pulsipher | 1 | 1 | 0 | 0 | 0 | 0 | 0 | 0 | 0 | 0.000 | 0.000 | 0.000 | 0.000 |
| J.J. Putz | 4 | 4 | 1 | 1 | 0 | 0 | 2 | 0 | 0 | 0.250 | 0.250 | 0.500 | 0.750 |
| Chad Qualls | 2 | 2 | 1 | 1 | 0 | 0 | 0 | 0 | 1 | 0.500 | 0.500 | 1.000 | 1.500 |
| Paul Quantrill | 2 | 1 | 0 | 0 | 0 | 0 | 0 | 1 | 0 | 0.000 | 0.500 | 0.000 | 0.500 |
| Brad Radke | 29 | 27 | 11 | 4 | 0 | 1 | 5 | 1 | 0 | 0.407 | 0.448 | 0.667 | 1.115 |
| Aaron Rakers | 1 | 1 | 0 | 0 | 0 | 0 | 0 | 0 | 0 | 0.000 | 0.000 | 0.000 | 0.000 |
| Edward Ramirez | 1 | 1 | 1 | 0 | 0 | 0 | 0 | 0 | 0 | 1.000 | 1.000 | 1.000 | 2.000 |

| Cat vs. | PA | AB | H | 2B | 3B | HR | RBI | BB | SO | BA | OBP | SLG | OPS |
|---|---|---|---|---|---|---|---|---|---|---|---|---|---|
| Ramon Ramirez | 1 | 1 | 1 | 0 | 0 | 0 | 0 | 0 | 0 | 1.000 | 1.000 | 1.000 | 2.000 |
| Steve Randolph | 2 | 1 | 0 | 0 | 0 | 0 | 0 | 1 | 1 | 0.000 | 0.500 | 0.000 | 0.500 |
| Pat Rapp | 13 | 12 | 2 | 0 | 0 | 0 | 2 | 1 | 2 | 0.167 | 0.231 | 0.167 | 0.397 |
| Darrell Rasner | 3 | 3 | 1 | 1 | 0 | 0 | 0 | 0 | 0 | 0.333 | 0.333 | 0.667 | 1.000 |
| Jon Rauch | 1 | 1 | 1 | 0 | 0 | 0 | 0 | 0 | 0 | 1.000 | 1.000 | 1.000 | 2.000 |
| Chris Ray | 5 | 4 | 2 | 0 | 0 | 0 | 2 | 1 | 0 | 0.500 | 0.600 | 0.500 | 1.100 |
| Ken Ray | 2 | 2 | 0 | 0 | 0 | 0 | 1 | 0 | 0 | 0.000 | 0.000 | 0.000 | 0.000 |
| Tim Redding | 3 | 3 | 1 | 0 | 0 | 0 | 0 | 0 | 0 | 0.333 | 0.333 | 0.333 | 0.667 |
| Rick Reed | 8 | 8 | 4 | 0 | 1 | 1 | 1 | 0 | 1 | 0.500 | 0.500 | 1.125 | 1.625 |
| Steve Reed | 3 | 3 | 1 | 0 | 0 | 1 | 1 | 0 | 1 | 0.333 | 0.333 | 1.333 | 1.667 |
| Dan Reichert | 8 | 7 | 4 | 0 | 0 | 1 | 1 | 1 | 0 | 0.571 | 0.625 | 1.000 | 1.625 |
| Chris Reitsma | 1 | 1 | 0 | 0 | 0 | 0 | 0 | 0 | 0 | 0.000 | 0.000 | 0.000 | 0.000 |
| Bryan Rekar | 16 | 15 | 7 | 2 | 0 | 2 | 6 | 0 | 1 | 0.467 | 0.438 | 1.000 | 1.438 |
| Chris Resop | 1 | 1 | 1 | 0 | 0 | 0 | 0 | 0 | 0 | 1.000 | 1.000 | 1.000 | 2.000 |
| Alberto Reyes | 2 | 2 | 0 | 0 | 0 | 0 | 0 | 0 | 0 | 0.000 | 0.000 | 0.000 | 0.000 |
| Anthony Reyes | 4 | 4 | 0 | 0 | 0 | 0 | 0 | 0 | 0 | 0.000 | 0.000 | 0.000 | 0.000 |
| Dennys Reyes | 5 | 4 | 0 | 0 | 0 | 0 | 0 | 0 | 1 | 0.000 | 0.000 | 0.000 | 0.000 |
| Armando Reynoso | 4 | 4 | 0 | 0 | 0 | 0 | 0 | 0 | 0 | 0.000 | 0.000 | 0.000 | 0.000 |
| Arthur Rhodes | 6 | 4 | 1 | 0 | 1 | 0 | 3 | 0 | 1 | 0.250 | 0.200 | 0.750 | 0.950 |
| Jeff Ridgway | 1 | 1 | 1 | 1 | 0 | 0 | 0 | 0 | 0 | 1.000 | 1.000 | 2.000 | 3.000 |
| John Riedling | 2 | 2 | 2 | 0 | 1 | 0 | 1 | 0 | 0 | 1.000 | 1.000 | 2.000 | 3.000 |
| Brad Rigby | 1 | 1 | 0 | 0 | 0 | 0 | 0 | 0 | 0 | 0.000 | 0.000 | 0.000 | 0.000 |
| Juan Rincon | 12 | 10 | 2 | 1 | 0 | 0 | 2 | 2 | 2 | 0.200 | 0.333 | 0.300 | 0.633 |
| Ricardo Rincon | 1 | 1 | 1 | 0 | 0 | 0 | 1 | 0 | 0 | 1.000 | 1.000 | 1.000 | 2.000 |

273

| Cat vs. | PA | AB | H | 2B | 3B | HR | RBI | BB | SO | BA | OBP | SLG | OPS |
|---|---|---|---|---|---|---|---|---|---|---|---|---|---|
| David Riske | 7 | 6 | 2 | 1 | 0 | 0 | 0 | 1 | 1 | 0.333 | 0.429 | 0.500 | 0.929 |
| Todd Ritchie | 4 | 4 | 1 | 0 | 0 | 1 | 1 | 0 | 0 | 0.250 | 0.250 | 1.000 | 1.250 |
| Mariano Rivera | 12 | 11 | 3 | 0 | 0 | 0 | 1 | 0 | 1 | 0.273 | 0.250 | 0.273 | 0.523 |
| Saul Rivera | 2 | 2 | 2 | 0 | 0 | 0 | 0 | 0 | 0 | 1.000 | 1.000 | 1.000 | 2.000 |
| Willis Roberts | 1 | 1 | 0 | 0 | 0 | 0 | 0 | 0 | 0 | 0.000 | 0.000 | 0.000 | 0.000 |
| Nate Robertson | 1 | 1 | 0 | 0 | 0 | 0 | 0 | 0 | 1 | 0.000 | 0.000 | 0.000 | 0.000 |
| John Rocker | 1 | 0 | 0 | 0 | 0 | 0 | 0 | 1 | 0 |  | 1.000 |  |  |
| Fernando Rodney | 3 | 3 | 1 | 0 | 0 | 0 | 0 | 0 | 0 | 0.333 | 0.333 | 0.333 | 0.667 |
| Eddy Rodriguez | 1 | 0 | 0 | 0 | 0 | 0 | 1 | 1 | 0 |  | 1.000 |  |  |
| Felix Rodriguez | 2 | 2 | 1 | 0 | 0 | 0 | 0 | 0 | 0 | 0.500 | 0.500 | 0.500 | 1.000 |
| Francisco Rodriguez | 12 | 10 | 3 | 0 | 0 | 0 | 3 | 1 | 2 | 0.300 | 0.333 | 0.300 | 0.633 |
| Frankie Rodriguez | 1 | 1 | 0 | 0 | 0 | 0 | 0 | 0 | 0 | 0.000 | 0.000 | 0.000 | 0.000 |
| Jose Rodriguez | 1 | 1 | 1 | 0 | 0 | 0 | 0 | 0 | 0 | 1.000 | 1.000 | 1.000 | 2.000 |
| Nerio Rodriguez | 1 | 1 | 1 | 0 | 0 | 0 | 0 | 0 | 0 | 1.000 | 1.000 | 1.000 | 2.000 |
| Ricardo Rodriguez | 1 | 1 | 0 | 0 | 0 | 0 | 0 | 0 | 0 | 0.000 | 0.000 | 0.000 | 0.000 |
| Rich Rodriguez | 2 | 2 | 1 | 0 | 0 | 0 | 0 | 0 | 0 | 0.500 | 0.500 | 0.500 | 1.000 |
| Wandy Rodriguez | 2 | 1 | 0 | 0 | 0 | 0 | 0 | 1 | 1 | 0.000 | 0.500 | 0.000 | 0.500 |
| Esmil Rogers | 1 | 1 | 0 | 0 | 0 | 0 | 0 | 0 | 0 | 0.000 | 0.000 | 0.000 | 0.000 |
| Kenny Rogers | 9 | 7 | 2 | 1 | 0 | 0 | 2 | 1 | 2 | 0.286 | 0.333 | 0.429 | 0.762 |
| J.C. Romero | 3 | 2 | 0 | 0 | 0 | 0 | 0 | 0 | 0 | 0.000 | 0.000 | 0.000 | 0.000 |
| Sergio Romo | 1 | 1 | 0 | 0 | 0 | 0 | 0 | 0 | 1 | 0.000 | 0.000 | 0.000 | 0.000 |
| Matt Roney | 4 | 4 | 1 | 0 | 0 | 0 | 0 | 0 | 0 | 0.250 | 0.250 | 0.250 | 0.500 |
| Brian Rose | 7 | 5 | 1 | 0 | 0 | 0 | 0 | 2 | 0 | 0.200 | 0.429 | 0.200 | 0.629 |
| Ryan Rupe | 4 | 4 | 0 | 0 | 0 | 0 | 0 | 0 | 0 | 0.000 | 0.000 | 0.000 | 0.000 |

| Cat vs. | PA | AB | H | 2B | 3B | HR | RBI | BB | SO | BA | OBP | SLG | OPS |
|---|---|---|---|---|---|---|---|---|---|---|---|---|---|
| B.J. Ryan | 5 | 5 | 0 | 0 | 0 | 0 | 0 | 0 | 2 | 0.000 | 0.000 | 0.000 | 0.000 |
| Jae Kuk Ryu | 1 | 1 | 0 | 0 | 0 | 0 | 0 | 0 | 0 | 0.000 | 0.000 | 0.000 | 0.000 |
| Kirk Saarloos | 11 | 7 | 3 | 0 | 1 | 1 | 5 | 2 | 1 | 0.429 | 0.545 | 1.143 | 1.688 |
| Bret Saberhagen | 4 | 4 | 1 | 1 | 0 | 0 | 0 | 0 | 0 | 0.250 | 0.250 | 0.500 | 0.750 |
| Takashi Saito | 1 | 1 | 0 | 0 | 0 | 0 | 0 | 0 | 0 | 0.000 | 0.000 | 0.000 | 0.000 |
| Juan Salas | 2 | 2 | 1 | 0 | 0 | 0 | 1 | 0 | 0 | 0.500 | 0.500 | 0.500 | 1.000 |
| Brad Salmon | 1 | 1 | 0 | 0 | 0 | 0 | 0 | 0 | 0 | 0.000 | 0.000 | 0.000 | 0.000 |
| Jeff Samardzija | 1 | 1 | 1 | 0 | 1 | 0 | 1 | 0 | 0 | 1.000 | 1.000 | 3.000 | 4.000 |
| Benj Sampson | 2 | 1 | 1 | 0 | 0 | 0 | 1 | 0 | 0 | 1.000 | 0.500 | 1.000 | 1.500 |
| Chris Sampson | 4 | 4 | 1 | 0 | 0 | 0 | 0 | 0 | 0 | 0.250 | 0.250 | 0.250 | 0.500 |
| Brian Sanches | 1 | 1 | 1 | 0 | 0 | 0 | 0 | 0 | 0 | 1.000 | 1.000 | 1.000 | 2.000 |
| Anibal Sanchez | 2 | 2 | 0 | 0 | 0 | 0 | 0 | 0 | 0 | 0.000 | 0.000 | 0.000 | 0.000 |
| Duaner Sanchez | 3 | 2 | 0 | 0 | 0 | 0 | 0 | 1 | 0 | 0.000 | 0.333 | 0.000 | 0.333 |
| David Sanders | 2 | 2 | 1 | 0 | 1 | 0 | 1 | 0 | 0 | 0.500 | 0.500 | 1.500 | 2.000 |
| Ervin Santana | 22 | 19 | 5 | 1 | 0 | 0 | 0 | 2 | 4 | 0.263 | 0.364 | 0.316 | 0.679 |
| Johan Santana | 1 | 1 | 0 | 0 | 0 | 0 | 0 | 0 | 0 | 0.000 | 0.000 | 0.000 | 0.000 |
| Julio Santana | 6 | 6 | 2 | 0 | 0 | 0 | 0 | 0 | 1 | 0.333 | 0.333 | 0.333 | 0.667 |
| Marino Santana | 1 | 1 | 0 | 0 | 0 | 0 | 0 | 0 | 1 | 0.000 | 0.000 | 0.000 | 0.000 |
| Jose Santiago | 4 | 4 | 1 | 0 | 0 | 0 | 0 | 0 | 1 | 0.250 | 0.250 | 0.250 | 0.500 |
| Victor Santos | 3 | 2 | 1 | 0 | 0 | 0 | 0 | 0 | 0 | 0.500 | 0.667 | 0.500 | 1.167 |
| Kazuhiro Sasaki | 11 | 11 | 2 | 0 | 0 | 0 | 0 | 0 | 2 | 0.182 | 0.182 | 0.182 | 0.364 |
| Scott Sauerbeck | 3 | 2 | 2 | 0 | 0 | 0 | 0 | 1 | 0 | 1.000 | 1.000 | 1.000 | 2.000 |
| Max Scherzer | 1 | 1 | 0 | 0 | 0 | 0 | 0 | 0 | 0 | 0.000 | 0.000 | 0.000 | 0.000 |
| Curt Schilling | 22 | 22 | 11 | 4 | 0 | 1 | 6 | 0 | 2 | 0.500 | 0.500 | 0.818 | 1.318 |

| Cat vs. | PA | AB | H | 2B | 3B | HR | RBI | BB | SO | BA | OBP | SLG | OPS |
|---|---|---|---|---|---|---|---|---|---|---|---|---|---|
| Jason Schmidt | 8 | 7 | 3 | 0 | 0 | 0 | 0 | 1 | 1 | 0.429 | 0.500 | 0.429 | 0.929 |
| Rudy Seanez | 1 | 1 | 0 | 0 | 0 | 0 | 0 | 0 | 0 | 0.000 | 0.000 | 0.000 | 0.000 |
| Bobby Seay | 1 | 1 | 1 | 0 | 0 | 0 | 0 | 0 | 0 | 1.000 | 1.000 | 1.000 | 2.000 |
| Shawn Sedlacek | 3 | 3 | 2 | 0 | 0 | 0 | 0 | 0 | 0 | 0.667 | 0.667 | 0.667 | 1.333 |
| Aaron Sele | 29 | 27 | 7 | 1 | 1 | 0 | 1 | 2 | 4 | 0.259 | 0.310 | 0.370 | 0.681 |
| Jae Weong Seo | 10 | 10 | 3 | 0 | 1 | 1 | 3 | 0 | 0 | 0.300 | 0.300 | 0.800 | 1.100 |
| Scott Service | 2 | 2 | 0 | 0 | 0 | 0 | 1 | 0 | 0 | 0.000 | 0.000 | 0.000 | 0.000 |
| Ben Sheets | 7 | 6 | 2 | 1 | 0 | 0 | 0 | 1 | 1 | 0.333 | 0.429 | 0.500 | 0.929 |
| George Sherrill | 6 | 5 | 0 | 0 | 0 | 0 | 0 | 0 | 4 | 0.000 | 0.000 | 0.000 | 0.000 |
| James Shields | 6 | 6 | 2 | 1 | 0 | 0 | 2 | 0 | 2 | 0.333 | 0.333 | 0.500 | 0.833 |
| Scot Shields | 13 | 11 | 0 | 0 | 0 | 0 | 1 | 0 | 0 | 0.000 | 0.077 | 0.000 | 0.077 |
| Jason Shiell | 1 | 1 | 1 | 1 | 0 | 0 | 0 | 0 | 0 | 1.000 | 1.000 | 2.000 | 3.000 |
| Brian Shouse | 4 | 4 | 1 | 0 | 0 | 0 | 0 | 0 | 0 | 0.250 | 0.250 | 0.250 | 0.500 |
| Paul Shuey | 8 | 6 | 1 | 0 | 0 | 1 | 2 | 2 | 1 | 0.167 | 0.375 | 0.667 | 1.042 |
| Carlos Silva | 20 | 20 | 6 | 3 | 0 | 1 | 1 | 0 | 3 | 0.300 | 0.300 | 0.600 | 0.900 |
| Bill Simas | 6 | 6 | 1 | 0 | 0 | 1 | 2 | 0 | 1 | 0.167 | 0.167 | 0.667 | 0.833 |
| Jason Simontacchi | 3 | 3 | 1 | 0 | 0 | 0 | 0 | 0 | 0 | 0.333 | 0.333 | 0.333 | 0.667 |
| Andy Sisco | 1 | 0 | 0 | 0 | 0 | 0 | 0 | 1 | 0 |  | 1.000 |  |  |
| Heathcliff Slocumb | 1 | 1 | 1 | 1 | 0 | 0 | 1 | 0 | 0 | 1.000 | 1.000 | 2.000 | 3.000 |
| Kevin Slowey | 3 | 3 | 0 | 0 | 0 | 0 | 0 | 0 | 1 | 0.000 | 0.000 | 0.000 | 0.000 |
| Joe Slusarski | 4 | 4 | 2 | 0 | 0 | 0 | 2 | 0 | 0 | 0.500 | 0.500 | 0.500 | 1.000 |
| Aaron Small | 5 | 5 | 0 | 0 | 0 | 0 | 0 | 0 | 1 | 0.000 | 0.000 | 0.000 | 0.000 |
| Chris Smith | 1 | 1 | 0 | 0 | 0 | 0 | 0 | 0 | 0 | 0.000 | 0.000 | 0.000 | 0.000 |
| Dan Smith | 1 | 1 | 0 | 0 | 0 | 0 | 0 | 0 | 1 | 0.000 | 0.000 | 0.000 | 0.000 |

| Cat vs. | PA | AB | H | 2B | 3B | HR | RBI | BB | SO | BA | OBP | SLG | OPS |
|---|---|---|---|---|---|---|---|---|---|---|---|---|---|
| Mike Smith | 3 | 2 | 1 | 1 | 0 | 0 | 1 | 1 | 0 | 0.500 | 0.667 | 1.000 | 1.667 |
| John Smoltz | 3 | 3 | 1 | 0 | 0 | 0 | 0 | 0 | 0 | 0.333 | 0.333 | 0.333 | 0.667 |
| Ian Snell | 4 | 3 | 2 | 0 | 0 | 0 | 0 | 1 | 0 | 0.667 | 0.750 | 0.667 | 1.417 |
| John Snyder | 8 | 7 | 2 | 0 | 0 | 0 | 2 | 1 | 0 | 0.286 | 0.375 | 0.286 | 0.661 |
| Kyle Snyder | 13 | 12 | 3 | 1 | 0 | 0 | 3 | 1 | 0 | 0.250 | 0.308 | 0.500 | 0.808 |
| Andy Sonnanstine | 8 | 8 | 3 | 0 | 0 | 1 | 3 | 0 | 1 | 0.375 | 0.375 | 0.750 | 1.125 |
| Rafael Soriano | 2 | 1 | 0 | 0 | 0 | 0 | 0 | 1 | 0 | 0.000 | 0.500 | 0.000 | 0.500 |
| Jorge Sosa | 14 | 10 | 3 | 0 | 0 | 0 | 0 | 4 | 1 | 0.300 | 0.500 | 0.300 | 0.800 |
| Steve Sparks | 22 | 22 | 9 | 2 | 0 | 1 | 2 | 0 | 2 | 0.409 | 0.409 | 0.636 | 1.045 |
| Justin Speier | 4 | 4 | 0 | 0 | 0 | 0 | 0 | 0 | 0 | 0.000 | 0.000 | 0.000 | 0.000 |
| Paul Spoljaric | 2 | 1 | 0 | 0 | 0 | 0 | 0 | 1 | 0 | 0.000 | 0.500 | 0.000 | 0.500 |
| Jerry Spradlin | 1 | 1 | 0 | 0 | 0 | 0 | 0 | 0 | 1 | 0.000 | 0.000 | 0.000 | 0.000 |
| Dennis Springer | 3 | 3 | 0 | 0 | 0 | 0 | 0 | 0 | 1 | 0.000 | 0.000 | 0.000 | 0.000 |
| Jay Spurgeon | 3 | 1 | 0 | 0 | 0 | 0 | 0 | 2 | 1 | 0.000 | 0.667 | 0.000 | 0.667 |
| Chris Spurling | 1 | 1 | 0 | 0 | 0 | 0 | 0 | 0 | 0 | 0.000 | 0.000 | 0.000 | 0.000 |
| Craig Stammen | 2 | 2 | 0 | 0 | 0 | 0 | 0 | 0 | 0 | 0.000 | 0.000 | 0.000 | 0.000 |
| Mike Stanton | 6 | 4 | 3 | 1 | 0 | 0 | 3 | 2 | 0 | 0.750 | 0.833 | 1.000 | 1.833 |
| Denny Stark | 4 | 4 | 1 | 0 | 0 | 0 | 0 | 0 | 0 | 0.250 | 0.250 | 0.250 | 0.500 |
| Blake Stein | 13 | 10 | 4 | 1 | 0 | 0 | 2 | 2 | 1 | 0.400 | 0.538 | 0.500 | 1.038 |
| Jeff Stevens | 1 | 1 | 0 | 0 | 0 | 0 | 0 | 0 | 0 | 0.000 | 0.000 | 0.000 | 0.000 |
| Scott Stewart | 1 | 1 | 0 | 0 | 0 | 0 | 0 | 0 | 0 | 0.000 | 0.000 | 0.000 | 0.000 |
| Brian Stokes | 4 | 3 | 1 | 1 | 0 | 0 | 0 | 1 | 0 | 0.333 | 0.500 | 0.667 | 1.167 |
| Ricky Stone | 1 | 0 | 0 | 0 | 0 | 0 | 0 | 1 | 0 |  | 1.000 |  |  |
| Todd Stottlemyre | 2 | 2 | 1 | 1 | 0 | 0 | 1 | 0 | 0 | 0.500 | 0.500 | 1.000 | 1.500 |

| Cat vs. | PA | AB | H | 2B | 3B | HR | RBI | BB | SO | BA | OBP | SLG | OPS |
|---|---|---|---|---|---|---|---|---|---|---|---|---|---|
| Huston Street | 5 | 5 | 1 | 0 | 0 | 0 | 0 | 0 | 2 | 0.200 | 0.200 | 0.200 | 0.400 |
| Tanyon Sturtze | 19 | 17 | 4 | 2 | 0 | 0 | 0 | 1 | 1 | 0.235 | 0.278 | 0.353 | 0.631 |
| Jeff Suppan | 18 | 15 | 6 | 1 | 0 | 0 | 0 | 2 | 1 | 0.400 | 0.471 | 0.467 | 0.937 |
| Mac Suzuki | 7 | 6 | 1 | 0 | 0 | 0 | 0 | 0 | 1 | 0.167 | 0.286 | 0.167 | 0.452 |
| Bill Swift | 5 | 4 | 0 | 0 | 0 | 0 | 1 | 0 | 0 | 0.000 | 0.000 | 0.000 | 0.000 |
| Greg Swindell | 1 | 1 | 0 | 0 | 0 | 0 | 0 | 0 | 0 | 0.000 | 0.000 | 0.000 | 0.000 |
| Jon Switzer | 3 | 3 | 0 | 0 | 0 | 0 | 0 | 0 | 0 | 0.000 | 0.000 | 0.000 | 0.000 |
| Shingo Takatsu | 1 | 1 | 1 | 0 | 0 | 0 | 0 | 0 | 0 | 1.000 | 1.000 | 1.000 | 2.000 |
| Brian Tallet | 2 | 1 | 0 | 0 | 0 | 0 | 0 | 1 | 0 | 0.000 | 0.500 | 0.000 | 0.500 |
| Jeff Tam | 4 | 2 | 0 | 0 | 0 | 0 | 0 | 2 | 0 | 0.000 | 0.500 | 0.000 | 0.500 |
| Julian Tavarez | 15 | 12 | 3 | 1 | 0 | 0 | 1 | 2 | 1 | 0.250 | 0.400 | 0.333 | 0.733 |
| Billy Taylor | 5 | 5 | 1 | 0 | 0 | 0 | 0 | 0 | 0 | 0.200 | 0.200 | 0.200 | 0.400 |
| Joe Thatcher | 1 | 1 | 1 | 0 | 0 | 0 | 1 | 0 | 0 | 1.000 | 1.000 | 1.000 | 2.000 |
| Brad Thompson | 1 | 1 | 1 | 0 | 0 | 0 | 0 | 0 | 0 | 1.000 | 1.000 | 1.000 | 2.000 |
| John Thomson | 3 | 3 | 2 | 0 | 0 | 0 | 0 | 0 | 0 | 0.667 | 0.667 | 0.667 | 1.333 |
| Corey Thurman | 1 | 1 | 0 | 0 | 0 | 0 | 0 | 0 | 1 | 0.000 | 0.000 | 0.000 | 0.000 |
| Mike Thurman | 1 | 0 | 0 | 0 | 0 | 0 | 0 | 1 | 0 | | 1.000 | | |
| Mike Timlin | 12 | 12 | 8 | 3 | 0 | 0 | 3 | 0 | 2 | 0.667 | 0.667 | 0.917 | 1.583 |
| Brett Tomko | 6 | 5 | 0 | 0 | 0 | 0 | 0 | 1 | 0 | 0.000 | 0.167 | 0.000 | 0.167 |
| Salomon Torres | 1 | 1 | 0 | 0 | 0 | 0 | 0 | 0 | 0 | 0.000 | 0.000 | 0.000 | 0.000 |
| Josh Towers | 8 | 8 | 3 | 0 | 0 | 2 | 2 | 0 | 0 | 0.375 | 0.375 | 1.125 | 1.500 |
| Steve Trachsel | 12 | 11 | 1 | 0 | 0 | 0 | 3 | 1 | 2 | 0.091 | 0.167 | 0.091 | 0.258 |
| Mike Trombley | 7 | 6 | 3 | 2 | 0 | 0 | 3 | 1 | 1 | 0.500 | 0.571 | 0.833 | 1.405 |
| Ramon Troncoso | 2 | 2 | 2 | 0 | 0 | 0 | 0 | 0 | 0 | 1.000 | 1.000 | 1.000 | 2.000 |

| Cat vs. | PA | AB | H | 2B | 3B | HR | RBI | BB | SO | BA | OBP | SLG | OPS |
|---|---|---|---|---|---|---|---|---|---|---|---|---|---|
| T.J. Tucker | 2 | 2 | 0 | 0 | 0 | 0 | 0 | 0 | 1 | 0.000 | 0.000 | 0.000 | 0.000 |
| Derrick Turnbow | 5 | 5 | 0 | 0 | 0 | 0 | 0 | 0 | 0 | 0.000 | 0.000 | 0.000 | 0.000 |
| Ugueth Urbina | 1 | 1 | 0 | 0 | 0 | 0 | 0 | 0 | 0 | 0.000 | 0.000 | 0.000 | 0.000 |
| Ismael Valdez | 6 | 5 | 3 | 0 | 0 | 0 | 0 | 1 | 1 | 0.600 | 0.667 | 0.600 | 1.267 |
| Jose Valverde | 1 | 1 | 1 | 1 | 0 | 0 | 1 | 0 | 0 | 1.000 | 1.000 | 2.000 | 3.000 |
| Jermaine Van Buren | 2 | 2 | 0 | 0 | 0 | 0 | 0 | 0 | 1 | 0.000 | 0.000 | 0.000 | 0.000 |
| Todd Van Poppel | 1 | 1 | 1 | 1 | 0 | 0 | 0 | 0 | 0 | 1.000 | 1.000 | 2.000 | 3.000 |
| Claudio Vargas | 5 | 4 | 1 | 1 | 0 | 0 | 0 | 1 | 0 | 0.250 | 0.400 | 0.500 | 0.900 |
| Javier Vazquez | 27 | 27 | 10 | 2 | 0 | 1 | 2 | 0 | 4 | 0.370 | 0.370 | 0.556 | 0.926 |
| Mike Venafro | 1 | 0 | 0 | 0 | 0 | 0 | 0 | 0 | 0 | | 1.000 | | |
| Jose Veras | 2 | 2 | 0 | 0 | 0 | 0 | 0 | 0 | 1 | 0.000 | 0.000 | 0.000 | 0.000 |
| Justin Verlander | 13 | 13 | 1 | 0 | 0 | 1 | 1 | 0 | 3 | 0.077 | 0.077 | 0.308 | 0.385 |
| Carlos Villanueva | 2 | 1 | 0 | 0 | 0 | 0 | 0 | 1 | 1 | 0.000 | 0.500 | 0.000 | 0.500 |
| Ron Villone | 3 | 3 | 0 | 0 | 0 | 0 | 0 | 0 | 2 | 0.000 | 0.000 | 0.000 | 0.000 |
| Luis Vizcaino | 4 | 4 | 2 | 0 | 0 | 1 | 2 | 0 | 0 | 0.500 | 0.500 | 1.250 | 1.750 |
| Doug Waechter | 17 | 16 | 6 | 1 | 0 | 1 | 4 | 0 | 1 | 0.375 | 0.412 | 0.625 | 1.037 |
| Adam Wainwright | 5 | 4 | 1 | 0 | 0 | 0 | 0 | 1 | 0 | 0.250 | 0.400 | 0.250 | 0.650 |
| Tim Wakefield | 64 | 55 | 16 | 4 | 0 | 3 | 9 | 6 | 7 | 0.291 | 0.391 | 0.527 | 0.918 |
| Jamie Walker | 4 | 4 | 0 | 0 | 0 | 0 | 0 | 0 | 0 | 0.000 | 0.000 | 0.000 | 0.000 |
| Tyler Walker | 2 | 2 | 0 | 0 | 0 | 0 | 0 | 0 | 1 | 0.000 | 0.000 | 0.000 | 0.000 |
| Jeff Wallace | 2 | 0 | 0 | 0 | 0 | 0 | 0 | 2 | 0 | | 1.000 | | |
| Chien-Ming Wang | 14 | 14 | 3 | 0 | 0 | 0 | 1 | 0 | 0 | 0.214 | 0.214 | 0.214 | 0.429 |
| Bryan Ward | 2 | 2 | 1 | 0 | 0 | 0 | 0 | 0 | 0 | 0.500 | 0.500 | 0.500 | 1.000 |
| John Wasdin | 7 | 5 | 2 | 0 | 0 | 0 | 2 | 1 | 1 | 0.400 | 0.429 | 0.400 | 0.829 |

279

| Cat vs. | PA | AB | H | 2B | 3B | HR | RBI | BB | SO | BA | OBP | SLG | OPS |
|---|---|---|---|---|---|---|---|---|---|---|---|---|---|
| David Weathers | 2 | 2 | 0 | 0 | 0 | 0 | 0 | 0 | 0 | 0.000 | 0.000 | 0.000 | 0.000 |
| Jeff Weaver | 34 | 31 | 7 | 4 | 0 | 1 | 2 | 2 | 4 | 0.226 | 0.273 | 0.452 | 0.724 |
| Jered Weaver | 12 | 9 | 2 | 0 | 0 | 0 | 0 | 1 | 1 | 0.222 | 0.364 | 0.222 | 0.586 |
| Ryan Webb | 1 | 1 | 1 | 1 | 0 | 0 | 0 | 0 | 0 | 1.000 | 1.000 | 2.000 | 3.000 |
| Ben Weber | 7 | 5 | 1 | 0 | 0 | 0 | 0 | 2 | 1 | 0.200 | 0.429 | 0.200 | 0.629 |
| Todd Wellemeyer | 4 | 4 | 3 | 0 | 1 | 0 | 2 | 0 | 0 | 0.750 | 0.750 | 1.250 | 2.000 |
| Bob Wells | 5 | 5 | 1 | 1 | 0 | 0 | 0 | 0 | 0 | 0.200 | 0.200 | 0.400 | 0.600 |
| David Wells | 3 | 3 | 2 | 2 | 0 | 0 | 0 | 0 | 1 | 0.667 | 0.667 | 1.333 | 2.000 |
| Kip Wells | 9 | 7 | 2 | 0 | 0 | 0 | 0 | 2 | 1 | 0.286 | 0.444 | 0.286 | 0.730 |
| Jake Westbrook | 17 | 15 | 5 | 1 | 0 | 0 | 0 | 2 | 2 | 0.333 | 0.412 | 0.400 | 0.812 |
| John Wetteland | 5 | 5 | 1 | 0 | 0 | 0 | 0 | 0 | 2 | 0.200 | 0.200 | 0.200 | 0.400 |
| Dan Wheeler | 3 | 3 | 2 | 0 | 0 | 1 | 3 | 0 | 0 | 0.667 | 0.667 | 1.667 | 2.333 |
| Gabe White | 2 | 2 | 0 | 0 | 0 | 0 | 0 | 0 | 1 | 0.000 | 0.000 | 0.000 | 0.000 |
| Matt White | 2 | 2 | 2 | 1 | 0 | 1 | 3 | 0 | 0 | 1.000 | 1.000 | 3.000 | 4.000 |
| Rick White | 9 | 8 | 3 | 0 | 0 | 0 | 0 | 1 | 2 | 0.375 | 0.444 | 0.375 | 0.819 |
| Matt Whiteside | 1 | 1 | 1 | 1 | 0 | 0 | 0 | 0 | 0 | 1.000 | 1.000 | 2.000 | 3.000 |
| Bob Wickman | 9 | 8 | 3 | 0 | 0 | 1 | 1 | 1 | 1 | 0.375 | 0.444 | 0.750 | 1.194 |
| Marc Wilkins | 1 | 1 | 0 | 0 | 0 | 0 | 0 | 0 | 0 | 0.000 | 0.000 | 0.000 | 0.000 |
| Todd Williams | 6 | 6 | 3 | 0 | 0 | 0 | 2 | 0 | 0 | 0.500 | 0.500 | 0.500 | 1.000 |
| Woody Williams | 11 | 9 | 1 | 0 | 0 | 1 | 1 | 2 | 4 | 0.111 | 0.273 | 0.444 | 0.717 |
| Scott Williamson | 3 | 3 | 2 | 1 | 0 | 0 | 2 | 0 | 1 | 0.667 | 0.667 | 1.000 | 1.667 |
| Brian Wilson | 1 | 1 | 0 | 0 | 0 | 0 | 0 | 0 | 1 | 0.000 | 0.000 | 0.000 | 0.000 |
| Kris Wilson | 9 | 9 | 2 | 0 | 0 | 1 | 1 | 0 | 1 | 0.222 | 0.222 | 0.556 | 0.778 |
| Matt Wise | 11 | 11 | 1 | 0 | 0 | 0 | 0 | 0 | 2 | 0.091 | 0.091 | 0.091 | 0.182 |

| Cat vs. | PA | AB | H | 2B | 3B | HR | RBI | BB | SO | BA | OBP | SLG | OPS |
|---|---|---|---|---|---|---|---|---|---|---|---|---|---|
| Jay Witasick | 2 | 2 | 1 | 0 | 0 | 0 | 0 | 0 | 1 | 0.500 | 0.500 | 0.500 | 1.000 |
| Mark Wohlers | 4 | 3 | 0 | 0 | 0 | 0 | 1 | 0 | 3 | 0.000 | 0.250 | 0.000 | 0.250 |
| Brian Wolfe | 1 | 1 | 0 | 0 | 0 | 0 | 0 | 0 | 0 | 0.000 | 0.000 | 0.000 | 0.000 |
| Kerry Wood | 3 | 3 | 1 | 0 | 0 | 0 | 0 | 0 | 0 | 0.333 | 0.333 | 0.333 | 0.667 |
| Mike Wood | 2 | 2 | 0 | 0 | 0 | 0 | 0 | 0 | 0 | 0.000 | 0.000 | 0.000 | 0.000 |
| Steve Woodard | 11 | 11 | 4 | 2 | 0 | 0 | 1 | 0 | 1 | 0.364 | 0.364 | 0.545 | 0.909 |
| Jake Woods | 6 | 4 | 2 | 0 | 0 | 1 | 1 | 1 | 0 | 0.500 | 0.600 | 1.250 | 1.850 |
| Tim Worrell | 2 | 2 | 1 | 0 | 0 | 0 | 0 | 0 | 0 | 0.500 | 0.500 | 0.500 | 1.000 |
| Dan Wright | 5 | 5 | 5 | 1 | 0 | 1 | 2 | 0 | 0 | 1.000 | 1.000 | 1.800 | 2.800 |
| Jaret Wright | 32 | 26 | 10 | 4 | 0 | 1 | 3 | 5 | 4 | 0.385 | 0.500 | 0.654 | 1.154 |
| Michael Wuertz | 1 | 1 | 1 | 0 | 0 | 0 | 1 | 0 | 0 | 1.000 | 1.000 | 1.000 | 2.000 |
| Kelly Wunsch | 1 | 1 | 0 | 0 | 0 | 0 | 0 | 0 | 0 | 0.000 | 0.000 | 0.000 | 0.000 |
| Keiichi Yabu | 1 | 1 | 0 | 0 | 0 | 0 | 0 | 0 | 0 | 0.000 | 0.000 | 0.000 | 0.000 |
| Yasuhiko Yabuta | 2 | 0 | 0 | 0 | 0 | 0 | 0 | 1 | 0 |  | 1.000 |  |  |
| Esteban Yan | 13 | 11 | 5 | 0 | 0 | 2 | 5 | 1 | 0 | 0.455 | 0.462 | 1.000 | 1.462 |
| Chris Young | 6 | 5 | 1 | 0 | 0 | 0 | 0 | 1 | 1 | 0.200 | 0.333 | 0.200 | 0.533 |
| Victor Zambrano | 9 | 8 | 2 | 0 | 0 | 0 | 0 | 1 | 0 | 0.250 | 0.333 | 0.250 | 0.583 |
| Brad Ziegler | 1 | 1 | 1 | 0 | 1 | 0 | 0 | 0 | 0 | 1.000 | 1.000 | 3.000 | 4.000 |
| Jeff Zimmerman | 2 | 2 | 1 | 0 | 0 | 0 | 0 | 0 | 0 | 0.500 | 0.500 | 0.500 | 1.000 |
| Charlie Zink | 3 | 3 | 1 | 1 | 0 | 0 | 2 | 0 | 0 | 0.333 | 0.333 | 0.667 | 1.000 |
| Barry Zito | 4 | 2 | 1 | 0 | 0 | 0 | 0 | 2 | 0 | 0.500 | 0.750 | 0.500 | 1.250 |
| Joel Zumaya | 2 | 1 | 1 | 0 | 0 | 0 | 1 | 1 | 0 | 1.000 | 1.000 | 1.000 | 2.000 |
| TOTALS | 4292 | 3824 | 1113 | 262 | 37 | 84 | 457 | 331 | 492 | .291 | .357 | .445 | .802 |

When our first daughter, Morgan, was about two weeks old, a discoloration of her skin began to develop on her left nostril. A week later, it was larger and we took her to a doctor. When it was diagnosed as a type of vascular birthmark called a hemangioma, we were devastated. We were also full of questions, including: Would it get bigger, and how big? Would it go away? The first doctor we consulted told us to wait for it to go away on its own. That wasn't good enough. We knew how harsh kids could be on someone who looks different or has something that causes them to stick out. Not wanting Morgan to feel ostracized by her peers, we sought treatment options.

Fortunately, we discovered the Vascular Birthmark Foundation. Through its resources we contacted Dr. Edwin Williams, who performed two laser procedures and one reconstructive surgery on Morgan's hemangioma. After several years, there were still traces of the birthmark, so when Morgan was ten we visited Dr. Roy Geronemus in New York City. He did laser surgery, which further reduced the birthmark's color and size.

What we realized during our experiences, and the reason we created The Frank Catalanotto Foundation, is that many doctors are not being taught the proper methods of treating these birthmarks. There are several varieties and some may be life threatening, growing internally or near the mouth and eyes. In addition, birthmarks can cause emotional stress to children and parents. Thankfully, there are organizations such as the Vascular Birthmark Foundation, which can help connect patients with doctors who are well versed in appropriate medical procedures. Linda Rozell Shannon, the founder and president of the VBF, encouraged us to be proactive with Morgan's hemangioma. Since she started the VBP in 1994, the organization has networked over 50,000 people into treatment all over the world.

We are proud to be Honorary Chairpersons of the Vascular Birthmark Foundation and to assist in its efforts to help families receive an accurate diagnosis, a proper treatment plan and, just as important, hope.

Each May, as baseball is in full swing, is Vascular Birthmark Awareness Month. Our entire family urges you to get involved in whatever way you can.

Please visit www.fcatalanotto.org.

Thank you,

Barbara and Frank

As an athlete, I always had three goals when it came to my supplements. First, I wanted to optimize my workouts and game performances by using a pre-workout formula, which gave me the extra push I needed to finish strong. Second, getting sustained energy throughout three-hour games was always a challenge for me as well as most athletes. Third, feeding my muscles after a hard workout or long game was critical for my body's recovery before the next game.

My vision for our brand took root when I developed a strong desire to know exactly what I was putting in my body. As a professional athlete, I had to. I had to know then and still want to know now that what I'm taking is safe, so it's important to me to have supplements that are clean, pure and certified by NSF . These supplements are put through a rigorous screening process to ensure the integrity of the product. I know firsthand that athletes today need to make good decisions about what they put in their bodies. Taking a contaminated product could affect their health as well as their career, so it's vital that what it says on the label is what's in the container.

I know that the Proven4Sport supplements contain exactly what each label claims, and that's why I'm able to recommend them to you.

Please visit our website for more information: www.proven4.com

Thank you,

Frank